VOICE AND ARTICULATION DRILLBOOK

by

GRANT FAIRBANKS, Ph. D.

Professor of Speech
University of Illinois

Published by

HARPER & BROTHERS

New York and London

CONTENTS

CONTENTS

PREFACE

When this book of voice and articulation practice materials was first conceived, the author's plan was to experiment with the book in actual clinical and teaching situations of various types, and to modify it until the materials were known to be satisfactory. This program has been carried out. A preliminary edition appeared in 1937, followed by two tentative revisions in 1938 and 1939, and these years composed a period of experimentation, not only by the author personally at the State University of Iowa, but also by teachers at several other institutions. During this period the book was used and scrutinized as a basic source of drill materials for individual clinical work, for small groups and self-help programs, for the retraining of defectives and the improvement of skilled speakers, for courses in speech improvement, speech correction, voice and phonetics, voice and articulation, fundamentals of speech, and others. On the basis of this trial the book has again been revised and enlarged for the present edition.

The author is conscious of obligations to many individuals. Among his colleagues at the State University of Iowa he is especially indebted to Professors Edward C. Mabie and Carl E. Seashore for their unfailing support, to Professor Harry G. Barnes for many suggestions and for permission to use his own previously unpublished research, to Professor Milton Cowan for valuable criticisms of the manuscript. Major debts also are owed to a number of teachers who experimented with the preliminary editions at other universities, and particularly to Professors Spencer F. Brown, Jack C. Cotton, Ernest C. Fossum, Giles W. Gray and Ernest H. Henrickson, whose recommendations have been invaluable. In many ways the most important specific contributions have come from the imaginative suggestions and research of the author's students. He is grateful in particular to his graduate assistants, E. Thayer Curry, Fred L. Darley, Phyllis Franke, David L. Johnson, C. W. McIntosh, Jr., Dorothy Oliver, W. L. Pronovost, John C. Snidecor and Caryl Spriestersbach.

INTRODUCTION

EXAMINATION OF VOICE AND ARTICULATION

Almost all speech clinicians and teachers find it necessary to record the results of voice and articulation examinations in some systematic way. The forms presented on the two succeeding pages are valuable for this purpose and a brief description of their use is included.

Voice can be observed most satisfactorily in some type of connected speech, and probably the most convenient performance for this purpose is oral reading of simple, factual prose. Any observations should be confirmed, however, in conversation and speaking. If the form headed Voice and Connected Speech is used, the following examination procedure is recommended: (1) Note deviations from acceptable performance, checking the appropriate descriptive terms, writing in others, and recording observations and explanations. Let the attention paid to articulation at this point be determined by whether or not a detailed speech sound analysis is to be made later. (2) Compare the individual's use of each of the six major aspects listed on the blank to average standards of performance. Encircle the proper number after each heading to indicate a rating on a 1-to-5 scale, where 3 represents average performance, with 2 and 1 scaling down to inferiority and 4 and 5 scaling up to superiority. (3) If several disorders have been observed and noted, indicate in some manner their relative importance in an improvement program.

The nature of an articulation examination is usually determined by the purpose of the examination. In some instances this purpose is served by general observations during a connected speech performance, as in the voice examination described above, while in many cases a detailed phonetic inventory is desirable. At other times only a partial analysis is possible or necessary. The examination form headed Articulation provides

VOICE AND CONNECTED SPEECH

PITCH:

1 2 3 4 5

Too High Level.............

Too Low Level.............

Monotony.................

Pitch Pattern..............

Other.....................

VOICE QUALITY:

1 2 3 4 5

Nasality...................

Breathiness................

Harshness..................

Hoarseness.................

Other.....................

TIME:

1 2 3 4 5

Too Rapid Rate............

Too Slow Rate.............

Staccato Phonations........

Prolonged Phonations.......

Monotony.................

Jerkiness..................

Faulty Phrasing...........

Time Pattern..............

Other.....................

ARTICULATION:

1 2 3 4 5

Generally Inaccurate........

Fricatives Inaccurate........

Substitutions...............

Voicing Errors..............

Distortions.................

Slighting...................

Omissions..................

Other.....................

LOUDNESS:

1 2 3 4 5

Too Loud Level............

Too Weak.................

Monotony.................

Too Flexible...............

Loudness Pattern...........

Other.....................

COMPLEX ATTRIBUTES:

1 2 3 4 5

Mispronunciation...........

Faulty Emphasis............

Too Even Stress............

Affectation................

Regional Dialect............

Foreign Dialect.............

Other.....................

ARTICULATION

	Substitution	Voicing Error	Distortion	Slighting	Omission
1. [i]	..	..	..	..	..
2. [ɪ]	..	..	..	..	..
3. [ɛ]	..	..	..	..	..
4. [æ]	..	..	..	..	..
5. [ʌ]	..	..	..	..	..
6. [ɑ]	..	..	..	..	..
7. [ɔ]	..	..	..	..	..
8. [ʊ]	..	..	..	..	..
9. [u]	..	..	..	..	..
10. [ju]	..	..	..	..	..
11. [oʊ]	..	..	..	..	..
12. [ɑʊ]	..	..	..	..	..
13. [eɪ]	..	..	..	..	..
14. [ɑɪ]	..	..	..	..	..
15. [ɔɪ]	..	..	..	..	..
16. [m]	..	..	..	..	..
17. [n]	..	..	..	..	..
18. [ŋ]	..	..	..	..	..

	Substitution	Voicing Error	Distortion	Slighting	Omission
19. [p]	..	..	..	..	..
20. [b]	..	..	..	..	..
21. [t]	..	..	..	..	..
22. [d]	..	..	..	..	..
23. [k]	..	..	..	..	..
24. [g]	..	..	..	..	..
*25. [r]	..	..	..	..	..
*26. [l]	..	..	..	..	..
27. [f]	..	..	..	..	..
28. [v]	..	..	..	..	..
*29. [θ]	..	..	..	..	..
*30. [ð]	..	..	..	..	..
*31. [s]	..	..	..	..	..
*32. [z]	..	..	..	..	..
*33. [ʃ]	..	..	..	..	..
*34. [ʒ]	..	..	..	..	..
35. [h]	..	..	..	..	..
*36. [ʍ]	..	..	..	..	..
37. [w]	..	..	..	..	..
38. [j]	..	..	..	..	..
*39. [tʃ]	..	..	..	..	..
*40. [dʒ]	..	..	..	..	..

space for noting errors on all the common sounds of General American speech (excepting [ə], which is almost never defective and is adequately surveyed when [ʌ] is examined). When testing articulation, the exact nature of the deviations should be recorded; it is not sufficient merely to indicate that sounds are faulty. To facilitate this process, spaces are provided after each symbol under headings that describe the major articulatory errors, so that the examiner can write in his observation, e.g., a phonetic symbol or a descriptive term, in the proper column. It is necessary to employ materials that are adapted to the age and reading level of the subject. For that reason separate sets of sentences are provided below for adult and primary readers, and a list of words for picture-test construction is added. The materials are numbered to correspond to the symbols on the examination form.

SENTENCES FOR ARTICULATION EXAMINATION: ADULT READERS

These sentences are long and somewhat difficult, but they make possible a detailed analysis. The vowel and diphthong sentences contain words in which vowel errors are common; the consonant sentences illustrate each sound in all positions.

1. Some people reason that "seeing is believing." They feel that they are frequently deceived.

2. Bill saw a big pickerel swimming in the ripples. He licked his lips in anticipation of a delicious fish dinner.

3. Several veteran members of the Senate expressed displeasure. Special legislation to regulate the selling of eggs was not necessary, they said.

4. Sally banged the black Packard into a taxicab. It was badly damaged by the crash.

5. I am unable to understand my Uncle Gus. He mutters and mumbles about nothing.

6. John started across the yard toward the barn. His father remarked calmly that he'd better not wander too far.

7. Is Shaw the author of "Walking on the Lawn"? I thought it was Walter Hall.

8. Captain Hook pushed through the bushes to the brook. From where he stood it looked like an ambush.

9. As a rule we go canoeing in the forenoon. The pool is too cool in June.

10. Hugh refused to join the musicians' union. His excuse was viewed with amusement.

11. Don't go home alone in the snow. You'll be cold and soaked and half frozen.

12. Fowler wants to plow all the ground around his house. Somehow I doubt if the council will allow it.

13. The agent remained away all day. Late at night he made his way to the place where the sailors stayed.

14. The tile workers were fighting for higher prices and more time off. They tried to drive back the strike breakers.

15. The boys toiled noisily in the boiling sun. They enjoyed the work that Roy avoided.

16. Mr. Miller had climbed many mountains. But the bottomless chasm that he glimpsed dimly before him was the mightiest in his memory.

17. Laden down by their burdens, Dan and Ned ran from the barn into the open. Their keen senses warned them that the tornado was not far distant.

18. The monks singing in the evening light had no inkling that anything was wrong. Suddenly the strong tones of the gong rang out.

19. Part way up the slope above the pool was a popular camping spot. Many people stopped there for picnic suppers among the pines.

20. The British were not bothered about the robbery. They believed that they could bribe the Arab to betray his tribe.

21. After waiting for twenty minutes the train left the station for the western front. The veterans went to sleep, but the excited recruits sat and talked all night.

22. The doll's red dress was soiled and muddy, but the ragged child hugged it adoringly.

23. Old Katy had a particular dislike for hawks and crows. She called them "wicked creatures."

24. As the big dog began to dig under the log, Gary forgot his hunger and grabbed his gun.

*25. Early every summer our barn is covered with brilliant red roses. The broad crimson roof draws admiring crowds from far and near.

*26. Lawyer Clark held his little felt hat and his black gloves in his lap. He silently placed the valise containing the wills on the table.

27. "For breakfast," said father, "I find that coffee is the staff of life. I refuse to be softened by all this foolishness about half a grapefruit."

28. I believe I'll save this heavy veil. The vogue might be revived eventually.

*29. We thought that the theory about the death of the author was pathetic. But we had faith that something would lead to the truth.

*30. My father finds it hard to breathe in this weather. Even the heather withers.

*31. The successful student of voice in speech does not assume that class exercise is sufficient. He also practices by himself outside of class.

*32. My cousin's play "The Zero Zone" is pleasant and amusing. But it won't be chosen for a prize because it doesn't deserve it.

*33. A flash of lightning showed the fishing ship in the shallows close to shore. With one great crushing motion the ocean dashed it against the shoal.

*34. Even before the explosion at the garage the Persian made a casual allusion to sabotage.

35. Hurry back anyhow, Harry. It will help if you only hear half of the rehearsal.

*36. "What is that?" he whispered. Somewhere from the left came the whistle of a bobwhite.

37. Wait until the weather is warm. Then everyone will want to walk in the woods.

38. Did you ever speculate on the comparative uses and values of onions and yellow yams?

*39. Mitchell was a righteous old bachelor. He watched for a chance to chase the children out of his cherry orchard.

*40. All but Judge Johnson pledged allegiance to the new legislation. He objected because it was unjust to the soldiers in his region.

SENTENCES FOR ARTICULATION EXAMINATION: PRIMARY READERS

The following sentences contain only words that are to be found in the vocabularies of average first- and second-grade children, according to at least one of the investigations summarized by Buckingham and Dolch in *A Combined Word List* (see Bibliography). The only exceptions are the few proper names and the sentence for [ʒ], which consonant is rare in the primary vocabulary except in the combination [dʒ]. This group of sentences is also suitable for the testing of poor adult readers.

1. She feeds the three geese. They eat peas and beans and seeds.

2. Give Dick the tin dish. It is filled with pins and rings.

3. Ted spent ten cents for eggs. He left them under the red bed.

4. The black cat sat on the hat. Dan patted him on the back.

5. Mother said, "Run and get some butter. We must not eat mud for supper."

6. Don wanted a car. Bob wanted a doll.

7. Walk along the wall. Can you see the ball on the lawn?

8. Our cook hit her foot on the wood. So she put the book on the table.

9. Ruth had two shoes. One was blue.

10. Do you like music? A few boys do not.

11. Oh, it is so cold in the snow. Let us go home by the stove.

12. The brown cow looked at the house. Out came a mouse.

13. James ate the cake. But he stayed away from the table.

14. I have a white kite. It can fly high in the sky.

15. The boy saw Roy. So Roy hid his toys.

16. When summer comes, Mary moves to the farm. We stay home and swim.

17. Guess what the man with the gun found in the nest. A spoon, a penny and ten nuts.

18. The king had a ring on his finger. He rang the bell a long time.

19. Peter drew an apple and a pig. Then he put the pencil on top of the paper.

20. Bobby was a big boy. He had a black bird, two rabbits and a boat.

21. Ted had a little cat with white feet. He fed it meat on a plate.

22. Old Ed got down off the red ladder. He called his dog and went away into the woods.

23. Dick filled his pockets with cookies and crackers. When the clock struck he ran out the back door.

24. The girl found a big dog in her wagon. "Go away! Go away!" she said.

*25. Harry read a story about a rabbit. A bird who had no feathers was in the same story.

*26. Little girls like to play with dolls. Boys like to play ball.

27. Fred found a calf on the farm. He also found five goldfish and saw a butterfly.

28. I have put on my gloves. Now we can shovel coal into the seven stoves.

*29. The trees are thick on both sides of the path. Do you think you can see anything?

*30. My brother likes this red feather but not that one. So do father and mother.

*31. Sister eats soup and ice cream with a spoon. She also likes to sew her dress.

*32. The bees are always buzzing in my ears. Their music makes me lazy.

*33. While she washed the dishes the men fished. Then she looked for shells along the shore.

*34. On this occasion the treasure was found in the usual place.

.35. Harry held his hat in one hand. He said, "I have a horse at my house."

*36. Which wheel came off? Was it the white one? Where did it go?

37. We wash our windows with soap and water. Are we doing it the right way?

38. You may not play in the yard yet. You may play there next year.

*39. The child sat in a chair in the kitchen. He watched the teacher choose some matches and a piece of cheese.

*40. Jimmy ate bread and jam and two oranges. He put a jar of jelly in his pocket.

ARTICULATION TEST FOR NON-READERS

All words in the following list are from an investigation of pre-school vocabulary by the Child Study Committee of the International Kindergarten Union (see Bibliography), in which the verbal responses of children to pictures were tabulated. By choosing a set of pictures that will elicit at least one word from each group a picture test can be constructed which permits a complete inventory of the articulation of a non-reading child, with the possible exception of [ju] and [ʒ] in all positions, initial [z], medial [ʍ], [w], [j], and final [ð], sounds that are difficult to obtain from all children by reason of their infrequency. It is desirable to test the consonants in all positions and words are provided for this purpose, but if a shorter form is necessary the medial positions are advised. Since responses cannot be predicted in all cases, several words should be prepared for each sound. The testing procedure usually can be turned into a game in which the child identifies objects pointed out in the pictures. The examiner should speak as little as possible, and during an attempt to elicit any word he should avoid stimulating the child with the sound that he wants to observe.

1. [i]:   trees, green, feet, sleep, meat, cheese
2. [ɪ]:   pig, fish, pink, chicken, pillow
3. [ɛ]:   bed, red, steps, head, sled, feather, dress
4. [æ]:   hat, black, Santa, basket, grass, can
5. [ʌ]:   butterfly, rug, tub, running, nuts, gun, gloves, button
6. [ɑ]:   clock, block, stocking, arms, stars, yard

7. [ɔ]: ball, horse, saw, horn, auto
8. [ʊ]: book, foot, football, cooking
9. [u]: blue, shoe, tooth, spoon, stool, two, moon
10. [ju]: Infrequent and difficult to elicit. Omit, or try *mew* from picture of small cat.
11. [oʊ]: comb, stove, coat, boat, soldier, snow
12. [aʊ]: house, towel, flower, brown, clown, mouse
13. [eɪ]: cake, skates, baby, plate, grapes, tail, table
14. [ɑɪ]: ice cream, pipe, tire, white, knife, kite, eye
15. [ɔɪ]: boy, toys
16. [m] Initial: mouse, meat, mother, man, matches, moon
      Medial: tomatoes, watermelon, woman, Christmas tree, hammer
      Final: arm, swim, comb, ice cream
17. [n] Initial: nuts, knife, nest, neck
      Medial: candle, raining, running, doughnuts
      Final: man, Indian, apron, woman, gun, spoon, wagon
18. [ŋ] Medial: finger, blanket, singing, swinging, drinking, donkey
      Final: swing, ring, tongue, string
19. [p] Initial: paper, puppy, pillow, pig, pencil, pail
      Medial: airplane, apple, apron, jumping rope, sleeping
      Final: pipe, jumping rope, cap
20. [b] Initial: bird, baby, butter, bed, boat, boy
      Medial: rabbit, umbrella, ribbon, table, baby
      Final: tub, bib
21. [t] Initial: tooth, tub, tire, tree, tail, table
      Medial: butter, kitten, kitty, letter, button
      Final: toothpaste, white, feet, meat, cat
22. [d] Initial: dog, doll, dress, drink, duck
      Medial: radio, teddy bear, candle, Indian, ladder
      Final: head, sled, hand, red, bed, bird, bread, wood
23. [k] Initial: cake, cookie, candle, can, comb, key
      Medial: chicken, basket, crackers, cookie, pocket, stockings

	Final:	cake, black, clock, book, rake
24. [g]	Initial:	gun, green, grass, gloves, grapes
	Medial:	wagon, doggie, buggy, digging
	Final:	dog, rug, pig, egg, flag
*25. [r]	Initial:	rabbit, rug, red, running, raining, radio, rake
	Medial:	apron, umbrella, carrots, barrel, carrying
	Final:	soldier, car, tire, teddy bear
	Stressed Syllabic:	bird, shirt, girl, skirt, worm
	Unstressed Syllabic:	butter, feather, watermelon, finger, paper, ladder
*26. [l]	Initial:	letter, ladder, leaf, lips, lady, leg
	Medial:	telephone, pillow, yellow
	Final:	ball, stool, tail, wheel, pail, doll
	Unstressed Syllabic:	candle, table, bicycle, bottle
27. [f]	Initial:	fire, flowers, finger, flag, foot, feather, fence
	Medial:	butterfly, laughing, telephone, elephant
	Final:	leaf, knife, roof, golf, half
28. [v]	Initial:	vase, violin, valentine, violet, Victrola
	Medial:	seven, shovel, cover, covers, driving, river
	Final:	stove, drive, five, sleeve
*29. [θ]	Initial:	thread, three, thimble, thumb
	Medial:	toothbrush, bathtub, birthday
	Final:	teeth, tooth, bath, mouth
*30. [ð]	Initial:	that one, this one, the bird, these, those
	Medial:	feather, father, mother, brother
	Final:	Infrequent and difficult to elicit.
*31. [s]	Initial:	soup, sister, sleep, sled, saw, stove, spoon
	Medial:	basket, ice cream, glasses, bicycle, sister
	Final:	glass, face, grass, mouse, house, dress
*32. [z]	Initial:	Infrequent and difficult to elicit. Omit, or try *zebra* or *zoo*.
	Medial:	roses, scissors, music, raisins
	Final:	cheese, nose, ears, eyes
*33. [ʃ]	Initial:	shoe, shirt, sheep, shelf, shoulder
	Medial:	washing, fishing, dishes, pushing
	Final·	fish, dish, brush

*34. [ʒ]   Medial: Infrequent and difficult to elicit. Omit, or try *measure*.

            Final: Infrequent and difficult to elicit.

35. [h]   Initial: hand, hair, head, hat, house

            Medial: yellow hair, birdhouse, playhouse

*36. [ʍ]   Initial: wheel, whistle, wheelbarrow, white

            Medial: Infrequent and difficult to elicit. Omit, or try *black and white* or *horsewhip*.

37. [w]   Initial: wagon, water, watermelon, washing, waves

            Medial: Infrequent and difficult to elicit. Omit, or try *sandwich* or *bow-wow*.

38. [j]   Initial: yellow, yesterday, yard

            Medial: Infrequent and difficult to elicit. Omit, or try *onions* or *barnyard*.

*39. [tʃ]   Initial: church, chair, chicken, cheese

            Medial: kitchen, matches, teacher

            Final: match, watch, catch

*40. [dʒ]   Initial: juice, jumping

            Medial: oranges, engine

            Final: orange, bridge, badge

A "SHORT" ARTICULATION TEST

When examining large groups it is sometimes necessary to give short tests that concentrate on those sounds that are most likely to be defective. This can be done with some validity by observing the vowels, diphthongs, nasals and stop-plosives in an oral reading performance and, if they are not obviously defective, restricting the detailed articulation examination to the consonants [r], [l], [θ], [ð], [s], [z], [ʃ], [ʒ], [ʍ], [tʃ], and [dʒ]. On the examination form and in the corresponding test materials these consonants are marked with asterisks.

DIRECTIONS FOR DRILL PROCEDURE

Although certain principles are common to the training and retraining of all aspects of audible speech, the specific methods may differ greatly. Thus certain disorders of voice seem to yield most readily to practice on sustained tones, while others can be approached successfully only in connected speech. Because of this lack of uniformity a general statement of directions would appear to be impractical for the materials on phonetic transcription, pronunciation, breathing and the various aspects of voice. Instead, specific directions are given where they are needed throughout the text.

In working on the individual speech sounds, however, the differences in procedure are less marked, and it will be observed that the drill materials on vowels, diphthongs and consonants in Chapters II, III and IV follow outlines that are essentially similar. These similarities make the following general suggestions and directions feasible, and considerable unnecessary repetition is thereby avoided.

In the chapters mentioned the materials on each speech sound are arranged in ascending order of complexity, beginning with isolated articulation and working up to use in connected speech. When articulating a sound in *isolation* it is valuable to start with prolonged examples, since you can listen carefully, make the necessary adjustments and perceive the positions of your articulators. Sustain the sound as long as possible on one breath each time and repeat until you have produced at least ten successful prolongations. Then articulate at least 25 accurate staccato examples of the sound. When working on non-continuant sounds, i.e., sounds that cannot be sustained, attempt only staccato examples.

In the *writing-sounding* technique you articulate the sound and simultaneously write its phonetic symbol, a further step in identifying and isolating the sound. The most important aspects of the process are accuracy of articulation, simultaneity of writing and sounding, and rhythmical repetition. Begin to articulate the sound at the instant that you begin to write the symbol and stop articulating just as you finish the symbol. Repeat this rhythmically many times, listening carefully to the sound. Produce a series of prolonged examples first; then a series of staccato articulations. Write the symbol as slowly or as rapidly as you articulate. The process of writing-sounding diphthongs, stopplosives, glides and combinations is slightly different from the procedure described. Instructions are given in the appropriate chapters.

The major aim in the construction of *nonsense syllables* is practice in joining one sound to other sounds. Routines will be found in which each vowel and diphthong is combined with five of the less difficult consonants and each consonant with five typical vowels. In these routines the dashes indicate pauses. Taking initial [i] joined to [p] as an example, the form [i-i-p] calls for [i], pause, [i], pause, [p]; [i-p] for [i], pause, [p]; [ip] for [i] joined to [p] normally, as in a word such as *sleep*. Ordinarily it is best to practice one position at a time and to work in order of increasing difficulty. Usually the initial position is easiest, the final position next, and the medial position most difficult, but this order is not invariable, and the procedure should be adapted to suit individual needs. No nonsense syllable drills are given for initial [ŋ] and [ʒ] or for final [h], [ʍ], [w] and [j], since they never occur in these positions in words.

Separate *word lists* are provided to illustrate the various positions in which the speech sounds occur. Attention should be called to the fact that usually the first ten words in each list are suitable for work with children, since they were selected from the first- and second-grade vocabulary list of Buckingham and Dolch (see above: Sentences for Articulation Examination: Primary Readers). Certain sounds are rare in the primary vocabulary, however, and because of that fact children's lists have not been attempted for initial [ju], [ɑɪ], [z], medial [ju], [ʒ], [h], [ʍ], [j], final [ə], [ju], [ɑʊ], [ɔɪ], [ð], [ʒ], and syllabic [m]. In addition to the basic word lists for both children and adults the consonants [r], [l], [s] and [ʃ] have special lists, designed to place these consonants before the various vowels and diphthongs so that they may be practiced systematically in varied environments. It is a common finding, for example, that an accurate [s] is more readily produced before a front vowel than before a back vowel, while the reverse appears to be true for [ʃ]. Also included at appropriate places in the consonant chapter are short lists of the common consonant blends.

The act of *distinguishing* a given sound from other sounds is facilitated by practice on words that are similar except for the sounds under consideration. Thus, for example, the consonants [d] and [t] in *wading-waiting* have identical phonetic environments, and the distinctive qualities of the similar sounds stand out clearly. Wherever possible such double lists of "word pairs" are given for the common substitutions.

The first five *sentences* for each sound were constructed from the same first- and second-grade vocabulary that was used for the primary articulation examination and the children's word lists. A few common proper names have been added. For the consonant [ʒ] only adult sentences were written, since this sound is infrequent at the younger reading level.

Although no specific directions are given in the chapters on articulation, there are numerous devices which assist the student to *habituate* the use of a newly learned correct sound in his casual speech. Useful for this purpose are assignments such as oral reading of simple material with all occurrences of the sound underlined, followed by oral reading of unmarked material; speaking before a small group on a topic that will necessitate frequent use of the sound, e.g., the person with [s] difficulty may speak on voiceless consonants, the Mississippi, success, selecting subjects for speeches, etc.; conversing with friends on such topics; asking information from a stranger; deliberately "faking" the error in each of the above situations.

Since the speaker's check on the accuracy of his articulation is his own auditory perception, it is obvious that a keen auditory image of the distinctive characteristics of any sound, and of the limits within which it may vary before it is confused with some other sound, is of primary importance in any of the above practice situations. In this regard the concept of the *phoneme* is helpful. Variations may be heard between different examples of the same speech sound, but if these variations are small enough so that there is no confusion as to what speech sound is being produced, all of the sounds are said to belong to the same phoneme. Wide variations within the phoneme are acceptable as far as intelligibility is concerned, but from the aesthetic standpoint it is desirable that each speech sound be as *typical* of its phoneme as possible. For example, in a given instance the vowel [æ] in *sat* may approach the [ɛ] phoneme, i.e., it stays within the [æ] phoneme but is somewhat similar in sound to [ɛ]. In spite of the fact that the variation is non-distinctive, that the word still sounds more like *sat* than *set*, this particular variant of [æ] is not so typical of its phoneme as an example of [æ] which bears no resemblance to [ɛ] or to any vowel other than [æ]. A few such variations in the speech of an individual may be unimportant, but when they occur in large numbers they produce a cumulative effect that is unpleasant to many listeners. Accepting the fact that it is impossible to produce consciously two examples of a speech sound that are absolutely identical, try to make all practice repetitions of any given sound as representative of the phoneme to which that sound belongs as possible.

BIBLIOGRAPHY

1. Bender, J. F., and Kleinfeld, V. M., *Speech Correction Manual*, Farrar & Rinehart, Inc., New York, 1936.

2. Buckingham, B. R., and Dolch, E. W., *A Combined Word List*, Ginn and Company, Boston, 1936.

3. International Kindergarten Union, Child Study Committee, *A Study of the Vocabulary of Children before Entering the First Grade*, Baltimore, 1928.

4. Travis, L. E., *Speech Pathology*, D. Appleton-Century Company, Inc., New York, 1931.

5. Van Riper, C., *Speech Correction Principles and Methods*, Prentice-Hall, Inc., New York, 1930.

6. West, R., Kennedy, L., and Carr, A., *The Rehabilitation of Speech*, Harper & Brothers, New York, 1937.

CHAPTER I

PHONETIC TRANSCRIPTION

A phonetic alphabet is a device to provide partial indication of how language sounds when it is spoken. It employs for this purpose a number of symbols which represent by agreement relatively fixed speech sounds or phonemes, and its essential principle is that one and only one symbol represents one and only one phoneme. It avoids to a large degree the ambiguities of ordinary spelling.

Unfortunately, however, scrutiny of the alphabets presented in the literature reveals that this principle has broken down in practice, and that there are almost as many phonetic alphabets as there are textbooks which present them. In order that this drillbook may be as universally intelligible as possible to students acquainted with other alphabets, the alphabet given below is the result of a survey of the speech sounds and phonetic symbols presented by 21 current textbooks of speech which employ forms of the International Phonetic Alphabet. With a few exceptions each sound included in the resulting alphabet was deemed necessary of symbolization by at least half, and usually all, of the texts surveyed; the phonetic symbols are those used most frequently by the texts to represent the sounds. Exceptions to these criteria are as follows:

1. Duration modifiers, i.e., dots following vowels to indicate varying degrees of length, although frequently used, were found to be superfluous, since only one instance occurred in which two different sounds were represented most frequently by symbols which were alike except for the modifier. For purposes of this book, therefore, modifiers are not used, the one case of confusion being reconciled in a manner described immediately below.

2. The symbol [ə], unmodified, was employed universally to

represent the first vowel of *ago*, while the same symbol, plus a duration modifier, was found to be the most frequent transcription of the vowel in British *bird*. Since it was deemed desirable to eliminate modifiers, for reasons already explained, the symbol [ɜ], the second most frequent transcription of the latter sound, was adopted.

3. The consonant-vowel combination [ju] was listed separately by fewer than one-half of the texts, its transcription being provided for by the symbols [j] and [u]. Since it deserves individual recognition in drill, it is presented below together with the other symbols.

4. In the case of the diphthong of *die* the survey showed [aɪ] to be listed most frequently. It will be noted that a departure from this most frequent practice is made here, it being the general observation that [ɑɪ] is more common in General American speech. It may be added that diphthongs should not, of course, be regarded as fixed, invariable combinations of certain vowels. In the transcription of any diphthong, vowel symbols should be used which represent as accurately as possible the vowels which compose the particular example under consideration.

PHONETIC ALPHABET

Vowels		Diphthongs		Consonants			
[i]	beat	[oʊ]	foal	[m]	sum, prism	[s]	seal
[ɪ]	bit	[aʊ]	fowl	[n]	sun, prison	[z]	zeal
[ɛ]	bet	[eɪ]	fail	[ŋ]	sung	[ʃ]	mesh
[æ]	bat	[ɑɪ]	file	[p]	pole	[ʒ]	measure
[ʌ]	above	[ɔɪ]	foil	[b]	bowl	[h]	how
[ə]	above	*[ɪə]	beer	[t]	toll	[ʍ]	whet
[ɑ]	calm	*[ɛə]	bear	[d]	dole	[w]	wet
[ɔ]	fall	*[ɔə]	bore	[k]	coal	[j]	yet
[ʊ]	full	*[ʊə]	boor	[g]	goal		
[u]	fool			[r]	red, batter, bird		
*[e]	bait			[l]	led, battle		
*[o]	boat			[f]	fat	Combinations	
*[a]	ask			[v]	vat	[ju]	fuel
*[ɜ]	bird			[θ]	thigh	[tʃ]	choke
*[ɒ]	hot			[ð]	thy	[dʒ]	joke

This alphabet includes all symbols that are required for broad transcription of American speech. Those preceded by asterisks will be needed only rarely in the transcription of General American. In this dialect [e] and [o] are commonly diphthongized to [eɪ] and [oʊ]; [a], intermediate in sound between [æ] and [ɑ], is infrequent; [ɜ], a middle vowel somewhat similar to [ə], is likewise uncommon, being heard chiefly in those dialect regions where it replaces the stressed syllabic [r̩] or [ər] of General American; [ɒ], which combines the qualities of [ɑ] and [ɔ], is rare; [ɪə], [ɛə], [ɔə] and [ʊə], also heard as [iə], [eə], [oə] and [uə], are diphthongs formed in regions where final [r] is replaced by [ə].

The phonetic alphabet uses 16 of the 21 consonants of the written English alphabet to symbolize the same sounds that they commonly represent in spelled words. These letters are as follows: m, n, p, b, t, d, k, g, r, l, f, v, s, z, h and w. In the case of such letters as g and s, which are pronounced in two or more different ways in spelled words, that one of the sounds which the symbol has been chosen to represent is made clear by the examples above. Of the remaining five consonants of the written alphabet, c, q, x and y are omitted entirely, since all the sounds that they symbolize in spelling are represented by other phonetic symbols, e.g., x as in *exercise* by [ks], etc. The pronunciation of written English j likewise is adequately represented by other symbols, but this letter is retained as a phonetic symbol to represent the first consonant of *yes*. In addition to the 16 consonants which are taken over directly from the written alphabet, six consonant symbols that are new to the English student are used: [ŋ], [θ], [ð], [ʃ], [ʒ], and [ʍ]. The sounds which they represent are exemplified above by the key-words of the phonetic alphabet. The five written vowel letters all are used as phonetic symbols, but they represent only the five phonemes that are specified by the examples above, and these five are not the ones that an American ordinarily associates with the letters a, e, i, o, u. Other symbols are added to represent the rest of the spoken vowels. The diphthongs and combinations are constructed from the vowel and consonant elements.

Phonetic transcription has two chief values. In the first place, it applies to the recording of spoken language a method that is much more exact than ordinary spelling, and is thus an important tool for the student of speech. Its other major contribution derives from the fact that in mastering the use of this technique the student necessarily develops increased attentiveness to his own speech and to that of others, both essential steps in the process of speech improvement. If you are to practice accurate transcription the first principle to learn is that you must *transcribe speech as it is spoken*, not necessarily as you think it should be spoken. Do not transcribe a word as if it were composed of sounds that can be predicted in advance from some idealized concept of the word's pronunciation; do not transcribe sentences as if they were simply strings of isolated words spoken one at a time, unless, of course, they are spoken in that manner. Sounds may be replaced or omitted, other sounds may be inserted, a word may have an entirely different phonetic structure in connected speech than it has when pronounced in isolation. As an example, pronounce the word *and* carefully and alone; then say *men and women* as you do in conversation and observe how the word changes phonetically when it is used in the phrase. Divorce phonetic transcription from spelling as soon as possible. Associate the phonetic symbol directly with the sound, not with some typical spelling and that in turn with the sound. Unless you can learn to ignore spelling, most of your transcriptions of such words as *board*, *care*, *coffee*, *fear*, *learn*, *misses*, *pure*, *raced* and *sink* will be incorrect, because in typical, connected American speech not one of these words is "pronounced the way it is spelled."

As you perform the drills of this chapter, however, and begin to learn the phonetic alphabet, do not allow your own particular pronunciations of the materials to prevent you from associating the right sounds with the right symbols. The materials will not necessarily agree with your own pronunciations, although they will approximate them closely, nor do they purport to exemplify the only possible correct pronunciation of the words. Rather do they take advantage of the relative consistency with which certain sounds are produced by the majority of General American speakers in certain words, as a device to illustrate, in the case of each symbol, that phoneme which is to be represented by that symbol. Therefore, as you transcribe the word lists you should attempt to use, *for purposes of learning the symbols*, pronunciations which exemplify the sounds.

In regard to the mechanics of phonetic transcription certain practices may be outlined as follows:

1. The script forms of the symbols that you will use in transcribing differ slightly from the printed symbols. Consult your instructor for these differences.

2. To indicate accent in polysyllabic words place short vertical strokes ['] *above* the line immediately before syllables having primary accent, i.e., the heaviest accent of the word; place similar marks [ˌ] *below* the line immediately before syllables having a secondary accent, i.e., the next to the heaviest accent of the word; leave unaccented syllables unmarked. Observe that the accent mark comes *before* the syllable, not after it.

3. To indicate an unstressed syllabic consonant place a dot under the consonant symbol, as [m̩], [n̩], [r̩], [l̩]; for stressed syllabic consonants, of which there is only one, [r̲], underline the symbol. In some systems [ɝ] is used to symbolize this vowel-like sound.

4. Differentiate transcriptions from other material by enclosing them in brackets.

5. Punctuate your transcriptions, but for obvious reasons attempt no capitalization.

In introducing the phonetic symbols one at a time, drills 1 to 5 employ the cumulative method. That is, after a given symbol has been introduced and a practice list has been provided, knowledge of that symbol is assumed and sounds which necessitate its use occur at random thereafter. However, no symbol will be needed for the transcription of any word until after an exercise has been provided for that symbol. For each symbol two lists of words are given. The first list, which is referred to hereafter as list 1, is presented in phonetic symbols and is designed to illustrate the phoneme under consideration; list 2 is printed in the written English alphabet and furnishes opportunities to use the symbol which represents that phoneme.

1. This exercise presents the vowel symbols. It assumes that the 16 consonant symbols [m], [n], [p], [b], [t], [d], [k], [g], [r], [l], [f], [v], [s], [z], [h], [w], are familiar from the written alphabet. As you consider each vowel symbol and its corresponding phoneme the following steps will help you to associate the two.[1]

a. Scrutinize the symbol; note how it differs from other similar symbols; practice writing it. Be especially careful to distinguish [ɪ] from [i] and [ʊ] from [u].

b. Read list 2 aloud, listening carefully to the vowel which is common to all words of the list. If you think you are producing it incorrectly consult your instructor for help. Don't expect all examples of the vowel to be absolutely identical; you couldn't make them so if you tried. Even though they differ slightly you will still use the same symbol in broad transcription, unless the differences are so great that another phoneme is involved. If that happens in the following lists your pronunciation is probably incorrect.

c. Translate list 1 aloud, observing how the symbol is used and attempting to associate it with the vowel phoneme under consideration. Record these translations in conventional spelling if you wish.

d. Lastly, write in the appropriate spaces your phonetic transcriptions of the words in list 2. One and only one vowel symbol will be needed for the words of each list, the only exceptions being the two-syllable words provided for [ə], where the vowels of the stressed syllables vary.

[1] If, in addition to the major vowels for which drills are provided, you wish to practice transcription of [a], [ɒ] and [ɜ], consult other sections of the book as follows: for [a] see the vowel [æ] in Chapter V, Alternatives and Errors Related to Phonetic Structure; for [ɒ] see the vowels [ɑ] and [ɔ] in the same chapter and section; for [ɜ] see stressed syllabic [r̩] below.

1. [i]

[wid]	need	_____
[bid]	reek	_____
[fit]	peak	_____
[did]	veal	_____
[gis]	zeal	_____
[hit]	team	_____
[kip]	feed	_____
[lis]	heel	_____
[mit]	mean	_____
[sid]	seep	_____

2. [ɪ]

[wɪt]	knit	_____
[sɪk]	tin	_____
[mɪl]	pick	_____
[lɪp]	vim	_____
[kɪd]	rip	_____
[hɪm]	lid	_____
[gɪv]	bib	_____
[dɪp]	miss	_____
[bɪn]	pin	_____
[fɪt]	dig	_____

3. [ɛ]

[gɛt]	hem	_____
[hɛn]	deck	_____
[dɛd]	tell	_____
[lɛd]	said	_____
[mɛs]	well	_____
[sɛt]	head	_____
[rɛk]	sell	_____
[bɛl]	guess	_____
[wɛd]	net	_____
[fɛd]	men	_____

4. [æ]

[sæd]	hag	_____
[hæm]	gap	_____
[mæp]	nab	_____
[ræk]	tack	_____
[sæk]	lag	_____
[sæt]	fan	_____
[kæn]	gnat	_____
[pæk]	pan	_____
[tæp]	rat	_____
[pæl]	bad	_____

5. [ɑ]

[pɑm]	psalm	_____
[tɑm]	mar	_____
[kɑm]	loll	_____
[bɑm]	con	_____
[pɑr]	don	_____

[dɑl]	far	_____
[hɑrd]	qualm	_____
[fɑrm]	mom	_____
[ɑrk]	harm	_____
[bɑr]	tar	_____

6. [ɔ]

[kɔ]	raw	_____
[lɔ]	flaw	_____
[ɔl]	gauze	_____
[bɔl]	hawk	_____
[pɔn]	tall	_____
[sɔs]	haul	_____
[dɔn]	fall	_____
[drɔ]	sawed	_____
[wɔl]	gnaw	_____
[kɔl]	salt	_____

7. [ʊ]

[hʊd]	cook	_____
[pʊt]	wood	_____
[krʊk]	could	_____
[nʊk]	hook	_____
[fʊt]	pull	_____
[brʊk]	would	_____
[gʊd]	full	_____
[tʊk]	rook	_____
[wʊl]	bull	_____
[bʊk]	took	_____

8. [u]

[fud]	soon	_____
[mun]	move	_____
[luz]	fool	_____
[rut]	cool	_____
[nun]	soup	_____
[but]	toot	_____
[swun]	loon	_____
[bun]	croon	_____
[spun]	tool	_____
[rum]	coon	_____

9. [ʌ]

[nʌt]	fun	_____
[sʌn]	love	_____
[slʌm]	numb	_____
[rʌnt]	stunt	_____
[klʌmzɪ]	punt	_____
[rʌb]	cut	_____
[blʌnt]	funny	_____
[bʌn]	sonny	_____
[hʌnt]	dove	_____
[mʌnɪ]	hut	_____

10. [ə]

[əlɑrm]	ado	_____
[ənʌl]	apart	_____
[ərɛst]	agree	_____
[əpɔl]	abed	_____
[əpis]	above	_____

[ərinə]	dogma	_____
[zibrə]	stanza	_____
[mɑmə]	vista	_____
[kæmərə]	manna	_____
[drɑmə]	tuba	_____

2. Knowledge of the 16 familiar consonant symbols and of the above ten vowel symbols is assumed in this exercise on diphthong transcription. Two new vowels, [e] and [o], which are heard only in diphthongs in most American speech, are introduced. Observe the following steps as you attempt to master each symbol.

    a. Scrutinize the symbol; compare it to the other symbols; practice writing it.

    b. Read list 2 aloud and listen carefully, noting the two vowel elements of which the diphthong is composed.

    c. Translate list 1 aloud.

    d. Record your transcriptions of the words in list 2.

1. [oʊ]			2. [aʊ]		
[roʊ]	sew	_____	[haʊnd]	gout	_____
[boʊt]	goad	_____	[gaʊn]	round	_____
[toʊd]	dote	_____	[saʊnd]	house	_____
[stoʊv]	poke	_____	[maʊs]	rowdy	_____
[loʊd]	home	_____	[fraʊn]	down	_____
[oʊd]	ghost	_____	[klaʊd]	found	_____
[toʊst]	cope	_____	[aʊl]	blouse	_____
[koʊl]	soak	_____	[əbaʊt]	pout	_____
[voʊg]	tote	_____	[staʊt]	now	_____
[woʊ]	soul	_____	[daʊdɪ]	foul	_____

3. [eɪ]					
[meɪ]	fate	_____	[keɪs]	trait	_____
[leɪt]	wait	_____	[deɪt]	race	_____
[steɪt]	gain	_____	[seɪm]	base	_____
[peɪn]	sale	_____	[neɪl]	came	_____
[heɪst]	weigh	_____	[kweɪl]	lace	_____

4. [aɪ]

[saɪ]	high	_____
[laɪn]	sign	_____
[raɪm]	wine	_____
[praɪd]	lime	_____
[haɪd]	prime	_____
[saɪt]	ride	_____
[kraɪm]	light	_____
[naɪ]	pine	_____
[əraɪ]	bite	_____
[taɪt]	guide	_____

5. [ɔɪ]

[əhɔɪ]	soil	_____
[tɔɪl]	annoy	_____
[lɔɪn]	coy	_____
[bɔɪ]	quoit	_____
[kɔɪn]	poise	_____
[bɔɪl]	coil	_____
[fɔɪl]	alloy	_____
[ədrɔɪt]	destroy	_____
[pɔɪnt]	void	_____
[nɔɪz]	toy	_____

3. This drill introduces seven new consonant symbols. It assumes knowledge of the 16 familiar consonants, the ten major vowels and the five major diphthongs. Before transcribing the words for [ʒ] it may be helpful to consult drill 5. As you learn each symbol adopt the following procedure:

a. Practice writing the symbol. Differentiate [ŋ] from [n], [ʃ] from [s], [ʍ] from [m].
b. Identify the phoneme by reading list 2 aloud.
c. Translate list 1.
d. Transcribe your pronunciations of the words in list 2.

1. [θ]

[tuθ]	thaw	_____
[kɪθ]	thane	_____
[riθ]	both	_____
[θɪk]	heath	_____
[θroʊ]	south	_____
[mɪθ]	health	_____
[θif]	thumb	_____
[θri]	thong	_____
[θʌg]	thought	_____
[θɪn]	thread	_____

2. [ð]

[raɪð]	thou	_____
[sið]	thee	_____
[ðoʊz]	soothe	_____
[ðaɪn]	thy	_____
[ðæn]	loathe	_____
[ðoʊ]	bathe	_____
[taɪð]	breathe	_____
[beɪð]	though	_____
[ðʌs]	this	_____
[ðɛm]	those	_____

3. [ʃ]

[ʃɪp]	shun	_____
[hæʃ]	shell	_____
[ʃɑɪn]	shag	_____
[ʃɪn]	sheik	_____
[ʃeɪv]	mush	_____
[ʃæm]	shame	_____
[hʌʃ]	shall	_____
[wɪʃ]	shape	_____
[ʃeɪk]	sheep	_____
[ʃɛd]	fish	_____

4. [ʒ]

[ruʒ]	menage	_____
[beɪʒ]	erosion	_____
[mɪrɑʒ]	derision	_____
[vɪʒn]	evasion	_____
[gərɑʒ]	casual	_____
[dɪluʒn]	rouging	_____
[dɪsɪʒn]	potage	_____
[kɔrsɑʒ]	intrusion	_____
[prɛstiʒ]	revision	_____
[liʒn]	adhesion	_____

5. [ʍ]

[ʍɪl]	whip	_____
[ʍɑɪl]	wheeze	_____
[ʍɪsk]	whet	_____
[ʍɪm]	white	_____
[ʍɑɪn]	whey	_____
[ʍɪst]	whelm	_____
[ʍɔrf]	whit	_____
[ʍɪz]	when	_____
[ʍæk]	whale	_____
[ʍɪt]	what	_____

6. [j]

[jɛt]	yen	_____
[jɑrd]	yaw	_____
[jæp]	yield	_____
[jɔrk]	yore	_____
[jɔn]	yowl	_____
[jist]	yew	_____
[joʊk]	yell	_____
[jul]	yam	_____
[jeɪ]	you	_____
[jɛs]	use	_____

7. [ŋ]

[lʌŋ]	wing	_____
[sɪŋ]	tongue	_____
[əmʌŋ]	song	_____
[bæŋ]	long	_____
[rʌŋ]	gang	_____

[rɔŋ]	tong	_____
[kɪŋ]	monk	_____
[pæŋ]	tang	_____
[gæŋ]	singer	_____
[bæŋk]	finger	_____

4. The following materials for the three combinations assume mastery of the vowel, diphthong and consonant symbols.

    a. Practice writing the symbol.

    b. Pronounce aloud the words in list 2, observing the two elements of each combination.

    c. Translate list 1 carefully.

    d. Transcribe list 2.

1. [tʃ]			2. [dʒ]		
[tʃip]	ditch	_____	[bʌdʒ]	hinge	_____
[tʃeɪn]	lunch	_____	[sɪndʒ]	lounge	_____
[pɪtʃ]	child	_____	[dʒeɪl]	fudge	_____
[rɛtʃ]	match	_____	[nʌdʒ]	huge	_____
[kætʃ]	touch	_____	[dʒoʊk]	jolly	_____
[mʌtʃ]	chop	_____	[lʌndʒ]	jig	_____
[tʃɛk]	chip	_____	[dʒɔɪ]	gem	_____
[tʃoʊk]	chess	_____	[dʒɑɪb]	ledge	_____
[frɪtʃ]	rich	_____	[dʒʌg]	judge	_____
[nɪtʃ]	chum	_____	[dʒɪn]	jot	_____

3. [ju]		
[mjut]	mule	_____
[fjuz]	mew	_____
[vjuz]	pews	_____
[kjʊ]	cube	_____
[bjutɪ]	hewn	_____
[fjum]	few	_____
[mjuz]	view	_____
[hju]	spume	_____
[fjud]	cute	_____
[bjut]	repute	_____

5. In many words of American speech the semi-vowels [r] and [l] and the nasals [n] and [m] are heard as *syllabic consonants*. The word *weasel*, for example, may be pronounced as [wizəl] or [wizḷ] with equal correctness. The latter pronunciation exemplifies an unstressed syllabic [ḷ] in the second syllable, the transition from [z] to [ḷ] having been made without an intervening indefinite [ə]. Most commonly this usage is found in unstressed syllables and is indicated by placing a dot under the symbol. The semi-vowel [r] is employed syllabically in stressed syllables also by most General American speakers, this being shown by underlining the consonant symbol. As you work on the following words do not forget the principle that you should transcribe speech as it is spoken, not necessarily as you think it should be spoken. For purposes of this drill, control what "is spoken" by pronouncing syllabic consonants in all of these words and transcribing them as such. It will seem strange at first to use no true vowel symbol in such words as *murder*, [mr̲dr̲], but that is because you are accustomed to the ordinary concept of one vowel per syllable in *spelled* words. Examples: [lɪsn̩], [fæsn̩]; [batm̩], [sɑrkæzm̩]; [mʌðr̲], [faðr̲]; [hr̲t], [lr̲n]; [bʌbḷ], [pɪkḷ].

[m̩]		[n̩]	
chasm	_____	harden	_____
fathom	_____	broaden	_____
balsam	_____	button	_____
anthem	_____	dozen	_____
rhythm	_____	ridden	_____
atom	_____	kitten	_____
emblem	_____	sudden	_____
blossom	_____	hasten	_____
spasm	_____	mitten	_____
bosom	_____	fasten	_____

[l̩]

marble _____

noodle _____

coddle _____

whistle _____

handle _____

battle _____

sickle _____

tassel _____

measles _____

simple _____

[r̩]		[ɝ]	
pervade	_____	bird	_____
permit	_____	word	_____
bitter	_____	heard	_____
butter	_____	curd	_____
sailor	_____	third	_____
Caesar	_____	firm	_____
record	_____	worm	_____
fettered	_____	term	_____
weather	_____	further	_____
southern	_____	worthy	_____

6. The past tenses and past participles of some verbs are indicated by the addition of *d* or *ed* to the stem as in *back, backed.* These suffixes are variously pronounced as [d], [əd] or [t] in different words. Similarly, the addition of *s* or *es* to the stem indicates the present third person singular of verbs (*give, he gives*) or the plural of nouns (*desk, desks*), and these suffixes also are heard variously in different words as [z], [əz] or [s]. All of these variations are systematic and depend upon phonetic, not grammatic, structure. Make very careful transcriptions of accurate pronunciations of the following words and attempt to determine the phonetic principles which account for the variations.

begged	_____	chooses	_____
bribed	_____	coins	_____
crossed	_____	crops	_____
crowded	_____	hats	_____
matted	_____	hides	_____
needed	_____	hisses	_____
rushed	_____	limbs	_____
saved	_____	packs	_____
slipped	_____	judges	_____
talked	_____	puffs	_____
teased	_____	rushes	_____
waited	_____	robes	_____

7. Because they are typically shorter in duration and weaker, the vowels of unstressed syllables are more difficult to identify with certainty than are those of stressed syllables. In addition they are much less predictable. For example, the first syllable of *believe* may be pronounced as [bi], [bɪ] or [bə], and it sometimes is very difficult to decide which vowel was used. As you consider the following two-syllable examples, pronounce each word, first, very carefully in isolation, and, second, rapidly in a short phrase. Transcribe both pronunciations, giving special attention to the unstressed syllables.

	Careful	Rapid
exit	_____	_____
ragged	_____	_____
rabbit	_____	_____
borax	_____	_____

	Careful	*Rapid*
manage	_____	_____
sonnet	_____	_____
silly	_____	_____
poem	_____	_____
pulpit	_____	_____
taxi	_____	_____
relieve	_____	_____
fatigue	_____	_____
consult	_____	_____
forbid	_____	_____
provide	_____	_____
evade	_____	_____
between	_____	_____
delay	_____	_____
pronounce	_____	_____
resent	_____	_____

8. When a speaker pronounces a word he does not ordinarily produce a series of isolated discrete sounds. Rather does he modify and interrupt a relatively continuous flow of tone and noise so that one speech sound blends into the next. A transcription problem sometimes arises when, in changing from one sound to the next, the speaker "moves through" other phonemes. In most instances the changes are so rapid that these intervening, unpurposeful sounds cannot be detected, but at other times they assume such prominence that controversies arise as to whether they should be omitted or included in accurate transcription. The purpose of drills 8, 9 and 10 is to indicate a few of these problems and to help you to establish your own point of view. Although these excrescent sounds vary in prominence, the problem is not resolved by attempting to include or exclude them on the basis of prominence alone, because sometimes they are more prominent than essential sounds. Probably you have three alternatives: (a) Transcribe them as such (*since*, [sɪnts]), on the grounds that they are part of the speech and should be included. (b) Omit them (*since*, [sɪns]), on the theory that they are only incidental, accidental or unpurposeful features of the speech. (c) Transcribe them, but indicate in some manner that they are unpurposeful, one method being that of enclosing them in parentheses (*since*, [sɪn(t)s]).

The list immediately below includes words in which the nasal consonants, [m], [n], [ŋ], are followed by certain voiceless sounds. In such words there is a tendency for an excrescent plosive to be introduced between the nasal and the following sound. For example, [p] may be heard between [m] and [θ] in *warmth*, [t] between [n] and [s] in *tinsel*, [k] between [ŋ] and [θ] in *strength*. These plosives result from the similarity between the articulatory positions for [p] and [m], [t] and [n], [k] and [ŋ]. The velum rises as the nasal sound is completed, leaving the mechanism in position for the corresponding plosive. When the articulators move into position for the following voiceless sound they go through the movements of the plosive even though it may not be intended. The perplexing feature is that much the same sound results in connected speech whether the plosive is intended or not; compare *sense* and *cents*, *prince* and *prints*, *tense* and *tents*. Problem: If you transcribe [t] in *cents* should you also transcribe it in *sense*, since the two words are identical in sound in most speech? Consider the following words carefully, record your transcriptions of both types of words, and attempt to arrive at an attitude toward the problem.

dreamt	_____	damped	_____
empty	_____	contempt	_____
warmth	_____	limped	_____
tempt	_____	tenth	_____
cramped	_____	ninth	_____
something	_____	fancy	_____
glimpse	_____	pencil	_____

mince	_____	instinct _____
mints	_____	linked _____
answer	_____	strength _____
comments	_____	function _____
commence	_____	banks _____
presence	_____	sanction _____
distinctive	_____	flunked _____
anxious	_____	length _____

9. In a second group of words the vowel [u] or [ʊ] is followed immediately in the same word by a different vowel or vowel-like consonant. This structure presents the requisite features for the glide consonant [w], which begins approximately at the position for [u] and moves immediately toward the following sound, this movement being characteristic of the glide. Problem: Should you transcribe *going* as [goʊɪŋ], [goʊwɪŋ] or [gowɪŋ], etc.? After listening intently to your pronunciations, record your transcriptions of the words below. As you pronounce such words as *vowel* and *flower* in this list employ two syllables, and if the [l] or [r] of the second syllable is syllabic indicate this with a dot underneath the symbol.

doing	_____	vowel _____
mewing	_____	towel _____
going	_____	flower _____
allowing	_____	ewer _____
towing	_____	blower _____

10. A similar situation arises in words in which an unstressed [ɪ] is followed immediately in the same word by a different vowel or vowel-like consonant. Here the glide [j], rather than [w], tends to intrude after [ɪ]. Study and transcribe the following words.

lion	_____	babying	_____
Indian	_____	dallying	_____
champion	_____	envying	_____
royal	_____	player	_____
loyal	_____	buyer	_____
portrayal	_____	employer	_____

11. In the following words the diphthongs [eɪ], [aɪ] and [ɔɪ] are followed by the suffix [ɪŋ]. Often in connected speech the [ɪ] of the diphthong and that of [ɪŋ] are combined into a single [ɪ], *saying* being pronounced [seɪŋ], etc. Transcribe your natural pronunciations of these examples.

saying	_____	sighing	_____
paying	_____	prying	_____
neighing	_____	toying	_____
playing	_____	enjoying	_____
buying	_____	annoying	_____
dying	_____	employing	_____

12. Write out a translation of the following transcribed paragraphs. Note that the transcription is of the material as it was read naturally. Hence, some of the words are transcribed differently from the way they would be if pronounced alone.

[ʃæŋhaɪ, ɔgəst fɪftin(t)θ (eɪ pi)—ə tʃaɪniz taɪfun tʊdeɪ swalɔʊd ðə wɔr hɔrərz əv ʃæŋhaɪ mɛr tʃaɪniz ɛr bɑmz kɪld eɪt hʌndrəd sɪkstɪ səvɪljənz, ɪnkludɪŋ θri əmɛrɪkn̩z, æn ɪndʒɪd ət list wʌn θaʊznd̩ wʌn hʌndrəd fɔrtɪ ɪn ðɪs timɪŋ ɪntr̩næʃənl̩ sɪtɪ.

pəlis əv ðɪ ɪntr̩næʃənl̩ kwɔrtr̩ sɛd fɔrtɪ fɔrənr̩z wr̩ əmʌŋ ðə dɛd, bət ðæt ə kəmplit tʃɛk hæd nɑt bɪn meɪd.

dʒæpəniz neɪvi gʌnz θʌndr̩d spæzmɑdɪklɪ frəm ʃɪps æŋkr̩d ɪn ðə mæŋpu rɪvr̩ æn məʃin gʌnz rætl̩d n̩ æn(t)sr̩ ɪn aɪsəleɪtəd sɛkʃn̩z.]

13. Transcribe your reading of the sentences for the adult articulation examination, Introduction, pages xii–xv. Since these sentences contain all of the major American sounds they afford excellent material for transcription practice.

14. Construct a sentence or paragraph which contains in as few words as possible all the speech sounds listed in the phonetic alphabet. Omit the sounds [a], [ɒ], [ɜ], [ɪə], [ɛə], [ʊə] and [ɔə], and attempt no distinction between [o] and [oʊ] or between [e] and [eɪ]. Transcribe your own reading of this paragraph, and present an analysis of the material which indicates for each sound the word or words in the material in which the sound should be heard.

15. Transcribe your pronunciation as you recite aloud the letters of the written alphabet.

16. Pronounce the following transcribed nonsense words one at a time, and attempt as carefully as possible to spell them out in the written English alphabet. (Example: [brætʃ], *bratch*.)
[əpʌks], [dæk], [blin], [nɛkroʊ], [ɪntʃḷ], [skiŋk], [fwæt], [trʌp], [rɛdʒ], [twɑrn], [grɔp], [kʌsk], [sluʒ], [ʃeɪʃt], [laɪbju], [rɔɪg], [glaʊflaʊ], [tjupwi], [dɛpḷpup], [mækənoʊbi], [gɪfḷfʌf], [wɔrtəpɪp], [tr̩grɑrk], [leɪloʊlɪgz], [jæsts], [æfənɪgu], [kwɑvjəl], [mɪθɪθɪpɪ], [ðʌðoʊð], [tʃʌz], [hihɑhu], [ʌɛgəru], [hɪʒ]tæpḷ], [tʃɛʃəθɔrɪ], [dʒukopleɪŋ], [lɔrmθɛg], [iŋglætʃ], [flɔntsr̩], [mædʒɪnts], [ɛŋkḷɪbḷfu].

17. Using all of the sounds listed in the phonetic alphabet, construct 50 spelled nonsense words such as those above, and write them out in ten nonsense sentences of five words each. Ask someone to read the sentences and transcribe his reading. Attempt to forget the spelled forms as you transcribe.

18. Attend a speech or lecture and transcribe on the spot 20 peculiarities of pronunciation that you observe.

19. Collect 50 such transcribed peculiarities that you have observed in your casual conversations during one week.

BIBLIOGRAPHY

1. Barrows, S. T., and Cordts, A. D., *The Teacher's Book of Phonetics*, Ginn and Company, Boston, 1926.

2. Bender, J. F., and Fields, V. A., *Phonetic Readings in American Speech*, Pitman Pub. Corp., New York, 1939.

3. Ettlinger, B. C., "A Survey of the Phonetic Alphabets Presented in Current Textbooks of Speech," *M.A. Thesis, State University of Iowa*, 1938.

4. Kenyon, J. S., *American Pronunciation*, George Wahr, Ann Arbor, Mich., 1937.

CHAPTER II

VOWEL ARTICULATION

beat [i]				[u] fool
bit [ɪ]			*[ɜ] bird	[ʊ] full
bait *[e]			[ə] above	*[o] boat
bet [ɛ]				[ɔ] fall
			[ʌ] above	*[ɒ] hot
bat [æ]		*[a] ask		[ɑ] calm
Front			**Middle**	**Back**

A vowel is a voiced speech sound in which the vocal cord tone is selectively modified as it passes through the resonance cavities of the throat and head. There is relatively little obstruction of the breath stream. Different vowels are produced by changing the characteristics of the cavities, and probably the most important factor in this process is variation of tongue position. Although any given vowel may be produced with a large number of different tongue positions, the variations from vowel to vowel are sufficiently systematic, on the average, to warrant classification on this basis. In the above arrangement the placement of the symbols indicates the approximate position of the highest point of the tongue in the articulation of each of the common American vowels. During [i], for example, this point tends to be forward and high in the mouth; during [ɑ] it usually is low and toward the rear. Thus, when we refer to *front*, *back* and *middle* (or *neutral*) vowels the general horizontal position of the highest point of the tongue is meant. We may outline the *typical* characteristics of these three classes as follows:

1. *Front vowels.*—Going up the series toward [i], the high point of the arched tongue shifts progressively upward and forward toward the anterior alveolar ridge, accompanied by a corresponding elevation of the jaw; the mouth opening becomes

progressively smaller and more slit-like, the lips being somewhat retracted. The tip of the tongue tends to remain immediately behind the lower front teeth; the velum is raised.

2. *Back vowels.*—Going up the series toward [u], the high point of the arched tongue shifts progressively upward toward the velum, accompanied by a corresponding elevation of the jaw; the lips are slightly rounded and protruded in a progressive manner, the mouth opening becoming smaller and more round for each successive vowel. The tip of the tongue tends to assume a position on the floor of the mouth, somewhat behind the lower front teeth; the velum is raised.

3. *Middle vowels.*—The tongue lies relatively relaxed on the floor of the mouth for [ə]; is lowered for [ʌ], raised for [ɜ]; typically the mouth opening is small, with lips and teeth approximately even; the velum is raised.

Errors in vowel production are of two general types:

1. Substitution, or tendency toward substitution, of another vowel or diphthong, e.g., [ɪ] or [eɪ] for [ɛ].
2. Diphthongization or triphthongization, e.g., [ɛə] or [ɛjə] for [ɛ].

In the present chapter exercises are provided for all of the vowels of American speech, except for those vowels that are marked with asterisks in the above diagram. Since [e] and [o] usually are diphthongized legitimately to [eɪ] and [oʊ], all materials on these sounds are to be found in the next chapter. Although it is true that [e] and [o], as vowels, are occasionally heard in unstressed syllables and before voiceless consonants, the differences between them and their corresponding diphthongs are not phonemic and need not be practiced. For [a], [ɒ] and [ɜ], and for consideration of such vowel problems as dialect variations, pronunciation alternatives and vowel errors related to adjacent consonants, the student is referred to the chapter on pronunciation.

The consonant-vowel combination [ju], sometimes classified as a diphthong, is included with the vowels in this chapter because substitution of [ju] for [u] and of [u] for [ju] are common errors.

Detailed directions for drill procedure will be found in the Introduction.

THE FRONT VOWELS

THE VOWEL [i]

[i] is spelled typically as in she, feed, repeat, receive, belief; also as in machine, key, people, debris, Caesar, Phoenix, quay.

1. Articulating [i] in Isolation.
2. Writing-sounding [i].
3. [i] Nonsense Syllables.

[i-i-p]	[i-p]	[ip]	[p-i-i]	[p-i]	[pi]	[p-i-i-p]	[p-i-p]	[pip]
[i-i-d]	[i-d]	[id]	[d-i-i]	[d-i]	[di]	[d-i-i-d]	[d-i-d]	[did]
[i-i-f]	[i-f]	[if]	[f-i-i]	[f-i]	[fi]	[f-i-i-f]	[f-i-f]	[fif]
[i-i-b]	[i-b]	[ib]	[b-i-i]	[b-i]	[bi]	[b-i-i-b]	[b-i-b]	[bib]
[i-i-k]	[i-k]	[ik]	[k-i-i]	[k-i]	[ki]	[k-i-i-k]	[k-i-k]	[kik]

4. [i] Words.

Initial		Final		Medial	
each	eager	be	agree	feet	bead
eagle	ease	flee	decree	green	bean
east	easel	he	fee	keep	deep
easy	Easter	knee	free	leave	heel
eat	eastern	me	glee	need	kneel
eaten	eaves	see	key	please	lease
eel	ego	she	lee	read	mean
either	eke	three	plea	sleep	seal
eve	Enid	tree	tea	teacher	sheep
even	equal	we	trustee	these	wheel

5. Distinguishing [ɪ] from [i].

bid – bead	dim – deem	bit – beet	bin – bean
dip – deep	did – deed	dill – deal	pick – peak
pill – peal	tin – teen	kin – keen	kill – keel
fit – feet	fill – feel	sin – seen	sip – seep

6. [i] Sentences.

1. He will feed my three geese when I leave.
2. Each of us needs to be neat.
3. Please read to me.
4. She would rather eat meat than peas or beans.
5. We brush our teeth to keep them clean.
6. I feel the need of deep sleep.
7. The eastern team was completely defeated.
8. The thieves made a plea for freedom.
9. She believed that she didn't need to please the teacher.
10. The trustees decreed that Seniors would be free from fees.

THE VOWEL [ɪ]

[ɪ] is spelled typically as in fit; also as in sieve, pretty, hymn, guilt, business, been, women; and it participates in [eɪ], [aɪ], [ɔɪ]. It is probably the most frequent vowel used in unaccented syllables that are spelled as in many, collie, coffee, money, Sunday, manage, knowledge, marriage. It is commonly used before [r] in the pronunciation of such spellings as hero, steer, fear, pier, weird. Consult Chapter V, Pronunciation, for alternatives.

1. Articulating [ɪ] in Isolation.

2. Writing-sounding [ɪ].

3. [ɪ] Nonsense Syllables.

[ɪ-ɪ-p]	[ɪ-p]	[ɪp]	[p-ɪ-ɪ]	[p-ɪ]	[pɪ]	[p-ɪ-ɪ-p]	[p-ɪ-p]	[pɪp]
[ɪ-ɪ-d]	[ɪ-d]	[ɪd]	[d-ɪ-ɪ]	[d-ɪ]	[dɪ]	[d-ɪ-ɪ-d]	[d-ɪ-d]	[dɪd]
[ɪ-ɪ-f]	[ɪ-f]	[ɪf]	[f-ɪ-ɪ]	[f-ɪ]	[fɪ]	[f-ɪ-ɪ-f]	[f-ɪ-f]	[fɪf]
[ɪ-ɪ-b]	[ɪ-b]	[ɪb]	[b-ɪ-ɪ]	[b-ɪ]	[bɪ]	[b-ɪ-ɪ-b]	[b-ɪ-b]	[bɪb]
[ɪ-ɪ-k]	[ɪ-k]	[ɪk]	[k-ɪ-ɪ]	[k-ɪ]	[kɪ]	[k-ɪ-ɪ-k]	[k-ɪ-k]	[kɪk]

4. [ɪ] Words.

Initial		Medial	
if	idiot	been	bill
ill	ignore	big	din
in	image	did	fish
inch	imbue	give	king

Initial		*Medial*	
ink	impact	him	lid
inside	impel	milk	mill
into	index	pig	pit
is	Indian	six	ship
it	insult	thing	sill
itch	irritate	will	wish

5. Distinguishing [i] from [ɪ].

bead – bid	deem – dim	beet – bit	bean – bin
deep – dip	deed – did	deal – dill	peak – pick
peal – pill	teen – tin	keen – kin	keel – kill
feet – fit	feel – fill	seen – sin	seep – sip

6. Distinguishing [ɛ] from [ɪ].

Ben – bin	beg – big	bet – bit	bell – bill
dead – did	pen – pin	peg – pig	peck – pick
ken – kin	fell – fill	set – sit	hem – him
head – hid	led – lid	red – rid	well – will

7. Distinguishing [ʌ] from [ɪ].

bun – bin	but – bit	mull – mill	dumb – dim
bug – big	pug – pig	fun – fin	tuck – tick
dud – did	hum – him	love – live	gull – gill
pun – pin	hull – hill	cull – kill	dun – din

8. [ɪ] Sentences.

1. His sister has six pigs.
2. The king gave a ring to the little boy.
3. Jim has spilled the ink.
4. Will you give the baby a drink of milk?
5. Bill should give this pin to his sister.
6. He was sick and didn't go fishing.
7. He thinks he is king of an Indian kingdom.
8. She quickly became chilled in the bitter wind.
9. The lower lip is lifted for the initial fricative in "fish."
10. You will not develop skill in articulation simply by wishing for it.

The Vowel [ɛ]

[ɛ] is spelled typically as in set; also as in weather, friend, says, said, heifer, heir, Geoffrey, bury, guess. It is commonly used before [r] in the pronunciation of such spellings as fare, hair, prayer, there, wear. Consult Chapter V, Pronunciation, for alternatives.

1. Articulating [ɛ] in Isolation.
2. Writing-sounding [ɛ].
3. [ɛ] Nonsense Syllables.

[ɛ-ɛ-p]	[ɛ-p]	[ɛp]	[p-ɛ-ɛ]	[p-ɛ]	[pɛ]	[p-ɛ-ɛ-p]	[p-ɛ-p]	[pɛp]
[ɛ-ɛ-d]	[ɛ-d]	[ɛd]	[d-ɛ-ɛ]	[d-ɛ]	[dɛ]	[d-ɛ-ɛ-d]	[d-ɛ-d]	[dɛd]
[ɛ-ɛ-f]	[ɛ-f]	[ɛf]	[f-ɛ-ɛ]	[f-ɛ]	[fɛ]	[f-ɛ-ɛ-f]	[f-ɛ-f]	[fɛf]
[ɛ-ɛ-b]	[ɛ-b]	[ɛb]	[b-ɛ-ɛ]	[b-ɛ]	[bɛ]	[b-ɛ-ɛ-b]	[b-ɛ-b]	[bɛb]
[ɛ-ɛ-k]	[ɛ-k]	[ɛk]	[k-ɛ-ɛ]	[k-ɛ]	[kɛ]	[k-ɛ-ɛ-k]	[k-ɛ-k]	[kɛk]

4. [ɛ] Words.

Initial		Medial	
any	ebony	bed	beg
edge	edit	dress	deck
egg	elegant	get	hen
elephant	elevate	guess	keg
elm	elk	help	leg
else	ending	let	met
end	enter	men	neck
engine	entry	said	pen
every	etch	them	shell
extra	excellent	well	web

5. Distinguishing [ɪ] from [ɛ].

bin – Ben	big – beg	bit – bet	bill – bell
did – dead	pin – pen	pig – peg	pick – peck
kin – ken	fill – fell	sit – set	him – hem
hid – head	lid – led	rid – red	will – well

6. Distinguishing [eɪ] from [ɛ].

bake – beck	bait – bet	bail – bell	date – debt
dale – dell	Yale – yell	tale – tell	fail – fell
sail – sell	laid – led	late – let	raid – red
wade – wed	wait – wet	mane – men	mate – met

7. Distinguishing [æ] from [ɛ].

bag – beg	back – beck	dad – dead	pan – pen
pack – peck	pat – pet	can – ken	sat – set
shall – shell	had – head	lag – leg	mat – met
bat – bet	bad – bed	than – then	tan – ten

8. Distinguishing [ʌ] from [ɛ].

buck – beck	muss – mess	pug – peg
mutt – met	sud – said	nut – net
hum – hem	but – bet	lug – leg
bud – bed	Gus – guess	pup – pep

9. [ɛ] Sentences.

1. Let the men help us get the bed.
2. I guess I left your engine under the elm tree.
3. Ted broke the eggs when he fell down the stairs.
4. Betty said to wear the red dress.
5. Anyone will lend them seven pennies.
6. They begged for rest before the extra session.
7. Everyone said it was an elegant dress.
8. His entry was an excellent etching of an elk.
9. It is better to consult Webster than to guess at the stress.
10. One method of determining intensity level is direct measurement of sound pressure.

THE VOWEL [æ]

[æ] is spelled typically as in h**a**t; also as in l**augh**, pl**ai**d. Consult Chapter V, Pronunciation, for alternatives.

1. Articulating [æ] in Isolation.
2. Writing-sounding [æ].

3. [æ] Nonsense Syllables.

[æ-æ-p]	[æ-p]	[æp]	[p-æ-æ]	[p-æ]	[pæ]	[p-æ-æ-p]	[p-æ-p]	[pæp]
[æ-æ-d]	[æ-d]	[æd]	[d-æ-æ]	[d-æ]	[dæ]	[d-æ-æ-d]	[d-æ-d]	[dæd]
[æ-æ-f]	[æ-f]	[æf]	[f-æ-æ]	[f-æ]	[fæ]	[f-æ-æ-f]	[f-æ-f]	[fæf]
[æ-æ-b]	[æ-b]	[æb]	[b-æ-æ]	[b-æ]	[bæ]	[b-æ-æ-b]	[b-æ-b]	[bæb]
[æ-æ-k]	[æ-k]	[æk]	[k-æ-æ]	[k-æ]	[kæ]	[k-æ-æ-k]	[k-æ-k]	[kæk]

4. [æ] Words.

Initial		*Medial*	
add	abbey	back	bag
am	absolute	began	cat
an	acrid	black	dash
animal	action	can	lack
apple	addle	catch	map
apt	agate	had	rap
as	agitate	has	sad
ashes	agony	rabbit	tack
at	atom	ran	tan
ax	avid	that	than

5. Distinguishing [ɛ] from [æ].

beg – bag	beck – back	dead – dad	pen – pan
peck – pack	pet – pat	ken – can	set – sat
shell – shall	head – had	leg – lag	met – mat
bet – bat	bed – bad	then – than	ten – tan

6. Distinguishing [ʌ] from [æ].

bug – bag	bud – bad	mutt – mat	mush – mash
but – bat	dud – dad	ton – tan	shuck – shack
buck – back	lug – lag	mud – mad	luck – lack
putt – pat	pun – pan	hug – hag	come – cam

7. Distinguishing [ɑ] from [æ].

don – Dan	sot – sat	tot – tat	shock – shack
cod – cad	pod – pad	not – gnat	pot – pat
cot – cat	hock – hack	rot – rat	cop – cap
sod – sad	hod – had	hot – hat	mop – map

8. [æ] Sentences.

1. Sam has a rabbit in his hat.
2. Jack ran to get an apple for Sally.
3. Ann patted the fat lamb.
4. Dan will catch cold if he doesn't have a hat.
5. The black cat ran in back of the wagon.
6. Jack sat on a tack.
7. The fat man grabbed madly for his hat.
8. He dashed to the back of the factory.
9. Dazzy Vance was sad about his batting average.
10. The soft palate hangs at the back of the oral cavity.

THE MIDDLE VOWELS

The Vowel [ʌ]

[ʌ] is spelled typically as in fun, above; also as in trouble, blood, does.

1. Articulating [ʌ] in Isolation.
2. Writing-sounding [ʌ].
3. [ʌ] Nonsense Syllables.

[ʌ-ʌ-p]	[ʌ-p]	[ʌp]	[p-ʌ-ʌ]	[p-ʌ]	[pʌ]	[p-ʌ-ʌ-p]	[p-ʌ-p]	[pʌp]
[ʌ-ʌ-d]	[ʌ-d]	[ʌd]	[d-ʌ-ʌ]	[d-ʌ]	[dʌ]	[d-ʌ-ʌ-d]	[d-ʌ-d]	[dʌd]
[ʌ-ʌ-f]	[ʌ-f]	[ʌf]	[f-ʌ-ʌ]	[f-ʌ]	[fʌ]	[f-ʌ-ʌ-f]	[f-ʌ-f]	[fʌf]
[ʌ-ʌ-b]	[ʌ-b]	[ʌb]	[b-ʌ-ʌ]	[b-ʌ]	[bʌ]	[b-ʌ-ʌ-b]	[b-ʌ-b]	[bʌb]
[ʌ-ʌ-k]	[ʌ-k]	[ʌk]	[k-ʌ-ʌ]	[k-ʌ]	[kʌ]	[k-ʌ-ʌ-k]	[k-ʌ-k]	[kʌk]

4. [ʌ] Words.

Initial		*Medial*	
other	oven	but	buzz
ugly	ultimate	come	done
umbrella	ultra	cut	dull
uncle	umpire	jump	gun
under	unction	just	mud
unless	upper	love	nut
until	upward	mother	rung
up	usher	much	sun
upstairs	utter	one	tongue
us	utmost	run	young

5. Distinguishing [ɑ] from [ʌ].

bomb – bum	dock – duck	pop – pup	pot – putt
calm – come	psalm – sum	wan – won	cop – cup
cot – cut	shock – shuck	shot – shut	hob – hub
hot – hut	lock – luck	rob – rub	knot – nut

6. Distinguishing [ʊ] from [ʌ].

book – buck	shook – shuck	hoof – huff
sook – suck	stood – stud	could – cud
rook – ruck	took – tuck	look – luck
put – putt	hook – Huck	crooks – crux

7. [ʌ] Sentences.

1. Your uncle took the umbrella upstairs.
2. My puppy loves to run.
3. You must go to lunch, but come back for supper.
4. The ugly duck is under the hut.
5. Put some honey on the bun, Mother.
6. Brush the dust off your cuff.
7. Mother shoved the buns into the oven.
8. When the sun came up the guns began to thunder.
9. Much of the tongue is muscle.
10. Southern pronunciation is sometimes lovely and sometimes slovenly.

THE VOWEL [ə]

[ə] is spelled typically as in soda, praises, possible, purpose, circus; also as in callous, tortoise, vehement.

1. Articulating [ə] in Isolation.
2. Writing-sounding [ə].
3. [ə] Nonsense Syllables.

[ə-ə-p]	[ə-p]	[əp]	[p-ə-ə]	[p-ə]	[pə]	[p-ə-ə-p]	[p-ə-p]	[pəp]
[ə-ə-d]	[ə-d]	[əd]	[d-ə-ə]	[d-ə]	[də]	[d-ə-ə-d]	[d-ə-d]	[dəd]
[ə-ə-f]	[ə-f]	[əf]	[f-ə-ə]	[f-ə]	[fə]	[f-ə-ə-f]	[f-ə-f]	[fəf]
[ə-ə-b]	[ə-b]	[əb]	[b-ə-ə]	[b-ə]	[bə]	[b-ə-ə-b]	[b-ə-b]	[bəb]
[ə-ə-k]	[ə-k]	[ək]	[k-ə-ə]	[k-ə]	[kə]	[k-ə-ə-k]	[k-ə-k]	[kək]

4. [ə] Words.

Initial		Final		Medial	
about	abate	arena	camera	accident	buffalo
above	ado	cinema	china	alphabet	cinnamon
ago	allow	dogma	data	arithmetic	element
alive	amass	mica	drama	balloon	emphasis
along	amaze	papa	gorilla	banana	filament
another	annoy	polka	mania	breakfast	necessary
around	appeal	soda	quota	chocolate	parachute
asleep	arouse	sofa	stanza	circus	relative
away	attach	tuba	vista	company	suffocate
awhile	await	vanilla	zebra	parasol	syllable

5. [ə] Sentences.

1. Papa bought me a balloon at the circus.
2. Anna has another parasol.
3. I had a banana for breakfast.
4. The elephant is a large animal.
5. She gave me some chocolate when I went away.
6. The pilot jumped from the balloon in a parachute.
7. I am amazed that you allow the man to annoy you.
8. A buffalo, a zebra and a gorilla escaped from the circus.
9. The famous attorney submitted an appeal.
10. He fell asleep on the sofa.

THE BACK VOWELS

The Vowel [ɑ]

[ɑ] is spelled typically as in **father, on**; also as in **ah, sergeant, hearth, guard, honest**; and it participates in [ɑɪ], [ɑʊ]. Consult Chapter V, Pronunciation, for alternatives.

1. Articulating [ɑ] in Isolation.
2. Writing-sounding [ɑ].
3. [ɑ] Nonsense Syllables.

[ɑ-ɑ-p]	[ɑ-p]	[ɑp]	[p-ɑ-ɑ]	[p-ɑ]	[pɑ]	[p-ɑ-ɑ-p]	[p-ɑ-p]	[pɑp]
[ɑ-ɑ-d]	[ɑ-d]	[ɑd]	[d-ɑ-ɑ]	[d-ɑ]	[dɑ]	[d-ɑ-ɑ-d]	[d-ɑ-d]	[dɑd]
[ɑ-ɑ-f]	[ɑ-f]	[ɑf]	[f-ɑ-ɑ]	[f-ɑ]	[fɑ]	[f-ɑ-ɑ-f]	[f-ɑ-f]	[fɑf]
[ɑ-ɑ-b]	[ɑ-b]	[ɑb]	[b-ɑ-ɑ]	[b-ɑ]	[bɑ]	[b-ɑ-ɑ-b]	[b-ɑ-b]	[bɑb]
[ɑ-ɑ-k]	[ɑ-k]	[ɑk]	[k-ɑ-ɑ]	[k-ɑ]	[kɑ]	[k-ɑ-ɑ-k]	[k-ɑ-k]	[kɑk]

4. [ɑ] Words.

Initial		*Medial*	
arch	arbor	bar	bomb
are	arc	barn	calm
ark	arcade	car	don
arm	ardent	doll	loll
army	argue	far	mar
art	arson	farm	palm
honest	ominous	father	psalm
honor	onset	heart	tar
olive	onward	upon	Tom
on	onyx	want	yon

5. Distinguishing [æ] from [ɑ].

Dan – don	sat – sot	tat – tot	shack – shock
cad – cod	pat – pot	gnat – not	knack – knock
cat – cot	hack – hock	rat – rot	cap – cop
sad – sod	had – hod	hat – hot	map – mop

6. Distinguishing [ʌ] from [ɑ].

bum – bomb	duck – dock	pup – pop	putt – pot
come – calm	sum – psalm	won – wan	cup – cop
cut – cot	shuck – shock	shut – shot	hub – hob
hut – hot	luck – lock	rub – rob	nut – knot

7. Distinguishing [ɔ] from [ɑ].

dawn – don	yawn – yon	pawed – pod	taught – tot
cawed – cod	sawed – sod	hawk – hock	naught – not
caught – cot	sought – sot	hawed – hod	wrought – rot
gnawed – nod	bore – bar	core – car	for – far

8. [ɑ] Sentences.

1. Tom wants to be in the army.
2. Are you going far from the farm?
3. I want to put my doll in the cart.
4. My father has a new car.

5. I hurt my arm on the iron bar.
6. Are the olives large?
7. Sergeant Garner was calm after the bombing.
8. Polly wanted to loll on the hearth.
9. John argued ardently about honesty.
10. Harsh quality is a common problem.

The Vowel [ɔ]

[ɔ] is spelled typically as in **saw**, **ball**, **Saul**, **bought**, **soft**; also as in **broad**; and it participates in [ɔɪ]. It is commonly used before [r] in the pronunciation of such spellings as **warm**, **lord**, **door**, **coarse**, **course**, **toward**, **George**. Consult Chapter V, Pronunciation, for alternatives.

1. Articulating [ɔ] in Isolation.
2. Writing-sounding [ɔ].
3. [ɔ] Nonsense Syllables.

[ɔ-ɔ-p]	[ɔ-p]	[ɔp]	[p-ɔ-ɔ]	[p-ɔ]	[pɔ]	[p-ɔ-ɔ-p]	[p-ɔ-p]	[pɔp]
[ɔ-ɔ-d]	[ɔ-d]	[ɔd]	[d-ɔ-ɔ]	[d-ɔ]	[dɔ]	[d-ɔ-ɔ-d]	[d-ɔ-d]	[dɔd]
[ɔ-ɔ-f]	[ɔ-f]	[ɔf]	[f-ɔ-ɔ]	[f-ɔ]	[fɔ]	[f-ɔ-ɔ-f]	[f-ɔ-f]	[fɔf]
[ɔ-ɔ-b]	[ɔ-b]	[ɔb]	[b-ɔ-ɔ]	[b-ɔ]	[bɔ]	[b-ɔ-ɔ-b]	[b-ɔ-b]	[bɔb]
[ɔ-ɔ-k]	[ɔ-k]	[ɔk]	[k-ɔ-ɔ]	[k-ɔ]	[kɔ]	[k-ɔ-ɔ-k]	[k-ɔ-k]	[kɔk]

4. [ɔ] Words.

Initial		Final		Medial	
all	auburn	caw	chaw	ball	cause
almost	auction	claw	craw	caught	daub
already	audible	draw	flaw	fall	dawn
also	auger	gnaw	guffaw	hawk	fawn
always	author	law	jaw	tall	fought
auto	autumn	paw	outlaw	taught	laws
automobile	awful	raw	seesaw	thought	naught
office	awkward	saw	Shaw	walk	pawed
often	awl	squaw	thaw	wall	sauce
ought	awning	straw	withdraw	warm	sawed

5. Distinguishing [ʌ] from [ɔ].

cut – caught	Huck – hawk	mud – Maude	tongue – tong
nut – naught	rut – wrought	mull – maul	tut – taught
dun – dawn	buck – balk	pun – pawn	gun – gone
cud – cawed	tuck – talk	but – bought	rung – wrong

6. Distinguishing [ɑ] from [ɔ].

don – dawn	yon – yawn	pod – pawed	tot – taught
cod – cawed	sod – sawed	hock – hawk	not – naught
cot – caught	sot – sought	hod – hawed	rot – wrought
nod – gnawed	bar – bore	car – core	far – for

7. [ɔ] Sentences.

1. Do not walk on the lawn.
2. The shawl is in the automobile.
3. Can you draw a horse?
4. The ball has fallen over the wall.
5. When it is warm I often sit in the orchard.
6. The hawk caught the ball in his claw.
7. The outlaws fought until dawn.
8. Paul's audience applauded warmly.
9. They sprawled awkwardly under the awning.
10. I thought Shaw was the author.

The Vowel [ʊ]

[ʊ] is spelled typically as in book, full; also as in would, woman, worsted; and it participates in [oʊ], [ɑʊ]. It is commonly used before [r] in the pronunciation of such spellings as sure, poor, pour, and it participates in cure. Consult Chapter V, Pronunciation, for alternatives.

1. Articulating [ʊ] in Isolation.
2. Writing-sounding [ʊ].
3. [ʊ] Nonsense Syllables.

[ʊ-ʊ-p]	[ʊ-p]	[ʊp]	[p-ʊ-ʊ]	[p-ʊ]	[pʊ]	[p-ʊ-ʊ-p]	[p-ʊ-p]	[pʊp]
[ʊ-ʊ-d]	[ʊ-d]	[ʊd]	[d-ʊ-ʊ]	[d-ʊ]	[dʊ]	[d-ʊ-ʊ-d]	[d-ʊ-d]	[dʊd]
[ʊ-ʊ-f]	[ʊ-f]	[ʊf]	[f-ʊ-ʊ]	[f-ʊ]	[fʊ]	[f-ʊ-ʊ-f]	[f-ʊ-f]	[fʊf]
[ʊ-ʊ-b]	[ʊ-b]	[ʊb]	[b-ʊ-ʊ]	[b-ʊ]	[bʊ]	[b-ʊ-ʊ-b]	[b-ʊ-b]	[bʊb]
[ʊ-ʊ-k]	[ʊ-k]	[ʊk]	[k-ʊ-ʊ]	[k-ʊ]	[kʊ]	[k-ʊ-ʊ-k]	[k-ʊ-k]	[kʊk]

4. [ʊ] Words.

Medial

book	brook
could	bush
good	cook
look	foot
looked	full
pull	nook
put	push
should	puss
took	rook
would	wool

5. Distinguishing [ʌ] from [ʊ].

buck – book	shuck – shook	huff – hoof
suck – sook	stud – stood	cud – could
ruck – rook	tuck – took	luck – look
putt – put	Huck – hook	crux – crooks

6. [ʊ] Sentences.

1. The cook pushed the crooked stick with her foot.
2. The cookies are good.
3. Look at the pussy near the brook.
4. The poor rabbit hid in the bushes.
5. Put the book on the wooden table.
6. Would you look for the cushion?
7. The rook stood on one foot.
8. He shook himself and pushed off into the woods.
9. I could eat a bushel full of cookies.
10. She is good-looking when she puts on the wool dress.

THE VOWEL [u]

[u] is spelled typically as in rude, do, flew, too; also as in blue, through, group, shoe, fruit, maneuver, lieu, rendezvous; and it participates in [ju]. Consult Chapter V, Pronunciation, for alternatives.

1. Articulating [u] in Isolation.

2. Writing-sounding [u].

3. [u] Nonsense Syllables.

[u-u-p]	[u-p]	[up]	[p-u-u]	[p-u]	[pu]	[p-u-u-p]	[p-u-p]	[pup]
[u-u-d]	[u-d]	[ud]	[d-u-u]	[d-u]	[du]	[d-u-u-d]	[d-u-d]	[dud]
[u-u-f]	[u-f]	[uf]	[f-u-u]	[f-u]	[fu]	[f-u-u-f]	[f-u-f]	[fuf]
[u-u-b]	[u-b]	[ub]	[b-u-u]	[b-u]	[bu]	[b-u-u-b]	[b-u-b]	[bub]
[u-u-k]	[u-k]	[uk]	[k-u-u]	[k-u]	[ku]	[k-u-u-k]	[k-u-k]	[kuk]

4. [u] Words.

Final		*Medial*	
blue	bamboo	cool	boom
chew	crew	goose	boot
do	flu	moon	doom
drew	igloo	move	ghoul
flew	moo	noon	hoot
grew	tattoo	rule	loop
shoe	true	school	lute
through	undo	soon	pool
to	voodoo	tooth	shoot
who	woo	whose	tomb

5. Distinguishing [ju] from [u].

butte – boot	mewed – mooed	cues	– coos
hues – whose	feud – food	Hume	– whom
mews – moos	cute – coot	cue	– coo
cued – cooed	mute – moot	beauty – booty

6. [u] Sentences.

1. My ruler is at school too.
2. Chew your food, Ruth.
3. My shoe is in the pool.
4. Does the moon shine into your room?
5. It is very cool this noon.
6. Do you eat soup with a soupspoon?

7. A group of schoolboys went through the zoo.
8. Her tooth came loose at school.
9. Soon it will be cool enough to move.
10. Whose goose did Rooney shoot?

The Consonant-vowel Combination [ju]

[ju] is spelled typically as in cute, you, ewe, few, review; also as in feud, argue, beauty, Pugh.

1. Articulating [ju] in Isolation.
2. Writing-sounding [ju].
3. [ju] Nonsense Syllables.

[ju-ju-p]	[ju-p]	[jup]	[p-ju-ju]	[p-ju]	[pju]
[ju-ju-d]	[ju-d]	[jud]	[d-ju-ju]	[d-ju]	[dju]
[ju-ju-f]	[ju-f]	[juf]	[f-ju-ju]	[f-ju]	[fju]
[ju-ju-b]	[ju-b]	[jub]	[b-ju-ju]	[b-ju]	[bju]
[ju-ju-k]	[ju-k]	[juk]	[k-ju-ju]	[k-ju]	[kju]

[p-ju-ju-p]	[p-ju-p]	[pjup]
[d-ju-ju-d]	[d-ju-d]	[djud]
[f-ju-ju-f]	[f-ju-f]	[fjuf]
[b-ju-ju-b]	[b-ju-b]	[bjub]
[k-ju-ju-k]	[k-ju-k]	[kjuk]

4. [ju] Words.

Initial	*Final*	*Medial*	
uke	cue	butte	beauty
unify	few	cube	cues
union	hue	cued	feud
unit	imbue	cute	fume
use	mew	fugue	fuse
usurp	pew	huge	hewed
utilize	review	mule	hues
yews	skew	muse	music
you	spew	mute	viewed
youth	view	pews	views

5. [ju] Sentences.

1. The cute kitten mewed and mewed.
2. Do you have a huge dog?
3. Are you using the music book?
4. Have you ever seen a mule?
5. Few people do not like music.
6. Unions have their uses.
7. She was beautiful and amusing.
8. The musician accused the reviewer of trying to be cute.
9. Some buttes in Utah are shaped like huge cubes.
10. The feud started over the use of the family pew.

BIBLIOGRAPHY

1. Gray, G. W., and Wise, C. M., *The Bases of Speech*, Harper & Brothers, New York, 1934.

2. Kelly, J. P., and Higley, L. B., "A Contribution to the X-Ray Study of Tongue Position in Certain Vowels," *Archives of Speech*, 1:84–95 (1934).

3. Kenyon, J. S., *American Pronunciation*, George Wahr, Ann Arbor, Mich., 1937.

4. Lewis, D., "Vocal Resonance," *Journal of the Acoustical Society of America*, 8:91–99 (1936).

5. Parmenter, C. E., and Treviño, S. N., "Vowel Positions as Shown by X-Ray," *Quarterly Journal of Speech*, 18:351–369 (1932).

6. Russell, G. O., *Speech and Voice*, The Macmillan Company, New York, 1931.

CHAPTER III

DIPHTHONG ARTICULATION

The five phonemic diphthongs of General American speech may be divided into two groups: (1) [ʊ] diphthongs: [oʊ], *foal;* [aʊ], *fowl;* (2) [ɪ] diphthongs: [eɪ], *fail;* [aɪ], *file;* [ɔɪ], *foil.* The vowels which compose these sounds may vary within limits and still be acceptable. Thus, [u] and [i] are heard frequently for [ʊ] and [ɪ], forming [ou], [au], [ei], [ai], [ɔi]. Likewise, [a] is a legitimate modification of [ɑ] in the diphthongs [ɑʊ] and [ɑɪ], which become [aʊ] and [aɪ].

In dialect regions where [ə] replaces final [r], four additional diphthongs are formed: [ɪɚ] or [iə], [ɛɚ] or [eə], [ɔɚ] or [oə], [ʊə] or [uə]. Since these sounds are uncommon in General American, materials are not provided in this chapter. Consult Chapter V, Pronunciation, for word lists.

It is evident that the basic difference between a diphthong and a vowel is that in a diphthong *two* vowel elements are blended in rapid succession. In addition to this essential feature, all five General American diphthongs have other characteristics as follows:

1. The two vowels blend in a smooth articulatory movement and without interruption of phonation.

2. The tongue movement from the first vowel element to the second is upward.

3. The mouth opening is smaller for the second vowel element than for the first.

4. The first vowel element is invariably stressed, i.e., is longer in duration and louder than the second element.

The most frequent errors in diphthong articulation are of four general types:

1. Substitution, or tendency toward substitution, of another vowel for the first vowel element, e.g., [æʊ] for [ɑʊ].
2. Over-prolongation of the first vowel element.
3. Slighting or omission of the second vowel element, e.g., [ɑ] for [ɑɪ].
4. Triphthongization, e.g., [eɪə] for [eɪ].

The major consideration in the production of a diphthong is accurate articulation of the constituent vowels. In practicing, therefore, it is suggested that the two vowel elements be reviewed in isolation first, then alternated rapidly several times, both in isolation and with continuous phonation, before the diphthong itself is approached. The materials will be seen to follow that outline. Since a diphthong, as such, cannot be sustained, the isolated articulation and writing-sounding of prolonged examples should consist of prolongation of the vowel elements, with the first blended into the second in the same phonation. For [ɑɪ] and [ɔɪ] additional practice in constructing the diphthong is afforded by word sequences such as *don-din-dine*, *top-tip-type*, etc., which involve the constituent vowels. A similar list is provided for [ɑʊ], except that the second word in each sequence involves the vowel [u] instead of [ʊ]. Certain word pairs, such as *run-roan*, *fun-phone*, etc., are intended to assist correction of such errors as [ʌʊ] for [oʊ] and [æʊ] for [ɑʊ].

Detailed directions for drill procedure will be found in the Introduction.

THE [ʊ] DIPHTHONGS

THE DIPHTHONG [oʊ]

[oʊ] is spelled typically as in so, goal, toe, blown, boulder; also as in oh, owe, though, sew, beau, chauffeur, yeoman, brooch, apropos. This sound is sometimes heard as a vowel, [o], before voiceless consonants and in unstressed syllables.

1. Articulating [oʊ] in Isolation.

    a. [o]
    b. [ʊ]

c. [o] and [ʊ] alternated, as in [o-ʊ-o-ʊ-o-ʊ-oʊ] and [oʊoʊoʊoʊoʊ].

d. [oʊ]

2. Writing-sounding [oʊ].

3. [oʊ] Nonsense Syllables.

[oʊ-oʊ-p]	[oʊ-p]	[oʊp]	[p-oʊ-oʊ]	[p-oʊ]	[poʊ]
[oʊ-oʊ-d]	[oʊ-d]	[oʊd]	[d-oʊ-oʊ]	[d-oʊ]	[doʊ]
[oʊ-oʊ-f]	[oʊ-f]	[oʊf]	[f-oʊ-oʊ]	[f-oʊ]	[foʊ]
[oʊ-oʊ-b]	[oʊ-b]	[oʊb]	[b-oʊ-oʊ]	[b-oʊ]	[boʊ]
[oʊ-oʊ-k]	[oʊ-k]	[oʊk]	[k-oʊ-oʊ]	[k-oʊ]	[koʊ]

[p-oʊ-oʊ-p]	[p-oʊ-p]	[poʊp]
[d-oʊ-oʊ-d]	[d-oʊ-d]	[doʊd]
[f-oʊ-oʊ-f]	[f-oʊ-f]	[foʊf]
[b-oʊ-oʊ-b]	[b-oʊ-b]	[boʊb]
[k-oʊ-oʊ-k]	[k-oʊ-k]	[koʊk]

4. [oʊ] Words.

Initial		Final		Medial	
oak	oaf	go	crow	boat	code
oat	oath	grow	doe	both	cold
oatmeal	oboe	hello	flow	don't	goes
oh	ocean	know	foe	home	moan
old	ode	show	hoe	known	note
only	odor	snow	low	loaf	robe
open	omen	so	though	pony	shone
over	opal	toe	throw	soap	soul
overalls	opus	window	whoa	those	stove
ɔwn	oval	yellow	woe	wrote	yoke

5. Distinguishing [ʌ] from [o] in [oʊ].

run – roan	cull – coal	nut – note	ton – tone
fun – phone	gull – goal	pun – pone	hum – home
hull – hole	mutt – moat	pup – pope	shut – shoat
cut – coat	none – known	bun – bone	sup – soap

6. Distinguishing [ɔ] from [o] in [oʊ].

bought – boat	bawl – bowl	pall – pole	paws – pose
taught – tote	caught – coat	cawed – code	call – coal
fawn – phone	fall – foal	shawl – shoal	hawed – hoed
haul – hole	lawn – loan	walk – woke	gall – goal

7. [oʊ] Sentences.

1. Don't throw snow at your pony.
2. Open the window and close the door.
3. The oatmeal is on the stove.
4. Don't go out in the boat alone.
5. We are both going home.
6. It was so cold that he froze a toe.
7. We won't go home until we know who stole the gold.
8. Many crows have grown old in that oat field.
9. They showed a polo pony in slow-motion.
10. Joseph Sloan wrote an ode to the ocean.

THE DIPHTHONG [ɑʊ]

[ɑʊ] is spelled typically as in cow, out; also as in sauerkraut, hour.

1. Articulating [ɑʊ] in Isolation.

    a. [ɑ]

    b. [ʊ]

    c. [ɑ] and [ʊ] alternated, as in [ɑ-ʊ-ɑ-ʊ-ɑ-ʊ-ɑʊ] and [ɑʊɑʊɑʊɑʊɑʊ].

    d. [ɑʊ].

2. Writing-sounding [ɑʊ].

3. [ɑʊ] Nonsense Syllables.

[ɑʊ-ɑʊ-p]	[ɑʊ-p]	[ɑʊp]	[p-ɑʊ-ɑʊ]	[p-ɑʊ]	[pɑʊ]
[ɑʊ-ɑʊ-d]	[ɑʊ-d]	[ɑʊd]	[d-ɑʊ-ɑʊ]	[d-ɑʊ]	[dɑʊ]
[ɑʊ-ɑʊ-f]	[ɑʊ-f]	[ɑʊf]	[f-ɑʊ-ɑʊ]	[f-ɑʊ]	[fɑʊ]
[ɑʊ-ɑʊ-b]	[ɑʊ-b]	[ɑʊb]	[b-ɑʊ-ɑʊ]	[b-ɑʊ]	[bɑʊ]
[ɑʊ-ɑʊ-k]	[ɑʊ-k]	[ɑʊk]	[k-ɑʊ-ɑʊ]	[k-ɑʊ]	[kɑʊ]

[p-ɑʊ-ɑʊ-p]	[p-ɑʊ-p]	[pɑʊp]
[d-ɑʊ-ɑʊ-d]	[d-ɑʊ-d]	[dɑʊd]
[f-ɑʊ-ɑʊ-f]	[f-ɑʊ-f]	[fɑʊf]
[b-ɑʊ-ɑʊ-b]	[b-ɑʊ-b]	[bɑʊb]
[k-ɑʊ-ɑʊ-k]	[k-ɑʊ-k]	[kɑʊk]

4. Constructing [ɑʊ] Words.

tot	– toot	– tout
cod	– cooed	– cowed
wad	– wooed	– wowed
lot	– loot	– lout

shot	– shoot	– shout
don	– dune	– down
ha	– who	– how
rot	– route	– rout

5. [ɑʊ] Words.

Initial		*Final*		*Medial*	
hour	oust	allow	avow	about	cowl
ouch	outcast	brow	bough	around	douse
ounce	outer	chow	bow-wow	brown	doubt
our	outfit	cow	eyebrow	count	gout
ours	outlaw	endow	mow	down	gown
ourselves	outlet	how	prow	flower	loud
out	outline	now	scow	found	mouth
outdoors	output	plow	somehow	house	noun
outside	outset	thou	sow	mouse	pout
owl	outward	vow	trow	round	town

6. Distinguishing [æ] from [ɑ] in [ɑʊ].

pat	– pout	gat	– gout	mass	– mouse	tan	– town
tat	– tout	rat	– rout	Nan	– noun	lad	– loud
Dan	– down	scat	– scout	bad	– bowed	lass	– louse
cad	– cowed	spat	– spout	bat	– bout	can't	– count

7. Distinguishing [ʌ] from [ɑ] in [ɑʊ].

muss – mouse	ton – town	shut – shout
nun – noun	dun – down	hull – howl
putt – pout	gun – gown	utter – outer
bud – bowed	rut – rout	butt – bout

8. Distinguishing [ɑ] from [ɑʊ].

pot – pout	cod – cowed	shot – shout
tot – tout	got – gout	Scott – scout
don – down	rot – rout	spot – spout
dot – doubt	lot – lout	trot – trout

9. [ɑʊ] Sentences.

1. Our brown cow has been found.
2. I have plowed the ground around the house.
3. She shouted loudly when she found a mouse among the flowers.
4. The owl came down from the mountain.
5. The boy scout bowed to the crowd.
6. Count me out for about an hour.
7. He scowled at the crowd that was shouting around town.
8. Somehow I doubt if it's a brown trout.
9. The mouth is usually rounded in shouting.
10. The sound was found to be a compound of vowels.

THE [ɪ] DIPHTHONGS

THE DIPHTHONG [eɪ]

[eɪ] is spelled typically as in sale, sail, pay; also as in great, survey, veil, neigh, fiancé, fiancée, crochet, gauge, gaol. This sound is sometimes heard as a vowel, [e], before voiceless consonants and in unstressed syllables.

1. Articulating [eɪ] in Isolation.

    a. [e]
    b. [ɪ]
    c. [e] and [ɪ] alternated, as in [e-ɪ-e-ɪ-e-ɪ-eɪ] and [eɪeɪeɪeɪeɪ].
    d. [eɪ]

2. Writing-sounding [eɪ].

3. [eɪ] Nonsense Syllables.

[eɪ-eɪ-p]	[eɪ-p]	[eɪp]	[p-eɪ-eɪ]	[p-eɪ]	[peɪ]
[eɪ-eɪ-d]	[eɪ-d]	[eɪd]	[d-eɪ-eɪ]	[d-eɪ]	[deɪ]
[eɪ-eɪ-f]	[eɪ-f]	[eɪf]	[f-eɪ-eɪ]	[f-eɪ]	[feɪ]
[eɪ-eɪ-b]	[eɪ-b]	[eɪb]	[b-eɪ-eɪ]	[b-eɪ]	[beɪ]
[eɪ-eɪ-k]	[eɪ-k]	[eɪk]	[k-eɪ-eɪ]	[k-eɪ]	[keɪ]

[p-eɪ-eɪ-p]	[p-eɪ-p]	[peɪp]
[d-eɪ-eɪ-d]	[d-eɪ-d]	[deɪd]
[f-eɪ-eɪ-f]	[f-eɪ-f]	[feɪf]
[b-eɪ-eɪ-b]	[b-eɪ-b]	[beɪb]
[k-eɪ-eɪ-k]	[k-eɪ-k]	[keɪk]

4. [eɪ] Words.

Initial		*Final*		*Medial*	
able	acre	away	bay	baby	cane
ace	agent	day	bray	cake	date
ache	ailment	gay	clay	came	face
age	aimless	may	hay	gave	laid
aid	alien	pay	jay	great	made
ail	amiable	play	neigh	name	pail
aim	ape	say	prey	paper	rail
apron	apex	stay	slay	place	rain
ate	Asia	they	spray	same	sail
eighty	atheist	way	stray	tail	tape

5. Distinguishing [ʌ] from [e] in [eɪ].

mum	– maim	numb	– name	buck	– bake	fun	– feign
muck	– make	pun	– pain	hull	– hail	luck	– lake
mud	– made	putt	– pate	shove	– shave	run	– rain
mutt	– mate	bun	– bane	son	– sane	won	– wane

6. Distinguishing [ɛ] from [eɪ].

beck	– bake	bet	– bait	bell	– bail	debt	– date
dell	– dale	yell	– Yale	tell	– tale	fell	– fail
sell	– sail	led	– laid	let	– late	red	– raid
wed	– wade	wet	– wait	men	– mane	met	– mate

7. [eɪ] Sentences.

1. Stay and play with the baby.
2. James paid for the apron.
3. May baked a cake yesterday.
4. He sailed eighty miles away from the bay.
5. The rain made me late.
6. I won't stay unless we can make it pay.
7. The favorite went lame before the race.
8. A grape becomes a raisin in its old age.
9. The player laid his ace face down on the table.
10. He gained his greatest fame in Asia.

THE DIPHTHONG [aɪ]

[aɪ] is spelled typically as in **I, fly, tie**; also as in **eye, aye** (yes), **rye, buy, guile, sigh, aisle, height**.

1. Articulating [aɪ] in Isolation.

    a. [ɑ]
    b. [ɪ]
    c. [ɑ] and [ɪ] alternated, as in [ɑ-ɪ-ɑ-ɪ-ɑ-ɪ-aɪ] and [aɪaɪaɪaɪaɪ].
    d. [aɪ]

2. Writing-sounding [aɪ].

3. [aɪ] Nonsense Syllables.

[aɪ-aɪ-p]	[aɪ-p]	[aɪp]	[p-aɪ-aɪ]	[p-aɪ]	[paɪ]
[aɪ-aɪ-d]	[aɪ-d]	[aɪd]	[d-aɪ-aɪ]	[d–aɪ]	[daɪ]
[aɪ-aɪ-f]	[aɪ-f]	[aɪf]	[f-aɪ-aɪ]	[f-aɪ]	[faɪ]
[aɪ-aɪ-b]	[aɪ-b]	[aɪb]	[b-aɪ-aɪ]	[b-aɪ]	[baɪ]
[aɪ-aɪ-k]	[aɪ-k]	[aɪk]	[k-aɪ-aɪ]	[k-aɪ]	[kaɪ]

[p-aɪ-aɪ-p]	[p-aɪ-p]	[paɪp]
[d-aɪ-aɪ-d]	[d-aɪ-d]	[daɪd]
[f-aɪ-aɪ-f]	[f-aɪ-f]	[faɪf]
[b-aɪ-aɪ-b]	[b-aɪ-b]	[baɪb]
[k-aɪ-aɪ-k]	[k-aɪ-k]	[kaɪk]

4. Constructing [aɪ] Words.

don	– din	– dine	pop	– pip	– pipe
top	– tip	– type	lock	– lick	– like
wan	– win	– wine	rod	– rid	– ride
hod	– hid	– hide	pock	– pick	– pike

5. [aɪ] Words.

Initial		*Final*		*Medial*	
eyes	aisle	by	guy	cried	dive
I	icicle	die	nigh	find	guide
ice	ideal	fly	pry	fine	line
iceberg	idolize	high	rye	five	mile
idea	iota	lie	shy	hide	mine
idle	ire	my	sigh	kind	night
iris	islet	pie	spy	light	pile
iron	item	sky	sty	like	shine
ironing	ivory	tie	thigh	ride	tire
island	ivy	why	thy	time	wise

6. Distinguishing [ʌ] from [a] in [aɪ].

dun	– dine	nut	– night	bud	– bide	cut	– kite
won	– wine	mutt	– might	ton	– tine	rut	– right
pup	– pipe	nun	– nine	shun	– shine	fun	– fine
luck	– like	pun	– pine	dove	– dive	sun	– sign

7. Distinguishing [a] from [aɪ].

don	– dine	sod	– side	pop	– pipe	pod	– pied
top	– type	tot	– tight	far	– fire	tar	– tire
shod	– shied	hod	– hide	lock	– like	rod	– ride
wan	– wine	wad	– wide	mar	– mire	knot	– night

8. [aɪ] Sentences.

1. Isn't it fine to fly a kite?
2. What kind of ice cream shall I buy?
3. Why do you hide?
4. I like my five pet mice.

5. Be kind to the crying child.
6. Irish eyes are smiling.
7. Blind Island is a mile wide.
8. My guide will buy us the right kind of line.
9. He tried to find some high-priced ivory.
10. If I were wise I'd change the tire tonight.

THE DIPHTHONG [ɔɪ]

[ɔɪ] is spelled typically as in toy, soil.

1. Articulating [ɔɪ] in Isolation.

    a. [ɔ]
    b. [ɪ]
    c. [ɔ] and [ɪ] alternated, as in [ɔ-ɪ-ɔ-ɪ-ɔ-ɪ-ɔɪ] and [ɔɪɔɪɔɪ].
    d. [ɔɪ]

2. Writing-sounding [ɔɪ].

3. [ɔɪ] Nonsense Syllables.

[ɔɪ-ɔɪ-p]	[ɔɪ-p]	[ɔɪp]	[p-ɔɪ-ɔɪ]	[p-ɔɪ]	[pɔɪ]
[ɔɪ-ɔɪ-d]	[ɔɪ-d]	[ɔɪd]	[d-ɔɪ-ɔɪ]	[d-ɔɪ]	[dɔɪ]
[ɔɪ-ɔɪ-f]	[ɔɪ-f]	[ɔɪf]	[f-ɔɪ-ɔɪ]	[f-ɔɪ]	[fɔɪ]
[ɔɪ-ɔɪ-b]	[ɔɪ-b]	[ɔɪb]	[b-ɔɪ-ɔɪ]	[b-ɔɪ]	[bɔɪ]
[ɔɪ-ɔɪ-k]	[ɔɪ-k]	[ɔɪk]	[k-ɔɪ-ɔɪ]	[k-ɔɪ]	[kɔɪ]

[p-ɔɪ-ɔɪ-p]	[p-ɔɪ-p]	[pɔɪp]
[d-ɔɪ-ɔɪ-d]	[d-ɔɪ-d]	[dɔɪd]
[f-ɔɪ-ɔɪ-f]	[f-ɔɪ-f]	[fɔɪf]
[b-ɔɪ-ɔɪ-b]	[b-ɔɪ-b]	[bɔɪb]
[k-ɔɪ-ɔɪ-k]	[k-ɔɪ-k]	[kɔɪk]

4. Constructing [ɔɪ] Words.

call	– kill	– coil	fall	– fill	– foil
maul	– mill	– moil	Saul	– sill	– soil
ball	– bill	– boil	all	– ill	– oil
tall	– till	– toil	lawn	– Linn	– loin

5. [ɔɪ] Words.

Final		Medial	
alloy	ahoy	boil	adroit
annoy	cloy	boys	coif
boy	convoy	coin	coil
decoy	corduroy	noise	foil
destroy	coy	point	joist
employ	deploy	poison	loin
enjoy	envoy	soil	poise
joy	Savoy	toil	toyed
Roy	soy	toys	void
toy	Troy	voice	voile

6. Distinguishing [ɑɪ] from [ɔɪ].

mile – moil	tied – toyed	line – loin
pies – poise	tile – toil	file – foil
bile – boil	ties – toys	vile – voile
buys – boys	kine – coin	vice – voice

7. Distinguishing [ɔ] from [ɔɪ].

maul – moil	gnaws – noise
ball – boil	lawn – loin
call – coil	pause – poise
tall – toil	fall – foil

8. [ɔɪ] Sentences.

1. The boy bought some oil.
2. Tom joined his noisy friends.
3. Roy likes oysters.
4. The boy was glad to hear his mother's voice.
5. He gave the boys money to buy toys.
6. Floy enjoyed the voile dress.
7. Mr. Boiler is employed at Detroit.
8. The point of the foil was poisoned.
9. He voiced his annoyance at the noise in the Savoy.
10. The Royal adroitly avoided the destroyer.

BIBLIOGRAPHY

1. Avery, E., Dorsey, J., and Sickels, V. A., *First Principles of Speech Training*, D. Appleton-Century Company, Inc., New York, 1931.
2. Gray, G. W., and Wise, C. M., *The Bases of Speech*, Harper & Brothers, New York, 1934.
3. Kenyon, J. S., *American Pronunciation*, George Wahr, Ann Arbor, Mich., 1937.
4. Krapp, G. P., *The Pronunciation of Standard English in America*, Oxford University Press, New York, 1919.

CHAPTER IV

CONSONANT ARTICULATION

	Nasal	Stop-plosive		Semi-vowel	Fricative		Glide	
	Voiced	Voiceless	Voiced	Voiced	Voiceless	Voiced	Voiceless	Voiced
Labial	[m]	[p]	[b]				[ʍ]	[w]
Labio-dental					[f]	[v]		
Lingua-dental					[θ]	[ð]		
Post-dental	[n]	[t]	[d]	[r] [l]	[s] [ʃ]	[z] [ʒ]		[j]
Velar	[ŋ]	[k]	[g]					
Glottal					[h]			

A consonant is a speech sound in which the expired breath stream is hindered, diverted or stopped during its emission. In the above table the 23 consonant elements of American speech are arranged in a threefold classification. The major headings at the top designate general perceptual properties; the anatomical terms at the left indicate the places in the speech mechanism where the characteristic articulatory positions are taken or movements are made; the terms *voiced* and *voiceless*, referring to presence or absence of vocal cord vibration, enlarge both the perceptual and the anatomical descriptions.

The classification into nasal, stop-plosive, semi-vowel, fricative and glide consonants furnishes an outline for the present chapter. The general characteristics of each of these types may be summarized as follows:

1. *Nasal consonants.*—Emission of sound is nasal, oral emission

being almost entirely precluded; all three of the nasal consonants have a typical nasal quality in common; all three are voiced. [m] and [n] frequently serve as syllabic consonants, resembling the semi-vowels in this respect.

2. *Stop-plosive consonants.*—Involve typically a stoppage, then an explosion of the breath, although the explosive phase is sometimes absent in American speech; occur in three voiced and voiceless pairs, the members of each pair having substantially identical positions and movements.

3. *Semi-vowel consonants.*—Vowel-like, both perceptually and physiologically; both are voiced; both serve frequently as syllabic consonants. [l] is frequently termed a *lateral*, because emission is over the sides of the tongue; [r] in some positions is sometimes classified as a glide, although it is by no means unique among non-glide consonants and vowels in having some glide-like features.

4. *Fricative consonants.*—Characteristic quality produced by forcing air through a restricted opening; occur in four voiced and voiceless pairs, plus one additional voiceless sound. The fricatives [s], [z], [ʃ] and [ʒ], along with [tʃ] and [dʒ], are sometimes termed *sibilants*.

5. *Glide consonants.*—Vary, both acoustically and physiologically, during their duration; one voiced and voiceless pair, plus one additional voiced sound.

Materials for the consonant combinations [tʃ] and [dʒ] are presented at the end of this chapter. In some schemes these sounds are considered as consonant elements, forming a sixth class, the *affricates*. Although phonemically there is considerable justification for this procedure in English, it is convenient for drill purposes to regard them as combinations.

When consonants are classified according to the characteristic places of articulatory position or movement, as in the rows of the above table, the groups are described as in the following paragraphs. Detailed descriptions of the articulation of the individual sounds are given in connection with the drill materials.

1. *Labial consonants.*—The breath stream is impeded, stopped

or diverted by the lips. This class includes one nasal, two stop-plosives and two glides.

2. *Labio-dental consonants.*—The breath stream is restricted by interaction of the lower lip and upper teeth. Both labio-dentals are fricatives.

3. *Lingua-dental consonants.*—The breath stream is restricted by interaction of the tongue and upper teeth. Two lingua-dentals, both fricatives, are found in English.

4. *Post-dental consonants.*—The breath stream is restricted, stopped or diverted by elevation of the tip or body of the tongue to the region behind the upper anterior teeth. This is the largest group of consonants, including as it does one nasal, two stop-plosives, two semi-vowels, four fricatives and one glide. The glide, [j], ordinarily is classified as the one English *palatal* consonant, but recent data indicate that there is little physiological justification for distinguishing between this sound and the other post-dentals.

5. *Velar consonants.*—The breath stream is stopped or diverted by elevation of the rear portion of the tongue to the raised or lowered velum. One nasal and two stop-plosives compose the velar consonants in English.

6. *Glottal consonants.*—The breath stream is impeded at the glottis, but not enough to produce vocal cord vibration. The voiceless fricative [h] is the only phonemic glottal consonant of American English, although a glottal stop-plosive sometimes intrudes.

Errors in consonant articulation are of five general types:

1. Substitution, or tendency toward substitution, of another consonant, e.g., [w] for [r], [θ] for [s].
2. Voicing error, or substitution of the voiced or voiceless correlative, e.g., [s] for [z], [d] for [t].
3. Distortion, e.g., lateral [s], hissing [s].
4. Slighting, i.e., the consonant is incomplete, too short, made with too little breath pressure.
5. Omission.

According to the studies of both Hall and Barnes, cited in the

Bibliography, the ten individual sounds most frequently defective in the speech of both adults and children are [s], [z], [ʃ], [ʒ], [tʃ], [dʒ], [θ], [ð], [ʍ] and [ŋ]. For children's speech [r] and [l] should be added to the list.

Exercises for consonant sounds may follow the same procedure used for vowels, except for a slight modification in the case of stop-plosives and glides, which are non-continuant consonants, i.e., consonants that cannot be sustained. During isolated articulation and writing-sounding of these sounds attempt only short, staccato examples, adding the indefinite vowel [ə] to [b], [d], [g], [w] and [j]. Remember, however, that this vowel is not part of the consonant. To preserve the rhythm of the writing-sounding drill without distorting the sound, always articulate the sound at the same point in the written symbol. The above changes are also necessary in practicing [tʃ] and [dʒ], except that the indefinite vowel need not be added.

Detailed directions for drill procedure will be found in the Introduction.

THE NASAL CONSONANTS

The Consonant [m]

[m] is a voiced, labial, nasal continuant, the nasal correlative of [p] and [b]. Most typical features: relaxed contact of the lips; lowered velum; nasal emission. Usually the tongue is relaxed on the floor of the mouth and the teeth are slightly parted. There is vocal cord vibration throughout.

[m] is spelled typically as in my, summer, home; also as in palm, lamb, hymn, phlegm; also as a syllabic consonant in prism, blossom, emblem, bedlam. Among the 23 consonants it ranks seventh in frequency of use. It is found in initial, medial, final and unstressed syllabic positions.

1. Articulating [m] in Isolation.
2. Writing-sounding [m].

3. [m] Nonsense Syllables.

[m-m-i] [m-i] [mi]   [i-m-m] [i-m] [im]   [i-m-m-i] [i-m-i] [imi]
[m-m-e] [m-e] [me]   [e-m-m] [e-m] [em]   [e-m-m-e] [e-m-e] [eme]
[m-m-ɑ] [m-ɑ] [mɑ]   [ɑ-m-m] [ɑ-m] [ɑm]   [ɑ-m-m-ɑ] [ɑ-m-ɑ] [ɑmɑ]
[m-m-o] [m-o] [mo]   [o-m-m] [o-m] [om]   [o-m-m-o] [o-m-o] [omo]
[m-m-u] [m-u] [mu]   [u-m-m] [u-m] [um]   [u-m-m-u] [u-m-u] [umu]

4. [m] Words.

Initial

made	map	
make	match	
man	mean	
may	meet	
me	mesh	
men	might	
mine	mob	
much	mood	
must	moss	
my	mouse	

Final

came	am
come	climb
farm	dim
him	dime
home	dome
name	from
same	gem
some	gum
them	lame
time	seem

Medial

almost	beaming
among	bombing
animal	famous
Christmas	foamy
coming	hammer
company	lemon
empty	memory
farmer	pommel
mamma	rumor
something	timber

Unstressed Syllabic

blossom	anthem
bosom	atom
chasm	balsam
fathom	bedlam
ism	emblem
prism	heroism
rhythm	phantom
spasm	problem
transom	random
truism	symptom

5. Distinguishing [b] from [m].

bean – mean	batch – match	bob – bomb	sob – psalm
bit – mitt	bill – mill	rub – rum	lobe – loam
bake – make	beet – meet	mob – mom	robe – roam
boss – moss	bug – mug	hub – hum	rib – rim

6. [m] Blend Words.

[-mp]	[-mpt]	[-mps]	[-md]
trump	camped	glimpse	hymned
primp	prompt	camps	slammed
hemp	tramped	scamps	boomed
lamp	bumped	imps	beamed
romp	vamped	blimps	rhymed
swamp	skimped	romps	trimmed
camp	limped	dumps	tamed
plump	pumped	stomps	bombed
stamp	romped	jumps	palmed
shrimp	slumped	stamps	drummed

7. [m] Sentences.

1. Will you come home with me tomorrow?
2. My mother is making some jam.
3. Mary has milk every morning.
4. Tom comes from a farm.
5. The tame mouse jumped on my arm.
6. Come to my summer home.
7. Sometimes I climb mountains in my dreams.
8. The farmer came humming through the timber.
9. Remember that men are merely animals.
10. The diaphragm is the dome-shaped muscle that surmounts the abdomen.

The Consonant [n]

[n] is a voiced, post-dental, nasal continuant, the nasal correlative of [t] and [d]. Most typical features: contact of the curved border of the tongue around the entire alveolar ridge; lowered velum; nasal emission. The lips are usually parted, as are the teeth. There is vocal cord vibration throughout.

[n] is spelled typically as in not, sunny, bone; also as in gnat, knife, pneumonia, Wednesday, champagne; also as a syllabic consonant in mason, sudden, raisin, curtain. It is found in initial, final, medial and unstressed syllabic positions, and ranks second in general frequency of use among the English consonants.

1. Articulating [n] in Isolation.
2. Writing-sounding [n].
3. [n] Nonsense Syllables.

[n-n-i]	[n-i]	[ni]	[i-n-n]	[i-n]	[in]	[i-n-n-i]	[i-n-i]	[ini]
[n-n-e]	[n-e]	[ne]	[e-n-n]	[e-n]	[en]	[e-n-n-e]	[e-n-e]	[ene]
[n-n-ɑ]	[n-ɑ]	[nɑ]	[ɑ-n-n]	[ɑ-n]	[ɑn]	[ɑ-n-n-ɑ]	[ɑ-n-ɑ]	[ɑnɑ]
[n-n-o]	[n-o]	[no]	[o-n-n]	[o-n]	[on]	[o-n-n-o]	[o-n-o]	[ono]
[n-n-u]	[n-u]	[nu]	[u-n-n]	[u-n]	[un]	[u-n-n-u]	[u-n-u]	[unu]

4. [n] Words.

Initial

know	knee
name	net
near	next
need	noise
nest	nook
never	noon
new	nor
nice	notch
night	noun
not	now

Final

again	in
barn	on
been	one
brown	own
can	ran
down	soon
fun	sun
fine	ten
green	than
hen	train

Medial

animal	dinner
another	downfall
any	fanning
funny	gunner
into	keener
many	panel
morning	raining
only	senses
pony	universe
under	window

Unstressed Syllabic

broken	deaden
button	deepen
chicken	dozen
curtain	flatten
eleven	haven
garden	laden
heaven	oven
kitten	portion
lemon	rotten
open	season

5. Distinguishing [d] from [n].

deed – need	dip – nip	keyed – keen	bead – bean
dun – nun	door – nor	pad – pan	paid – pain
dole – knoll	down – noun	code – cone	dead – den
dame – name	dab – nab	died – dine	raid – rain

6. [n] Blend Words.

[-nt]	[-nd]	[-nts]	[-ntʃ]	[-ndʒ]
tent	bend	tents	pinch	binge
rant	sand	dents	crunch	lunge
print	round	haunts	staunch	singe
runt	spend	rants	branch	range
pant	fund	grants	launch	sponge
paint	blonde	grunts	wench	tinge
joint	burned	bunts	ranch	avenge
daunt	joined	pants	bunch	strange
pint	behind	pints	cinch	twinge
sent	groaned	rents	lunch	lounge

7. [n] Sentences.

1. Dan, find your napkin before dinner.
2. Ned has many new plants in his garden.
3. It is fun to spend the night on a train.
4. The kitten cannot run in the garden.
5. Anne, there is a green animal in the sand.
6. Nell's nonsense is not funny.
7. The Chinese and Japanese are not friendly at present.
8. Nine fancy brown hens ran out of the barn into the rain.
9. Definite statements are commonly accompanied by downward inflections.
10. Clinical practice has no meaning unless you can transfer what you learn into conversation.

THE CONSONANT [ŋ]

[ŋ] is a voiced, velar, nasal continuant, the nasal correlative of [k] and [g]. Most typical features: contact between the elevated rear portion of the tongue and the lowered velum; nasal emission. Usually the tip of the tongue is on the floor of the mouth, slightly behind the lower anterior teeth, and the lips are slightly parted, as are the teeth. There is vocal cord vibration throughout.

[ŋ] is spelled typically as in ring; also as in tongue; and it participates in finger, sank, uncle, conquer, anxious, anxiety. Among the 23 consonants [ŋ] ranks nineteenth in general frequency of use. It is found only in final and medial positions, and approximately 20 per cent of all its occurrences are in a single blend, [ŋk]. It is one of the ten sounds most frequently defective.

1. Articulating [ŋ] in Isolation.
2. Writing-sounding [ŋ].
3. [ŋ] Nonsense Syllables.

[i-ŋ-ŋ]	[i-ŋ]	[iŋ]	[i-ŋ-ŋ-i]	[i-ŋ-i]	[iŋi]
[e-ŋ-ŋ]	[e-ŋ]	[eŋ]	[e-ŋ-ŋ-e]	[e-ŋ-e]	[eŋe]
[ɑ-ŋ-ŋ]	[ɑ-ŋ]	[ɑŋ]	[ɑ-ŋ-ŋ-ɑ]	[ɑ-ŋ-ɑ]	[ɑŋɑ]
[o-ŋ-ŋ]	[o-ŋ]	[oŋ]	[o-ŋ-ŋ-o]	[o-ŋ-o]	[oŋo]
[u-ŋ-ŋ]	[u-ŋ]	[uŋ]	[u-ŋ-ŋ-u]	[u-ŋ-u]	[uŋu]

4. [ŋ] Words.

Final		*Medial*	
bring	fling	angle	banging
coming	gong	banker	longer
going	king	blanket	mangle
long	lung	donkey	ringing
making	rang	finger	singer
morning	sang	hungry	sinking
playing	spring	kingdom	stronger
ring	strong	language	thinker
sing	wing	monkey	wrangle
thing	wrong	single	wronging

5. Distinguishing [g] from [ŋ].

rigging – ringing	fag – fang	tug – tongue	lug – lung
logging – longing	gag – gang	wig – wing	sag – sang
bagging – banging	tag – tang	rag – rang	hag – hang
gagging – ganging	tog – tong	rug – rung	hug – hung

6. [ŋ] Blend Words.

[-ŋk]	[-ŋks]	[-ŋkt]	[-ŋd]
slink	banks	cranked	wronged
trunk	links	kinked	winged
honk	shanks	flanked	hanged
swank	bunks	honked	longed
monk	sinks	bunked	ringed

7. [ŋ] Sentences.

1. Something stung my finger.
2. Bring me the ink and the longest pen.
3. They sang for the king every morning.
4. She is going to bring me a monkey.
5. Birds' wings must be strong for flying.
6. Is it wrong to sing in the spring?
7. Frank went walking along Long Island.
8. Playing ping-pong makes me hungry.
9. He clings to the language of long ago.
10. The lungs are essential in breathing, speaking, and singing.

THE STOP-PLOSIVE CONSONANTS

THE CONSONANT [p]

[p] is a voiceless, labial stop-plosive, the voiceless correlative of [b]. Most typical features: a sequence of positions and movements consisting of (1) firm contact of the lips, (2) impounding of air under pressure behind this closure, (3) sudden parting of the lips, releasing the impounded air. The velum is raised; tongue position is immaterial; the teeth usually are slightly parted; there is no vocal cord vibration.

[p] is spelled typically as in pie, supper, hope; also as in

shepherd, hiccough. Among the 23 consonants it ranks sixteenth in general frequency of use, and is found in initial, final and medial positions.

1. Articulating [p] in Isolation.
2. Writing-sounding [p].
3. [p] Nonsense Syllables.

[p-p-i]	[p-i]	[pi]	[i-p-p]	[i-p]	[ip]	[i-p-p-i]	[i-p-i]	[ipi]
[p-p-e]	[p-e]	[pe]	[e-p-p]	[e-p]	[ep]	[e-p-p-e]	[e-p-e]	[epe]
[p-p-α]	[p-α]	[pα]	[α-p-p]	[α-p]	[αp]	[α-p-p-α]	[α-p-α]	[αpα]
[p-p-o]	[p-o]	[po]	[o-p-p]	[o-p]	[op]	[o-p-p-o]	[o-p-o]	[opo]
[p-p-u]	[p-u]	[pu]	[u-p-p]	[u-p]	[up]	[u-p-p-u]	[u-p-u]	[upu]

4. [p] Words.

Initial		*Final*		*Medial*	
paper	pack	chop	cap	apple	keeper
party	pad	clap	cape	apron	oppose
people	palm	help	deep	carpet	pepper
pet	peak	hop	ripe	happy	rapid
picture	pin	jump	rope	open	report
pig	pine	keep	ship	paper	separate
place	pole	sleep	shop	people	stupid
pony	pool	steep	slap	stopped	superior
pull	pot	stop	stoop	surprise	suppose
put	puff	up	wipe	upon	typical

5. Distinguishing [b] from [p].

beak	– peak	rib	– rip	rabid	– rapid
beet	– peat	nib	– nip	nabbing	– napping
beer	– peer	jib	– gyp	tabbing	– tapping
bees	– peas	tab	– tap	ribbing	– ripping
bath	– path	cab	– cap	robing	– roping
bomb	– palm	gab	– gap	cabby	– Cappy
bop	– pop	lab	– lap	lobbing	– lopping
bar	– par	nab	– nap	mobbing	– mopping

6. [p] Blend Words.

[pl-]	[pr-]	[-lp]	[-rp]
plump	prim	yelp	warp
plaster	prattle	pulp	harp
plenty	prayer	scalp	carp
plow	precede	help	sharp
play	presto	gulp	corpus
please	predict	whelp	harpy
pliable	price	kelp	warping
plot	prodigy	Alp	corporal
plume	program	sculp	harper
place	proud	palp	carpenter

7. [p] Sentences.

1. She made a cap out of paper.
2. Pat is spinning his new top.
3. Keep the apple but give me the pear.
4. Please draw a picture on this piece of paper.
5. Polly played a piece at the party.
6. The pig stopped in surprise and pounced on the apple.
7. Do you suppose that Paul appreciates painting and sculpture?
8. After the party there was paper all over the carpet.
9. Some spellings represent speech very poorly.
10. Plan a speech improvement program and keep practicing.

The Consonant [b]

[b] is a voiced, labial stop-plosive, the voiced correlative of [p]. Most typical features: a sequence of positions and movements consisting of (1) firm contact of the lips, (2) impounding of air under pressure behind this closure, (3) sudden parting of the lips, releasing the impounded air. Vocal cord vibration may continue throughout. The velum is raised; tongue position is immaterial; the teeth usually are slightly parted.

[b] is spelled typically as in bag, rubber, tube; also as in cupboard. Among the 23 consonants it ranks seventeenth in general frequency of use, and is found in initial, final and medial

positions. Initial occurrences are approximately 11 times as frequent as final occurrences.

1. Articulating [b] in Isolation.
2. Writing-sounding [b].
3. [b] Nonsense Syllables.

[b-b-i]	[b-i]	[bi]	[i-b-b]	[i-b]	[ib]	[i-b-b-i]	[i-b-i]	[ibi]
[b-b-e]	[b-e]	[be]	[e-b-b]	[e-b]	[eb]	[e-b-b-e]	[e-b-e]	[ebe]
[b-b-ɑ]	[b-ɑ]	[bɑ]	[ɑ-b-b]	[ɑ-b]	[ɑb]	[ɑ-b-b-ɑ]	[ɑ-b-ɑ]	[ɑbɑ]
[b-b-o]	[b-o]	[bo]	[o-b-b]	[o-b]	[ob]	[o-b-b-o]	[o-b-o]	[obo]
[b-b-u]	[b-u]	[bu]	[u-b-b]	[u-b]	[ub]	[u-b-b-u]	[u-b-u]	[ubu]

4. [b] Words.

Initial		Final		Medial	
back	began	crib	bob	about	bribery
ball	big	cub	bribe	above	dubious
barn	bird	grab	cab	anybody	fabulous
basket	black	knob	daub	baby	labial
be	blue	rib	jab	cupboard	liberty
bear	boat	rob	jib	fable	nobility
because	book	sob	job	number	robber
bed	both	tab	robe	rabbit	rubbing
been	box	tub	scrub	ribbon	sober
before	boy	web	tube	table	tubing

5. Distinguishing [p] from [b].

peak – beak	path – bath	rip – rib	cap – cab
peat – beet	palm – bomb	nip – nib	gap – gab
peer – beer	pop – bop	gyp – jib	lap – lab
peas – bees	par – bar	tap – tab	nap – nab

6. [b] Blend Words.

[bl-]	[br-]	[-rb]
blame	brag	absorb
blunt	brown	barb
blot	breathe	orb
black	brawl	garb
bloom	brim	rhubarb

7. [b] Sentences.

1. The baby's bunny is in the blue crib.
2. The bread is in the big cupboard.
3. Will you buy me a brown rabbit?
4. The ball bounced into the tub.
5. The bear grabbed the box and broke it.
6. Behind the barn are both blackbirds and bluebirds.
7. Grab that scrubbing brush below the cupboard.
8. Bob built the biggest building in Columbus.
9. I am becoming a bit dubious about this business of liberty.
10. Anybody who believes that fable is as gullible as a baby.

THE CONSONANT [t]

[t] is a voiceless, post-dental stop-plosive, the voiceless correlative of [d]. Most typical features: a sequence of positions and
movements consisting of (1) firm contact of the curved border
of the tongue around the entire alveolar ridge, (2) impounding
of air under pressure behind this closure, (3) sudden lowering of
the tongue, releasing the impounded air. The velum is raised;
the lips usually are slightly parted, as are the teeth; there is
no vocal cord vibration.

[t] is spelled typically as in tell, butter, ate; also as in Thomas,
light, debt, receipt, yacht, indict, two; also as in passed, raced
(see [d] for the past-tense rule); it participates in [tʃ].

[t] is found in initial, final and medial positions, and is the
most frequent consonant of the language. It is of interest that
the tongue contact for this sound is the most commonly assumed articulatory position among the English consonants, the
correlatives of [t], namely [n] and [d], ranking second and fourth
respectively.

1. Articulating [t] in Isolation.
2. Writing-sounding [t].
3. [t] Nonsense Syllables.

[t-t-i]	[t-i]	[ti]	[i-t-t]	[i-t]	[it]	[i-t-t-i]	[i-t-i]	[iti]
[t-t-e]	[t-e]	[te]	[e-t-t]	[e-t]	[et]	[e-t-t-e]	[e-t-e]	[ete]
[t-t-ɑ]	[t-ɑ]	[tɑ]	[ɑ-t-t]	[ɑ-t]	[ɑt]	[ɑ-t-t-ɑ]	[ɑ-t-ɑ]	[ɑtɑ]

| [t-t-o] | [t-o] | [to] | [o-t-t] | [o-t] | [ot] | [o-t-t-o] | [o-t-o] | [oto] |
| [t-t-u] | [t-u] | [tu] | [u-t-t] | [u-t] | [ut] | [u-t-t-u] | [u-t-u] | [utu] |

4. [t] Words.

Initial		*Final*		*Medial*	
table	take	about	fast	after	butter
tail	taught	asked	feet	better	detail
take	teeth	at	first	kitten	later
teacher	tight	basket	get	letter	lattice
tell	tip	boat	great	mister	metal
ten	ton	but	just	party	motto
time	tool	cat	last	pretty	pitied
to	town	count	left	sister	pouting
today	train	cut	light	wanted	rotate
took	tree	eat	liked	water	totem

5. Distinguishing [d] from [t].

deam – team	bad – bat	medal – metal
dean – teen	cad – cat	riding – writing
dear – tear	gad – gat	pedal – petal
din – tin	mad – mat	biding – biting
dame – tame	node – note	herding – hurting
dale – tale	showed – shoat	wading – waiting
dare – tare	booed – boot	madder – matter
dime – time	cooed – coot	kiddy – kitty

6. [t] Blend Words.

[tr-]	[-pt]	[-kt]	[-lt]	[-rt]	[-st]
train	slept	backed	melt	heart	past
trinket	crypt	tucked	salt	sort	crossed
tram	slipped	tracked	wilt	retort	just
trunk	slapped	hooked	jilt	mart	moist
truce	flopped	locked	felt	smart	sliced
try	doped	peeked	pelt	tart	haste
trout	wiped	talked	halt	wart	boost
treat	draped	jerked	fault	quart	best
troll	looped	raked	colt	part	fist
trellis	erupt	tacked	malt	start	feast

7. [t] Sentences.

1. Ted laughed and laughed at the kitten.
2. There is water in the bottom of your boat.
3. The kitten tried to play with the cat's tail.
4. Let's put the nuts into a basket.
5. I just wrote a letter to my sister.
6. It is better to talk too little than to talk too much.
7. The teacher taught him to touch his teeth with the tip of his tongue.
8. Betty's little sister wanted to go to the party.
9. Students sometimes use the term "accent" to refer to dialect.
10. A child with a cleft palate tends to omit certain consonants.

THE CONSONANT [d]

[d] is a voiced, post-dental stop-plosive, the voiced correlative of [t]. Most typical features: a sequence of positions and movements consisting of (1) firm contact of the curved border of the tongue around the entire alveolar ridge, (2) impounding of air under pressure behind this closure, (3) sudden lowering of the tongue, releasing the impounded air. Vocal cord vibration may continue throughout. The velum is raised; the lips usually are slightly parted, as are the teeth.

[d] is spelled typically as in did, rudder, side; also as in would; and participates in [dʒ]. The letters d or ed, added to a verb stem to indicate a past tense or past participle, are pronounced according to whether the preceding sound is voiced or voiceless. If the preceding sound is voiced the suffix is pronounced [d], as in rolled, paved; if voiceless it is pronounced [t], as in packed, faced; if the verb stem ends in [d] or [t], however, the addition is always pronounced [əd], as in stated, baited, sided, aided. [d] is found in initial, final and medial positions, and ranks fourth in frequency of use among the consonants of English.

1. Articulating [d] in Isolation.
2. Writing-sounding [d].

3. [d] Nonsense Syllables.

[d-d-i]	[d-i]	[di]	[i-d-d]	[i-d]	[id]	[i-d-d-i]	[i-d-i]	[idi]
[d-d-e]	[d-e]	[de]	[e-d-d]	[e-d]	[ed]	[e-d-d-e]	[e-d-e]	[ede]
[d-d-ɑ]	[d-ɑ]	[dɑ]	[ɑ-d-d]	[ɑ-d]	[ɑd]	[ɑ-d-d-ɑ]	[ɑ-d-ɑ]	[ɑdɑ]
[d-d-o]	[d-o]	[do]	[o-d-d]	[o-d]	[od]	[o-d-d-o]	[o-d-o]	[odo]
[d-d-u]	[d-u]	[du]	[u-d-d]	[u-d]	[ud]	[u-d-d-u]	[u-d-u]	[udu]

4. [d] Words.

Initial		*Final*		*Medial*	
day	dab	and	heard	body	audible
dear	dawn	bed	hide	building	edible
did	daze	bread	kind	candy	louder
do	death	could	land	children	medial
dog	deem	did	made	garden	modify
doll	deep	find	need	hidden	muddier
door	dig	good	old	ready	radical
down	dine	had	read	today	radio
draw	ditch	hand	red	under	shady
dress	doom	head	ride	window	sudden

5. Distinguishing [t] from [d].

team	– deem	tame	– dame	bat	– bad	note	– node
teen	– dean	tale	– dale	cat	– cad	shoat	– showed
tear	– dear	tare	– dare	gat	– gad	boot	– booed
tin	– din	time	– dime	mat	– mad	coot	– cooed

6. [d] Blend Words.

[dr-]	[-bd]	[-gd]	[-ld]	[-vd]	[-zd]
dream	sobbed	bogged	rolled	saved	raised
dram	robed	bagged	filed	lived	prized
dress	dabbed	begged	squealed	peeved	seized
draw	ribbed	hugged	failed	loved	crazed
drought	bobbed	rigged	toiled	moved	buzzed
drink	bribed	tugged	weld	roved	noised
drove	cribbed	lugged	tilled	raved	teased
dray	jabbed	lagged	scald	dived	pleased
dry	lobed	sagged	mild	believed	razzed
drop	grabbed	fogged	wailed	shoved	nosed

7. [d] Sentences.

1. Today is Don's birthday.
2. Dave reads to the children every day.
3. Did you weed the garden yesterday?
4. I found some candy in the drawer.
5. Dick opened the window and listened to the bird.
6. Reading this drill indifferently will do you no good.
7. My head is bloody but unbowed.
8. It is hidden in the garden under the window.
9. The building was dedicated today.
10. The sound faded until it was just audible.

THE CONSONANT [k]

[k] is a voiceless, velar stop-plosive, the voiceless correlative of [g]. Most typical features: a sequence of positions and movements consisting of (1) firm contact between the elevated rear portion of the tongue and the raised velum, (2) impounding of air under pressure behind this closure, (3) sudden lowering of the tongue, releasing the impounded air. Usually the tip of the tongue is on the floor of the mouth, slightly behind the lower anterior teeth; the lips are slightly parted, as are the teeth; there is no vocal cord vibration.

[k] is spelled typically as in kill, bake, cap, account, back; also as in chorus, ache, talk, liquor, oblique; and it participates in quite, six, anxious. Among the 23 consonants it ranks eighth in frequency of use, and is found in initial, final and medial positions.

1. Articulating [k] in Isolation.
2. Writing-sounding [k].
3. [k] Nonsense Syllables.

[k-k-i]	[k-i]	[ki]	[i-k-k]	[i-k]	[ik]	[i-k-k-i]	[i-k-i]	[iki]
[k-k-e]	[k-e]	[ke]	[e-k-k]	[e-k]	[ek]	[e-k-k-e]	[e-k-e]	[eke]
[k-k-ɑ]	[k-ɑ]	[kɑ]	[ɑ-k-k]	[ɑ-k]	[ɑk]	[ɑ-k-k-ɑ]	[ɑ-k-ɑ]	[ɑkɑ]
[k-k-o]	[k-o]	[ko]	[o-k-k]	[o-k]	[ok]	[o-k-k-o]	[o-k-o]	[oko]
[k-k-u]	[k-u]	[ku]	[u-k-k]	[u-k]	[uk]	[u-k-k-u]	[u-k-u]	[uku}

4. [k] Words.

Initial		Final		Medial	
cake	cool	back	brick	accident	cookery
call	couch	black	cook	basket	decorate
came	cow	book	hawk	because	likeable
can	cried	cake	like	biscuit	likely
car	cut	look	luck	breakfast	local
cat	keep	make	neck	cocoa	occur
catch	keg	milk	seek	making	second
come	kick	take	took	o'clock	walking
could	kind	thank	walk	picnic	wicked
count	kitten	think	work	picture	working

5. Distinguishing [g] from [k].

gill	– kill	tag	– tack	meager	– meeker
gab	– cab	lag	– lack	tagging	– tacking
gap	– cap	rag	– rack	bagging	– backing
gad	– cad	nag	– knack	stagger	– stacker
goad	– code	lug	– luck	haggle	– hackle
goat	– coat	chug	– chuck	hogging	– hawking
goal	– coal	brig	– brick	Deagan	– deacon
gore	– core	prig	– prick	sagging	– sacking

6. [k] Blend Words.

[kl-]	[kr-]	[-lk]	[-rk]
clean	craft	silk	lark
cling	crew	sulk	fork
class	crown	bulk	ark
clatter	crow	milk	mark
claw	crucial	hulk	dark
climb	cross	whelk	cork
clutter	critical	elk	bark
cloister	crest	bilk	pork
clay	create	skulk	shark
clothes	cry	ilk	park

7. [k] Sentences.

1. Take the carrots and cabbages from the basket.
2. I like to drink cocoa for breakfast.
3. The cock crows at break of day.
4. Carl gave me a picture book for Christmas.
5. Dick took the milk to the kitchen.
6. Can you come when I call?
7. The cook baked a cake for the picnic.
8. The speaker with inactive lips rarely becomes skilled.
9. An octave is a fraction of the musical scale.
10. Correction of defective consonants comes through careful practice.

THE CONSONANT [g]

[g] is a voiced, velar stop-plosive, the voiced correlative of [k]. Most typical features: a sequence of positions and movements consisting of (1) firm contact between the elevated rear portion of the tongue and the raised velum, (2) impounding of air under pressure behind this closure, (3) sudden lowering of the tongue, releasing the impounded air. Vocal cord vibration may continue throughout. Usually the tip of the tongue is on the floor of the mouth, slightly behind the lower anterior teeth, and the lips are slightly parted, as are the teeth.

[g] is spelled typically as in get, egg; also as in ghost, plague; it participates in longer, examine. Among the 23 consonants it ranks eighteenth in general frequency of use, being, thus, much less common than its correlative [k]. It is found in initial, final and medial positions. Initial occurrences are approximately 11 times as frequent as final occurrences.

1. Articulating [g] in Isolation.
2. Writing-sounding [g].
3. [g] Nonsense Syllables.

[g-g-i]	[g-i]	[gi]	[i-g-g]	[i-g]	[ig]	[i-g-g-i]	[i-g-i]	[igi]
[g-g-e]	[g-e]	[ge]	[e-g-g]	[e-g]	[eg]	[e-g-g-e]	[e-g-e]	[ege]
[g-g-ɑ]	[g-ɑ]	[gɑ]	[ɑ-g-g]	[ɑ-g]	[ɑg]	[ɑ-g-g-ɑ]	[ɑ-g-ɑ]	[ɑgɑ]
[g-g-o]	[g-o]	[go]	[o-g-g]	[o-g]	[og]	[o-g-g-o]	[o-g-o]	[ogo]
[g-g-u]	[g-u]	[gu]	[u-g-g]	[u-g]	[ug]	[u-g-g-u]	[u-g-u]	[ugu]

4. [g] Words.

Initial		*Final*		*Medial*	
garden	gale	beg	bog	again	aghast
gave	game	big	fog	ago	brigade
get	gauze	bug	keg	began	cigar
girl	geese	dig	log	buggy	legal
go	gift	dog	rag	figure	magazine
good	goat	egg	rogue	finger	regard
got	gone	flag	snag	forget	regulate
great	gout	frog	sprig	hungry	stagger
green	gum	leg	stag	organ	trigger
guess	gun	pig	vague	sugar	vigorous

5. Distinguishing [k] from [g].

kill – gill	code – goad	tack	– tag	luck	– lug
cab – gab	coat – goat	lack	– lag	chuck – chug
cap – gap	coal – goal	rack	– rag	brick	– brig
cad – gad	core – gore	knack	– nag	prick	– prig

6. [g] Blend Words.

[gl-]	[gr-]
glow	grey
gloom	grasp
glad	greet
glider	groan
gleeful	grit
glum	ground
glue	group
glimmer	gross
glaze	grind
glottal	grab

7. [g] Sentences.

1. Grace has gone to the garden to get some grapes.
2. The girl gave the hungry pig his dinner.
3. My grandfather has a green buggy.
4. The dog began to growl at the goat.

5. My goose does not give golden eggs.
6. Guy grabbed his gun, but the goose was gone.
7. "Good," said Gregory. "Begin again."
8. The dog vigorously wagged his tail.
9. He forgot his hunger and staggered through the fog.
10. If you go, I'll give you a good cigar.

THE SEMI-VOWEL CONSONANTS

THE CONSONANT [r]

[r] is a voiced, post-dental, semi-vowel continuant. Most typical feature: elevation of the tongue so that its sides contact the upper side teeth and the adjacent portions of the alveolar ridge. Position of the tip of the tongue is variable; most typically it is pointed upward or forward. The velum is raised; the teeth are very slightly parted, as are the lips, which tend to be retracted laterally. There is vocal cord vibration throughout.

[r] is spelled typically as in red, horrid, care; also as in wrong, rheostat, mortgage, catarrh, corps. Unstressed syllabic [r̩] is spelled as in liar, never, tapir, record, survey, theatre, zephyr, measure, glamour, cupboard; stressed syllabic [r̩] as in term, third, word, turn, burr, learn, myrtle, journal, herb, colonel. In the Eastern and Southern American dialects the spelled r is usually sounded only when it precedes a vowel, being omitted when final and before consonants. When final after the vowels [i] or [ɪ], [ɛ] or [e], [ɔ] or [o], [ʊ] or [u], as in *fear, there, bore, poor,* respectively, the [r] of General American is replaced in most instances by [ə], thus forming a group of diphthongs. In these regions also the stressed syllabic [r̩] of General American tends to become the vowel [ɜ], while the indefinite [ə] supplants the unstressed syllabic [r̩].

[r] is found in initial, final, medial, stressed and unstressed syllabic positions, and in the General American dialect ranks third in frequency of use among the 23 consonants. The above-mentioned omissions and replacements of this very common sound are thus seen to be important features of the regional dialects in which they occur; actually they reduce the use of [r] in

these dialects to approximately one-seventh of its frequency in General American. Although [r] is not among the sounds most commonly defective in adult speech, it is frequently difficult for children.

1. Articulating [r] in Isolation.
2. Writing-sounding [r].
3. [r] Nonsense Syllables.

[r-r-i]	[r-i]	[ri]	[i-r-r]	[i-r]	[ir]	[i-r-r-i]	[i-r-i]	[iri]
[r-r-e]	[r-e]	[re]	[e-r-r]	[e-r]	[er]	[e-r-r-e]	[e-r-e]	[ere]
[r-r-α]	[r-α]	[rα]	[α-r-r]	[α-r]	[αr]	[α-r-r-α]	[α-r-α]	[αrα]
[r-r-o]	[r-o]	[ro]	[o-r-r]	[o-r]	[or]	[o-r-r-o]	[o-r-o]	[oro]
[r-r-u]	[r-u]	[ru]	[u-r-r]	[u-r]	[ur]	[u-r-r-u]	[u-r-u]	[uru]

4. [r] Words.

Initial		*Final*		*Medial*	
rabbit	rail	are	or	already	berate
race	rain	bear	our	around	carry
ran	rib	car	scar	every	deride
read	road	chair	sheer	harrow	glory
ready	roan	dear	stair	morning	horrid
red	rob	far	their	orange	morrow
ride	room	for	were	organ	perish
right	wrap	hear	where	parrot	pouring
round	wreck	her	year	story	terrible
run	wren	near	your	very	tyranny

Stressed Syllabic		*Unstressed Syllabic*	
bird	curb	after	better
burn	hurt	another	bigger
church	learn	farmer	joker
curtain	lurch	father	paper
dirt	serve	letter	robber
early	shirk	mister	slender
girl	shirt	mother	summer
heard	turf	never	teacher
word	turn	other	under
work	worm	over	water

5. Special [r] Words.

ream	rage	rush	robe
reap	wren	romp	wrote
read	rent	rob	road
reel	red	rot	rogue
reef	wreck	rod	role
reach	rest	rock	rose
rim	ran	raw	rue
ring	ranch	wrong	room
rip	rat	wrought	root
rib	rag	roar	rude
rich	raft	wroth	rule
rain	run	row	roof
rate	rub	roam	ruse
rave	rug	roan	roost
race	rough	rope	rouge

6. Distinguishing [w] from [r].

weep – reap	wed – red	wake – rake	wide – ride
week – reek	wad – rod	wait – rate	wise – rise
weed – read	watt – rot	wail – rail	wink – rink
weal – real	won – run	ware – rare	wench – wrench

7. [r] Blend Words.

[pr-]	[br-]	[tr-]	[dr-]
prim	brag	train	dream
prayer	brawl	trunk	dress
price	brim	truce	draw
proud	broom	try	drink
precede	brother	treat	drop

[kr-]	[gr-]	[fr-]	[-rm]
craft	group	frank	arm
crew	grind	fruit	swarm
crown	grasp	fry	charm
crow	greet	freak	warm
crest	ground	fresh	harm

[-rn]	[-rp]	[-rb]	[-rk]
barn	warp	orb	lark
warn	harp	garb	fork
darn	carp	absorb	ark
horn	sharp	barb	cork
corn	corpus	rhubarb	dark

[-rl]	[-rf]	[-rv]	[-rd]
whorl	dwarf	starve	hard
Carl	scarf	carve	steered
gnarl	wharf	marvel	roared
snarl	Garfield	larva	scared
darling	morphine	Marvin	lard

8. [r] Sentences.

1. Harry tried to rip the orange ribbon.
2. Do not run across the narrow bridge.
3. The rain helps the flowers grow.
4. Robert heard the organ in the church.
5. Mary, there is dirt on your dress.
6. The early bird catches the worm.
7. Other farms may be bigger, but not better.
8. He carried the parrot around everywhere.
9. Robert rode the roan right up the stairs.
10. Our three major dialect regions are Southern, Eastern and General American.

The Consonant [l]

[l] is a voiced, post-dental, semi-vowel continuant. Most typical feature: elevation of the tip of the tongue to the anterior alveolar ridge, with little or no lateral contact. Position of the body of the tongue is variable; most typically it is arched downward. The velum is raised; the teeth are slightly parted, as are the lips. There is vocal cord vibration throughout.

[l] is spelled typically as in leg, ill, sale; also as in isle; also as a syllabic consonant in bottle, civil, metal, panel. It is found in initial, final, medial and unstressed syllabic positions, and ranks

fifth among the consonants in general frequency of use. It is frequently defective in children's speech, but affords little difficulty to most adults.

1. Articulating [l] in Isolation.
2. Writing-sounding [l].
3. [l] Nonsense Syllables.

[l-l-i]	[l-i]	[li]	[i-l-l]	[i-l]	[il]	[i-l-l-i]	[i-l-i]	[ili]
[l-l-e]	[l-e]	[le]	[e-l-l]	[e-l]	[el]	[e-l-l-e]	[e-l-e]	[ele]
[l-l-ɑ]	[l-ɑ]	[lɑ]	[ɑ-l-l]	[ɑ-l]	[ɑl]	[ɑ-l-l-ɑ]	[ɑ-l-ɑ]	[ɑlɑ]
[l-l-o]	[l-o]	[lo]	[o-l-l]	[o-l]	[ol]	[o-l-l-o]	[o-l-o]	[olo]
[l-l-u]	[l-u]	[lu]	[u-l-l]	[u-l]	[ul]	[u-l-l-u]	[u-l-u]	[ulu]

4. [l] Words.

Initial

land	lad		
last	lame		
leave	lawn		
left	ledge		
let	limb		
letter	long		
light	look		
like	loot		
little	loss		
live	love		

Final

all	cell
ball	full
call	rule
doll	seal
fall	soil
girl	still
pull	tail
school	tell
shall	well
small	will

Medial

alarm	ability
alive	follow
asleep	frolic
believe	pallid
belong	relate
careless	relic
children	silence
hello	solid
only	solo
yellow	village

Unstressed Syllabic

apple	ample
barrel	baffle
bicycle	bundle
bottle	feeble
bubble	haggle
camel	novel
candle	paddle
little	pickle
people	saddle
table	tussle

5. Special [l] Words.

lean	laid	lump	long
leap	lake	lung	loft
lead	lace	luck	loss
leak	let	lug	low
leaf	led	lull	loam
leave	leg	love	loan
limb	left	lot	load
lip	less	lock	loaf
lit	ledge	lard	loath
lid	lamb	lark	loom
lick	lap	large	loon
live	lad	lodge	loop
lame	lack	law	loot
lane	lag	lawn	loose
late	latch	launch	lose

6. Distinguishing [w] from [l].

wean – lean	wed – led	wake – lake	wise – lies
weep – leap	wet – let	wade – laid	wink – link
week – leak	wag – lag	wait – late	winch – lynch
weed – lead	wop – lop	ware – lair	wisp – lisp

7. [l] Blend Words.

[pl-]	[bl-]	[kl-]	[gl-]	[fl-]
plump	blimp	clean	glow	fleet
plenty	blame	class	glad	flown
plow	blunt	claw	glee	float
play	black	climb	glue	flame
plot	bleed	clay	glaze	flat

[-lm]	[-lv]	[-lp]	[-lk]	[-lf]
film	solve	yelp	silk	golf
helm	valve	pulp	sulk	elf
realm	delve	scalp	bulk	gulf
elm	shelve	gulp	elk	shelf
helmet	twelve	help	milk	wolf

8. [l] Sentences.

1. He fell into the lake and yelled for help.
2. Nell is very careless with her doll.
3. I like to blow bubbles.
4. Light the candle on the table, please.
5. The little girls laughed when he fell off his bicycle.
6. I believe I belong in this village.
7. He carelessly left the letter on the table.
8. The lake is so still it is almost like glass.
9. Lee made a living by building special saddles for camels.
10. Drills to develop flexibility of the lips may help to relieve faulty articulation.

THE FRICATIVE CONSONANTS

The Consonant [f]

[f] is a voiceless, labio-dental, fricative continuant, the voice-less correlative of [v]. Most typical features: light contact between the elevated lower lip and the cutting edges of the upper anterior teeth; air is forced between these structures. The velum is raised; the teeth are slightly parted; the tongue position is immaterial; there is no vocal cord vibration.

[f] is spelled typically as in foe, muff, life; also as in calf, laugh, phase, soften. It is found in initial, final and medial positions, and ranks thirteenth among the 23 consonants in frequency of use.

1. Articulating [f] in Isolation.
2. Writing-sounding [f].
3. [f] Nonsense Syllables.

[f-f-i]	[f-i]	[fi]	[i-f-f]	[i-f]	[if]	[i-f-f-i]	[i-f-i]	[ifi]
[f-f-e]	[f-e]	[fe]	[e-f-f]	[e-f]	[ef]	[e-f-f-e]	[e-f-e]	[efe]
[f-f-ɑ]	[f-ɑ]	[fɑ]	[ɑ-f-f]	[ɑ-f]	[ɑf]	[ɑ-f-f-ɑ]	[ɑ-f-ɑ]	[ɑfɑ]
[f-f-o]	[f-o]	[fo]	[o-f-f]	[o-f]	[of]	[o-f-f-o]	[o-f-o]	[ofo]
[f-f-u]	[f-u]	[fu]	[u-f-f]	[u-f]	[uf]	[u-f-f-u]	[u-f-u]	[ufu]

4. [f] Words.

Initial		*Final*		*Medial*	
fall	faith	calf	beef	afraid	deafen
far	fan	cough	chief	after	laughable
fast	fat	enough	cuff	barefoot	loafing
father	feed	half	deaf	before	prophet
feet	feel	if	loaf	breakfast	refute
find	fool	knife	muff	careful	rifle
fine	found	leaf	safe	coffee	sofa
first	fox	life	skiff	different	soften
five	fun	off	tough	effort	suffer
for	fuss	staff	waif	fifteen	wafer

5. Distinguishing [v] from [f].

veal – feel	vase – face	sheave – sheaf	save – safe
veer – fear	vine – fine	thieve – thief	grieve – grief
vat – fat	vile – file	calve – calf	prove – proof
vane – feign	vast – fast	have – half	strive – strife

6. [f] Blend Words.

[fl-]	[fr-]	[-lf]	[-rf]
fleet	frank	golf	dwarf
float	fruit	elf	scarf
fly	fry	gulf	Garfield
flame	freak	wolf	morphine
flat	fresh	shelf	wharf

7. [f] Sentences.

1. Fanny will feed the calf.
2. Be careful not to frighten the butterflies.
3. My father takes me fishing every fall.
4. Did you ever find a four-leafed clover?
5. Freddie has five goldfish.
6. He felt footloose and fancy-free.
7. Did you find enough coffee for breakfast?
8. What seems fine at fifteen seems foolish at fifty.

9. A phoneme is often defined as a sound family.
10. A falling inflection frequently indicates finality.

THE CONSONANT [v]

[v] is a voiced, labio-dental, fricative continuant, the voiced correlative of [f]. Most typical features: light contact between the elevated lower lip and the cutting edges of the upper anterior teeth; air is forced between these structures. There is vocal cord vibration throughout. The velum is raised; the teeth are slightly parted; the tongue position is immaterial.

[v] is spelled typically as in very, dive; also as in of, salve, Stephen. It is found in initial, final and medial positions, and ranks fifteenth in general frequency of use among the 23 consonants.

1. Articulating [v] in Isolation.
2. Writing-sounding [v].
3. [v] Nonsense Syllables.

[v-v-i]	[v-i]	[vi]	[i-v-v]	[i-v]	[iv]	[i-v-v-i]	[i-v-i]	[ivi]
[v-v-e]	[v-e]	[ve]	[e-v-v]	[e-v]	[ev]	[e-v-v-e]	[e-v-e]	[eve]
[v-v-ɑ]	[v-ɑ]	[vɑ]	[ɑ-v-v]	[ɑ-v]	[ɑv]	[ɑ-v-v-ɑ]	[ɑ-v-ɑ]	[ɑvɑ]
[v-v-o]	[v-o]	[vo]	[o-v-v]	[o-v]	[ov]	[o-v-v-o]	[o-v-o]	[ovo]
[v-v-u]	[v-u]	[vu]	[u-v-v]	[u-v]	[uv]	[u-v-v-u]	[u-v-u]	[uvu]

4. [v] Words.

Initial		*Final*		*Medial*	
vacation	vase	above	dive	clover	diving
value	vault	believe	dove	cover	evil
vane	veil	drive	grieve	driver	jovial
variety	vent	five	groove	envelope	oval
very	vice	give	move	even	prevent
vest	view	glove	salve	ever	revive
vine	village	have	shove	every	rival
violet	vogue	leave	sleeve	gravy	savage
visit	vote	live	stove	never	seven
voice	vowel	love	weave	over	vivid

5. Distinguishing [f] from [v].

feel – veal	face – vase	sheaf – sheave	safe – save
fear – veer	fine – vine	thief – thieve	grief – grieve
fat – vat	file – vile	calf – calve	proof – prove
feign – vane	fast – vast	half – have	strife – strive

6. [v] Blend Words.

[-lv]	[-rv]
solve	starve
valve	carve
delve	marvel
involve	larva
shelve	Marvin

7. [v] Sentences.

1. You have spilled gravy on your gloves.
2. I believe I will visit my aunt this vacation.
3. Violets never grow on vines.
4. I love to drive through the village.
5. I believe I gave the envelope to Eva.
6. We have over seven varieties of clover.
7. He carved the veal and served the gravy.
8. I believe I'll visit Java on my vacation.
9. The driver moved over to the stove and voiced his approval.
10. Among the several varieties of voiced sounds are vowels and semi-vowels.

The Consonant [θ]

[θ] is a voiceless, lingua-dental, fricative continuant, the voiceless correlative of [ð]. Most typical features: light contact between the flattened, elevated, protruded tongue and the cutting edges of the upper anterior teeth; air is forced between these structures. The velum is raised; the lips are relaxed and parted; there is no vocal cord vibration.

[θ] is spelled typically as in **thing**. Although it is found in initial, final and medial positions, it ranks twenty-first in general frequency of use among the 23 consonants. It is used in the initial position approximately 50 times more frequently than in the final position. It is one of the ten sounds most frequently defective.

1. Articulating [θ] in Isolation.
2. Writing-sounding [θ].
3. [θ] Nonsense Syllables.

[θ-θ-i]	[θ-i]	[θi]	[i-θ-θ]	[i-θ]	[iθ]	[i-θ-θ-i]	[i-θ-i]	[iθi]
[θ-θ-e]	[θ-e]	[θe]	[e-θ-θ]	[e-θ]	[eθ]	[e-θ-θ-e]	[e-θ-e]	[eθe]
[θ-θ-α]	[θ-α]	[θα]	[α-θ-θ]	[α-θ]	[αθ]	[α-θ-θ-α]	[α-θ-α]	[αθα]
[θ-θ-o]	[θ-o]	[θo]	[o-θ-θ]	[o-θ]	[oθ]	[o-θ-θ-o]	[o-θ-o]	[oθo]
[θ-θ-u]	[θ-u]	[θu]	[u-θ-θ]	[u-θ]	[uθ]	[u-θ-θ-u]	[u-θ-u]	[uθu]

4. [θ] Words.

Initial		Final		Medial	
thank	thaw	bath	booth	anything	atheist
thick	theater	both	breath	arithmetic	author
thimble	theft	cloth	death	bathtub	cathedral
thing	theme	fourth	faith	birthday	ether
think	theory	month	growth	earthquake	ethical
thought	thick	mouth	moth	everything	mythical
thousand	thief	north	myth	faithful	pathetic
thread	thigh	path	oath	healthy	pathos
three	thin	south	sleuth	nothing	southward
through	thud	teeth	sloth	something	truthful

5. Distinguishing [ð] from [θ].

sheathe – sheath		wreathe – wreath
soothe – sooth		loathe – loath
teethe – teeth		either – ether

6. [θ] Blend Words.

[θr-]	[-θs]	[-n(t)θ]
threat	growths	tenth
throw	faiths	month
three	sheaths	ninth
thrash	myths	thirteenth
throne	deaths	labyrinth

7. [θ] Sentences.

1. It is not healthy to put your thumb in your mouth.
2. Do you think there is a path through the thick woods?
3. I think they both have a toothache.
4. A thimble will help you put the thread through the cloth.
5. Was the earthquake in the north or the south?
6. The sleuth had a theory about the theft.
7. The author's death occurred in a cathedral.
8. The theater was threatened by the earthquake.
9. Hawthorne wrote a thesis on thermometers.
10. Is knowing nothing about something like knowing something about nothing?

The Consonant [ð]

[ð] is a voiced, lingua-dental, fricative continuant, the voiced correlative of [θ]. Most typical features: light contact between the flattened, elevated, protruded tongue and the cutting edges of the upper anterior teeth; air is forced between these structures. There is vocal cord vibration throughout. The velum is raised; the lips are relaxed and parted.

[ð] is spelled as in them, soothe. It is found in initial, final and medial positions, and ranks tenth in frequency of use among the 23 consonants, being approximately four times as common as its correlative [θ]. It also is one of the ten sounds most frequently misarticulated by both children and adults.

1. Articulating [ð] in Isolation.
2. Writing-sounding [ð].
3. [ð] Nonsense Syllables.

[ð-ð-i]	[ð-i]	[ði]	[i-ð-ð]	[i-ð]	[ið]	[i-ð-ð-i]	[i-ð-i]	[iði]
[ð-ð-e]	[ð-e]	[ðe]	[e-ð-ð]	[e-ð]	[eð]	[e-ð-ð-e]	[e-ð-e]	[eðe]
[ð-ð-ɑ]	[ð-ɑ]	[ðɑ]	[ɑ-ð-ð]	[ɑ-ð]	[ɑð]	[ɑ-ð-ð-ɑ]	[ɑ-ð-ɑ]	[ɑðɑ]
[ð-ð-o]	[ð-o]	[ðo]	[o-ð-ð]	[o-ð]	[oð]	[o-ð-ð-o]	[o-ð-o]	[oðo]
[ð-ð-u]	[ð-u]	[ðu]	[u-ð-ð]	[u-ð]	[uð]	[u-ð-ð-u]	[u-ð-u]	[uðu]

4. [ð] Words.

Initial		Final		Medial	
than	thee	bathe	loathe	another	although
that	thine	breathe	scathe	bother	heathen
the	this	clothe	scythe	brother	lather
their	those	lathe	soothe	either	leather
them	thou	seethe	swathe	father	loathing
then	though	smooth	teethe	feather	rather
these	thus	tithe	unclothe	mother	weather
they	thy	with	wreathe	other	without

5. Distinguishing [θ] from [ð].

sheath	– sheathe	wreath	– wreathe
sooth	– soothe	loath	– loathe
teeth	– teethe	ether	– either

6. [ð] Blend Words.

[-ðr̩]	[-ðr̩d]	[-ðd]	[-ðz]
other	feathered	bathed	writhes
lather	gathered	clothed	lathes
weather	tethered	seethed	wreathes
father	smothered	soothed	tithes
wither	bothered	loathed	breathes

7. [ð] Sentences.

1. My brother has a coat of smooth leather.
2. It is hard to breathe in this air.
3. I want another feather for that hat.
4. Mother and father gave them a present.
5. They think that it is a bother to bathe every day.
6. They gathered all the brothers together.
7. My father was rather scathing about the heathen.
8. Birds of a feather flock together.
9. This time they didn't bother the bathers' clothing.
10. The heather withers in this weather.

The Consonant [s]

[s] is a voiceless, post-dental, fricative consonant, the voiceless correlative of [z]. Most typical features: the body of the tongue is grooved and arched toward the anterior alveolar ridge, forming a narrow fissure between these structures; air forced through this fissure hisses over the cutting edges of the upper and lower incisor teeth. Usually the lips are slightly parted and retracted laterally; the opening between the teeth is extremely narrow; the lower jaw is thrust forward so that the upper and lower anterior teeth assume almost an end-to-end relationship. The tip of the tongue is variable in position, pointing upward, downward or forward in different speakers; the velum is raised; there is no vocal cord vibration.

[s] is spelled typically as in so, essay, loose, city, rice; also as in scene, listen, psalm, answer, quartz; it participates in six. The letters s and es, added to a noun to indicate the plural form, or to a verb stem to indicate the first person singular, are pronounced according to whether the preceding sound is voiced or voiceless. If the preceding sound is voiced the suffix is pronounced [z], as in *girls*, *saves*; if voiceless it is pronounced [s], as in *packs*, *apes*; if the preceding sound is [s], [z], [ʃ], [ʒ], [tʃ] or [dʒ], however, the addition is always pronounced [əz], as in *masses*, *pleases*, *pushes*, *rouges*, *matches*, *bridges*.

[s] is found in initial, final and medial positions, and ranks sixth in frequency of use among the consonants of English. It is much more frequently misarticulated by both children and adults than any other speech sound. Research indicates that approximately 90 per cent of all clinical articulatory cases have difficulty with [s].

1. Articulating [s] in Isolation.
2. Writing-sounding [s].
3. [s] Nonsense Syllables.

[s-s-i]	[s-i]	[si]	[i-s-s]	[i-s]	[is]	[i-s-s-i]	[i-s-i]	[isi]
[s-s-e]	[s-e]	[se]	[e-s-s]	[e-s]	[es]	[e-s-s-e]	[e-s-e]	[ese]
[s-s-ɑ]	[s-ɑ]	[sɑ]	[ɑ-s-s]	[ɑ-s]	[ɑs]	[ɑ-s-s-ɑ]	[ɑ-s-ɑ]	[ɑsɑ]
[s-s-o]	[s-o]	[so]	[o-s-s]	[o-s]	[os]	[o-s-s-o]	[o-s-o]	[osɔ]
[s-s-u]	[s-u]	[su]	[u-s-s]	[u-s]	[us]	[u-s-s-u]	[u-s-u]	[ʃusu]

4. [s] Words.

Initial		Final		Medial	
said	small	box	hiss	asleep	classic
same	snow	dress	loss	basket	deceive
sat	so	horse	moss	Christmas	essay
saw	some	house	niece	eraser	icing
say	soon	miss	pace	fasten	lesson
school	stand	nice	pass	gasoline	license
see	stay	once	peace	handsome	massive
sing	still	place	us	history	missing
six	stop	six	voice	instead	possible
sleep	sun	this	wants	mister	recent

5. Special [s] Words.

see	sale	some	salt
seem	safe	sun	soft
seat	save	sung	sauce
seed	sent	sup	sew
seek	send	suds	soap
seal	set	such	sewed
sin	said	psalm	soak
sing	sell	sop	soul
sip	self	sob	sold
sit	sap	sod	sue
sick	sat	sock	soon
sill	sad	sox	soup
say	sack	saw	sued
sane	sag	sought	soothe
sake	sash	sawed	sues

6. Distinguishing [z] from [s].

zeal	– seal	lose	– loose	flees	– fleece	braise	– brace
zing	– sing	buzz	– bus	craws	– cross	graze	– grace
zip	– sip	lies	– lice	Jews	– juice	trays	– trace
zag	– sag	vies	– vice	sloughs	– sluice	prize	– price

7. Distinguishing [θ] from [s].

theme – seem	thud – sud	kith – kiss	math – mass
thin – sin	think – sink	myth – miss	truth – truce
thing – sing	thank – sank	path – pass	sleuth – sluice
thick – sick	thigh – sigh	bath – bass	lath – lass

8. Distinguishing [ʃ] from [s].

sheen – seen	shad – sad	swish – Swiss	gash – gas
sheep – seep	shop – sop	clash – class	lash – lass
sheik – seek	shock – sock	brash – brass	mash – mass
sheet – seat	shod – sod	plush – plus	mush – muss

9. [s] Blend Words.

[sm-]	[sn-]	[sp-]	[st-]	[sk-]
small	sneer	spell	stay	skim
smirk	snipe	span	stem	scant
smart	sneeze	spar	star	skate
smoke	sniff	speak	stop	scald

[sw-]	[sl-]	[spl-]	[spr-]	[str-]
sweep	slow	splash	sprig	strike
swine	slice	split	spray	stream
swell	sleep	splotch	spread	straw
swing	slot	splice	sprawl	strap

[skw-]	[skr-]	[-ps]	[-ts]	[-ks]
squeak	scram	lapse	hats	backs
squat	scroll	crops	bits	trucks
square	script	stoops	coats	shocks
squint	scratch	ropes	boots	cooks

[-fs]	[-sps]	[-sts]	[-sks]
stuffs	lisps	mists	tasks
loafs	gasps	lasts	husks
puffs	wisps	boasts	casks
staffs	grasps	beasts	risks

10. [s] Sentences.

1. Boys were singing songs outside of our house.
2. Does your sister still like to sew?
3. See, there's a horse across the street.
4. Sally fell asleep in the soft chair.
5. I saw six birds in that small nest.
6. The gasoline sign said "Sixteen Cents."
7. The isolation policy was suggested in a recent essay on peace.
8. Loudness is one of several aspects of stress.
9. The loudness of speech is determined for the most part by the intensity of the sound wave.
10. Breathiness is often associated with excessive softness in speech.

THE CONSONANT [z]

[z] is a voiced, post-dental, fricative continuant, the voiced correlative of [s]. Most typical features: the body of the tongue is grooved and arched toward the anterior alveolar ridge, forming a narrow fissure between these structures; air forced through this fissure hisses over the cutting edges of the upper and lower incisor teeth. There is vocal cord vibration throughout. Usually the lips are slightly parted and retracted laterally; the opening between the teeth is extremely narrow; the lower jaw is thrust forward so that the upper and lower anterior teeth assume almost an end-to-end relationship. The tip of the tongue is variable in position, pointing upward, downward or forward in different speakers; the velum is raised.

[z] is spelled typically as in zero, fuzz, prize, easy, lose; also as in discern, czar, xylophone, Missouri; also as in saves, bags (see [s] for the plural rule); it participates in exist, exhaust.

[z] is found in initial, final and medial positions. Although it ranks eleventh in frequency of general use among the 23 consonants, it is the most infrequent initial consonant. Occurrence in this position is approximately one-twentieth as frequent as occurrence in the final position. Along with its correlative [s] it

also is among the ten sounds most frequently in error in the speech of both adults and children.

1. Articulating [z] in Isolation.
2. Writing-sounding [z].
3. [z] Nonsense Syllables.

[z-z-i]	[z-i]	[zi]	[i-z-z]	[i-z]	[iz]	[i-z-z-i]	[i-z-i]	[izi]
[z-z-e]	[z-e]	[ze]	[e-z-z]	[e-z]	[ez]	[e-z-z-e]	[e-z-e]	[eze]
[z-z-ɑ]	[z-ɑ]	[zɑ]	[ɑ-z-z]	[ɑ-z]	[ɑz]	[ɑ-z-z-ɑ]	[ɑ-z-ɑ]	[ɑzɑ]
[z-z-o]	[z-o]	[zo]	[o-z-z]	[o-z]	[oz]	[o-z-z-o]	[o-z-o]	[ozo]
[z-z-u]	[z-u]	[zu]	[u-z-z]	[u-z]	[uz]	[u-z-z-u]	[u-z-u]	[uzu]

4. [z] Words.

Initial	*Final*		*Medial*	
zeal	as	buzz	busy	buzzing
zebra	because	choose	closet	deserve
zenith	eyes	ease	cousin	disaster
zephyr	has	lose	crazy	dizzy
zero	his	nose	daisy	fusing
zest	plays	rise	dozen	hazard
zinc	please	size	easy	pleasant
zone	surprise	tease	fuzzy	rosin
zoo	these	use	lazy	usable
zoology	those	was	music	weasel

5. Distinguishing [s] from [z].

seal – zeal	loose – lose	fleece – flees	brace – braise
sing – zing	bus – buzz	cross – craws	grace – graze
sip – zip	lice – lies	juice – Jews	trace – trays
sag – zag	vice – vies	sluice – sloughs	price – prize

6. Distinguishing [ð] from [z].

seethe – sees	bathe – bays
lathe – lays	breathe – breeze
swathe – sways	writhe – rise
tithe – ties	scythe – sighs
clothe – close	teethe – tease

7. [z] Blend Words.

[-mz]	[-nz]	[-bz]	[-dz]
limbs	bans	robs	beds
plums	coins	tubs	lids
clams	fines	robes	seeds
tames	canes	cribs	hides
stems	moons	cabs	toads

[-gz]	[-lz]	[-rz]	[-vz]
bags	rolls	cars	saves
bugs	hills	leers	sleeves
legs	walls	tires	loves
figs	foils	pears	lives
gags	gulls	doors	knives

8. [z] Sentences.

1. Do not lose the roses with the long stems.
2. My cousin has some daisies.
3. There are a dozen apples in the closet.
4. The bees buzzed around the busy boys.
5. What pleasant music comes across the hills!
6. Some music is pleasing, amusing and amazing.
7. His plays deserve to be chosen for the prize.
8. There are zebras, monkeys and weasels in the zoo.
9. Good readers inhale during pauses between phrases.
10. Nasality, which has two chief causes, is characterized by nasal resonance in non-nasal sounds.

THE CONSONANT [ʃ]

[ʃ] is a voiceless, post-dental, fricative continuant, the voiceless correlative of [ʒ]. Most typical features: the body of the tongue is flattened and arched toward the hard palate and anterior alveolar ridge, forming a rather broad fissure between these structures; air is forced through this fissure; usually the lips protrude characteristically to form a cavity between lips and teeth. The tip of the tongue is variable in position, pointing upward, downward or forward in different speakers; the teeth opening is narrow; the velum is raised; there is no vocal cord vibration.

[ʃ] is spelled typically as in sugar, tissue, pension, mission, shoe, conscious, motion, racial, ocean, chagrin; it participates in anxious and in [tʃ]. Although found in initial, final and medial positions, and in the combination [tʃ], [ʃ] ranks twentieth among the 23 consonants in general frequency of use. Even with this low rank it is over three times as frequent as its correlative [ʒ]. It is one of the ten sounds most frequently misarticulated.

1. Articulating [ʃ] in Isolation.
2. Writing-sounding [ʃ].
3. [ʃ] Nonsense Syllables.

[ʃ-ʃ-i]	[ʃ-i]	[ʃi]	[i-ʃ-ʃ]	[i-ʃ]	[iʃ]	[i-ʃ-ʃ-i]	[i-ʃ-i]	[iʃi]
[ʃ-ʃ-e]	[ʃ-e]	[ʃe]	[e-ʃ-ʃ]	[e-ʃ]	[eʃ]	[e-ʃ-ʃ-e]	[e-ʃ-e]	[eʃe]
[ʃ-ʃ-a]	[ʃ-a]	[ʃa]	[a-ʃ-ʃ]	[a-ʃ]	[aʃ]	[a-ʃ-ʃ-a]	[a-ʃ-a]	[aʃa]
[ʃ-ʃ-o]	[ʃ-o]	[ʃo]	[o-ʃ-ʃ]	[o-ʃ]	[oʃ]	[o-ʃ-ʃ-o]	[o-ʃ-o]	[oʃo]
[ʃ-ʃ-u]	[ʃ-u]	[ʃu]	[u-ʃ-ʃ]	[u-ʃ]	[uʃ]	[u-ʃ-ʃ-u]	[u-ʃ-u]	[uʃu]

4. [ʃ] Words.

Initial		Final		Medial	
shade	shack	brush	crush	addition	ashes
shadow	shawl	bush	dash	ashamed	bashful
shall	shine	cash	flash	bushel	cushion
she	ship	dish	flesh	fisher	devotion
sheep	shoal	finish	fresh	fishing	facial
shelf	shoot	fish	hush	machine	fissure
shell	shot	push	leash	motion	ocean
shop	shout	radish	mesh	national	pressure
should	shun	wash	plush	sunshine	seashore
show	shut	wish	sash	washing	session

5. Special [ʃ] Words.

she	shake	shalt	shawl
sheen	shale	shaft	show
sheep	shave	shun	shone
sheet	shays	shunt	showed

sheik	shed	shut	shoal
sheaf	shell	shuck	shows
sheath	shelf	shove	should
shim	chef	shop	shouldst
shin	shelve	shot	shook
ship	sham	shod	sure
shift	shank	shock	shoe
shay	shad	sharp	shoot
shame	shack	shore	shooed
shape	shag	shorn	shoes

6. Distinguishing [ʒ] from [ʃ].

delusion – dilution   glazier – glacier

allusion – Aleutian

7. Distinguishing [s] from [ʃ].

seen – sheen	sad – shad	Swiss – swish	gas – gash
seep – sheep	sob – shop	class – clash	lass – lash
seek – sheik	sock – shock	brass – brash	mass – mash
seat – sheet	sod – shod	plus – plush	muss – mush

8. Distinguishing [tʃ] from [ʃ].

cheek	– sheik	ditch – dish
chip	– ship	crutch – crush
cheap	– sheep	witch – wish
chew	– shoe	catch – cash
chin	– shin	match – mash
cheat	– sheet	leech – leash
Rachel	– racial	hutch – hush
watching	– washing	latch – lash

9. [ʃ] Blend Words.

[ʃr-]	[-ʃt]
shroud	rushed
shriek	washed
shrimp	pushed
shrine	hushed
shrew	crashed

10. [ʃ] Sentences.

1. The dishes should be kept on the shelf.
2. That shop has brushes and washing machines.
3. He was ashamed to show them just one fish.
4. Shall we hide in the shade of this bush?
5. The bashful girl gathered shells at the shore.
6. There are many species of fish in the ocean.
7. You should get official permission to shoot.
8. His devotion received partial compensation.
9. Racial persecution in some nations is especially vicious.
10. Emotion may be shown by facial expression.

The Consonant [ʒ]

[ʒ] is a voiced, post-dental, fricative continuant, the voiced correlative of [ʃ]. Most typical features: the body of the tongue is flattened and arched toward the hard palate and anterior alveolar ridge, forming a rather broad fissure between these structures; air is forced through this fissure; usually the lips protrude characteristically to form a cavity between lips and teeth. There is vocal cord vibration throughout. The tip of the tongue is variable in position, pointing upward, downward or forward in different speakers; the teeth opening is narrow; the velum is raised.

[ʒ] is spelled typically as in vision, pleasure, negligee, garage, azure, glazier, bijou; it participates in [dʒ]. It is found only in final and medial positions. In general frequency of use [ʒ] ranks twenty-second among the 23 consonants, and is approximately one-third as common as its correlative [ʃ]. It is one of the ten sounds most frequently defective.

1. Articulating [ʒ] in Isolation.
2. Writing-sounding [ʒ].
3. [ʒ] Nonsense Syllables.

[i-ʒ-ʒ]	[i-ʒ]	[iʒ]	[i-ʒ-ʒ-i]	[i-ʒ-i]	[iʒi]
[e-ʒ-ʒ]	[e-ʒ]	[eʒ]	[e-ʒ-ʒ-e]	[e-ʒ-e]	[eʒe]
[ɑ-ʒ-ʒ]	[ɑ-ʒ]	[ɑʒ]	[ɑ-ʒ-ʒ-ɑ]	[ɑ-ʒ-ɑ]	[ɑʒɑ]
[o-ʒ-ʒ]	[o-ʒ]	[oʒ]	[o-ʒ-ʒ-o]	[o-ʒ-o]	[oʒo]
[u-ʒ-ʒ]	[u-ʒ]	[uʒ]	[u-ʒ-ʒ-u]	[u-ʒ-u]	[uʒu]

4. [ʒ] Words.

Final	*Medial*	
beige	azure	casual
camouflage	derision	decision
corsage	evasion	division
garage	glazier	erosion
menage	measure	explosion
mirage	negligee	intrusion
persiflage	seizure	lesion
potage	usual	Persian
prestige	vision	pleasure
rouge	visual	rouging

5. Distinguishing [ʃ] from [ʒ].

dilution – delusion   glacier – glazier

Aleutian – allusion

6. [ʒ] Sentences.

1. The treasure hunt was the most pleasureable part of the occasion.
2. Camouflage employs visual illusions.
3. She envisioned herself in a beige negligee.
4. He made an allusion to the invasion of Persia.
5. He filled his leisure hours with casual pleasures.

The Consonant [h]

[h] is a voiceless, glottal, fricative continuant. Most typical features: partial closure of the glottis, but not enough to produce vocal cord vibration; frictional passage of air through cavities prepared for the speech sound which immediately follows. The articulatory positions thus are exceedingly variable, except for the raised velum.

[h] is spelled typically as in hat; also as in who. It is found only in initial and medial positions, and ranks fourteenth among the 23 consonants in frequency of use.

1. Articulating [h] in Isolation.
2. Writing-sounding [h].

3. [h] Nonsense Syllables.

[h-h-i]	[h-i]	[hi]	[i-h-h-i]	[i-h-i]	[ihi]
[h-h-e]	[h-e]	[he]	[e-h-h-e]	[e-h-e]	[ehe]
[h-h-ɑ]	[h-ɑ]	[hɑ]	[ɑ-h-h-ɑ]	[ɑ-h-ɑ]	[ɑhɑ]
[h-h-o]	[h-o]	[ho]	[o-h-h-o]	[o-h-o]	[oho]
[h-h-u]	[h-u]	[hu]	[u-h-h-u]	[u-h-u]	[uhu]

4. [h] Words.

Initial		*Medial*	
had	help	ahead	ahoy
half	hen	anyhow	babyhood
hand	her	behave	behead
happy	hide	behind	behold
has	high	grasshopper	behoove
have	him	lighthouse	cahoots
he	home	mayhem	mahogany
head	horse	mohair	overhaul
hear	how	perhaps	rehash
hello	who	rehearse	unhook

5. [h] Sentences.

1. He is hiding behind the house.
2. Hurry, Helen is far ahead.
3. He has gone home because he is hungry.
4. I have a friend whose home is a lighthouse.
5. Harry is happy because he has a new horse.
6. How can I help being happy?
7. Perhaps he can hide the horse behind the lighthouse.
8. During babyhood he had only half a head of hair.
9. Who says a mahogany highboy isn't heavy?
10. A high, harsh voice is a handicap.

THE GLIDE CONSONANTS

THE CONSONANT [ʍ]

[ʍ] is a voiceless, labial glide, the voiceless correlative of [w]. Most typical features: immediate and continuous articulatory movement toward the setting for the following sound from an initial position similar to that for [u], i.e., the rear of the tongue elevated toward the velum and the lips closely rounded. The velum is raised; there is no vocal cord vibration.

[ʍ] is spelled as in which, is found only in initial and medial positions, and is used less frequently in American English than any other sound. According to surveys of articulation [ʍ] is one of the ten sounds most frequently defective. But most of the errors that were counted for this sound probably were substitutions of [w], and it is an open question at the present time whether or not this particular replacement should always be regarded as an error. [w] is clearly growing in frequency among good American speakers, especially in such common words as why, where, what, etc. For the time being, however, [ʍ] is advocated for the pronunciation of wh words in careful American speech.

1. Articulating [ʍ] in Isolation.
2. Writing-sounding [ʍ].
3. [ʍ] Nonsense Syllables.

[ʍ-ʍ-i]	[ʍ-i]	[ʍi]	[i-ʍ-ʍ-i]	[i-ʍ-i]	[iʍi]
[ʍ-ʍ-e]	[ʍ-e]	[ʍe]	[e-ʍ-ʍ-e]	[e-ʍ-e]	[eʍe]
[ʍ-ʍ-ɑ]	[ʍ-ɑ]	[ʍɑ]	[ɑ-ʍ-ʍ-ɑ]	[ɑ-ʍ-ɑ]	[ɑʍɑ]
[ʍ-ʍ-o]	[ʍ-o]	[ʍo]	[o-ʍ-ʍ-o]	[o-ʍ-o]	[oʍo]
[ʍ-ʍ-u]	[ʍ-u]	[ʍu]	[u-ʍ-ʍ-u]	[u-ʍ-u]	[uʍu]

4. [ʍ] Words.

Initial		Medial
what	whale	anywhere
wheat	wheeze	awhile
wheel	whelp	awhirl
when	whence	bobwhite
where	whet	elsewhere
which	whey	everywhere
while	whiff	meanwhile
whip	whig	nowhere
whisper	whim	somewhat
why	whine	somewhere

5. Distinguishing [w] from [ʍ].

wither	– whither	weather	– whether
wig	– Whig	wary	– wherry
weal	– wheel	wail	– whale
wit	– whit	wine	– whine
wear	– where	wile	– while
word	– whirred	way	– whey
wet	– whet	wen	– when
watt	– what	witch	– which

6. [ʍ] Sentences.

1. Why isn't wheat grown everywhere?
2. Listen awhile to the bobwhite's song.
3. Who is whipping the white horse?
4. The wheel came off with a whistling sound.
5. Why do you whisper?
6. Why does he whine and whimper everywhere?
7. Somewhere from the left came the whistle of a bobwhite.
8. He whispered that Wheeler was on the wharf.
9. The whip whistled through his whiskers as he wheeled around.
10. Many questions begin with *which*, *what* and *when*.

The Consonant [w]

[w] is a voiced, labial glide, the voiced correlative of [ʍ]. Most typical features: immediate and continuous articulatory movement toward the setting for the following sound from an initial position similar to that for [u], i.e., the rear of the tongue elevated toward the velum and the lips closely rounded. The velum is raised; there is vocal cord vibration throughout.

[w] is spelled typically as in well; also as in distinguish, memoir; it is heard without spelling in *one*, [wʌn]; and it participates in quick, where it sometimes is partially or completely voiceless. Although it is found only in initial and medial positions, [w] ranks ninth among the 23 consonants in general frequency of use and is the most common initial consonant.

1. Articulating [w] in Isolation.
2. Writing-sounding [w].
3. [w] Nonsense Syllables.

[w-w-i]	[w-i]	[wi]	[i-w-w-i]	[i-w-i]	[iwi]
[w-w-e]	[w-e]	[we]	[e-w-w-e]	[e-w-e]	[ewe]
[w-w-ɑ]	[w-ɑ]	[wɑ]	[ɑ-w-w-ɑ]	[ɑ-w-ɑ]	[ɑwɑ]
[w-w-o]	[w-o]	[wo]	[o-w-w-o]	[o-w-o]	[owo]
[w-w-u]	[w-u]	[wu]	[u-w-w-u]	[u-w-u]	[uwu]

4. [w] Words.

Initial		Medial	
walk	wash	always	bewail
want	wax	anyway	onward
was	weed	awake	reward
water	wind	away	rewind
way	wish	backward	seaweed
we	with	between	stalwart
well	won	everyone	unwind
went	word	forward	unwise
were	work	inkwell	unworthy
will	would	sandwich	wayward

5. [w] Blend Words.

[kw-]	[tw-]	[sw-]
quest	twelve	sweep
quick	twice	swim
quiet	twig	swell
choir	twin	swan

6. [w] Sentences.

1. Willie is going to wash the windows.
2. I wish Mary would wake up.
3. Do not walk in the woods; they are wet.
4. Everyone will want a sandwich.
5. We are going away this winter.
6. We can win without a reward.
7. I wish he would watch his words.

8. He awakened at once and went to the well for water.
9. Wishing for wealth is one way to waste time unwisely.
10. The woman looked wistfully downward all during the waltz.

The Consonant [j]

[j] is a voiced, post-dental glide. Most typical features: immediate and continuous articulatory movement toward the setting for the following sound from an initial position similar to that for [i], i.e., the tongue arched toward the anterior alveolar ridge and the lips retracted laterally. The velum is raised; there is vocal cord vibration throughout.

[j] is spelled typically as in yes, familiar; also as in hallelujah; it participates in [ju]. It is found only in initial and medial positions. In frequency of occurrence it ranks twelfth among the 23 consonants during conversation, but it is somewhat less common in formal speech because of the decreased use of *you* and *yes*.

1. Articulating [j] in Isolation.
2. Writing-sounding [j].
3. [j] Nonsense Syllables.

[j-j-i]	[j-i]	[ji]	[i-j-j-i]	[i-j-i]	[iji]
[j-j-e]	[j-e]	[je]	[e-j-j-e]	[e-j-e]	[eje]
[j-j-ɑ]	[j-ɑ]	[jɑ]	[ɑ-j-j-ɑ]	[ɑ-j-ɑ]	[ɑjɑ]
[j-j-o]	[j-o]	[jo]	[o-j-j-o]	[o-j-o]	[ojo]
[j-j-u]	[j-u]	[ju]	[u-j-j-u]	[u-j-u]	[uju]

4. [j] Words.

Initial		*Medial*	
yard	yacht	abuse	adieu
yarn	yam	accuse	alien
year	yank	amuse	bullion
yellow	yawl	canyon	coalyard
yes	yawn	familiar	collier
yesterday	yeast	loyal	grunion
yet	yell	million	innyard
you	yen	onion	minion
young	yield	valiant	stallion
your	yoke	value	vineyard

5. [j] Sentences.

1. Where did you put your yellow sweater?
2. That young puppy will not bite you.
3. Did you lose your red ball of yarn?
4. Yesterday we had onion soup.
5. Yes, you may play in the yard.
6. You are not as young as you used to be.
7. Millions yearn to see New York.
8. Is the use of yeast familiar to you?
9. It would amuse you to know the value of that yellow yacht.
10. Yesterday he accused me of disloyalty.

THE CONSONANT COMBINATIONS

THE COMBINATION [tʃ]

[tʃ] is a voiceless, post-dental, consonant combination, the voiceless correlative of [dʒ]. Most typical features: combination of [t] and [ʃ] in a rapid sequence of positions and movements consisting of (1) firm contact of the curved border of the tongue around the entire alveolar ridge, as in the first phase of [t], (2) impounding of air under pressure behind this closure, as in the second phase of [t], (3) sudden assumption of the tongue position for [ʃ], releasing the impounded air. During the stopped phase the lips usually prepare for [ʃ] by taking a protruded position. The velum is raised; there is no vocal cord vibration.

[tʃ] is spelled typically as in **ch**air, ma**tch**, na**t**ure, sugges**t**ion, righ**te**ous. It is found in initial, final and medial positions, and is approximately as frequent as the two or three least common consonant elements. It is one of the ten sounds most frequently defective.

1. Articulating [tʃ] in Isolation.
2. Writing-sounding [tʃ].
3. [tʃ] Nonsense Syllables.

[tʃ-tʃ-i]	[tʃ-i]	[tʃi]	[i-tʃ-tʃ]	[i-tʃ]	[itʃ]
[tʃ-tʃ-e]	[tʃ-e]	[tʃe]	[e-tʃ-tʃ]	[e-tʃ]	[etʃ]
[tʃ-tʃ-ɑ]	[tʃ-ɑ]	[tʃɑ]	[ɑ-tʃ-tʃ]	[ɑ-tʃ]	[ɑtʃ]
[tʃ-tʃ-o]	[tʃ-o]	[tʃo]	[o-tʃ-tʃ]	[o-tʃ]	[otʃ]
[tʃ-tʃ-u]	[tʃ-u]	[tʃu]	[u-tʃ-tʃ]	[u-tʃ]	[utʃ]

[i-tʃ-tʃ-i] [i-tʃ-i] [itʃi]
[e-tʃ-tʃ-e] [e-tʃ-e] [etʃe]
[a-tʃ-tʃ-a] [a-tʃ-a] [atʃa]
[o-tʃ-tʃ-o] [o-tʃ-o] [otʃo]
[u-tʃ-tʃ-u] [u-tʃ-u] [utʃu]

4. [tʃ] Words.

Initial		*Final*		*Medial*	
chain	cheat	beach	coach	butcher	bachelor
chair	check	branch	latch	exchange	etcher
chalk	chess	bunch	leach	grandchild	ketchup
chance	chick	catch	match	hatchet	merchant
change	chill	church	pitch	kitchen	preaching
chase	chime	each	reach	matches	ratchet
cheese	chin	lunch	rich	orchard	richest
cherry	chip	march	speech	pitcher	righteous
chew	choke	much	watch	teacher	touchy
children	chore	which	wretch	teaching	wretched

5. Distinguishing [dʒ] from [tʃ].

gin	– chin		jeer	– cheer
Jess	– chess		jump	– chump
junk	– chunk		Jill	– chill
joke	– choke		jest	– chest
jar	– char		bridges	– breeches
jug	– chug		ledger	– lecher
Joyce	– choice		badge	– batch
Jane	– chain		ridge	– rich

6. Distinguishing [ʃ] from [tʃ].

sheik	– cheek		dish	– ditch
ship	– chip		crush	– crutch
sheep	– cheap		wish	– witch
shoe	– chew		cash	– catch
shin	– chin		mash	– match
sheet	– cheat		leash	– leech
racial	– Rachel		hush	– hutch
washing	– watching		lash	– latch

7. [tʃ] Blend Words.

[-tʃr]	[-rtʃ]	[-tʃt]
sketcher	smirch	watched
watcher	lurch	scratched
butcher	perch	crunched
preacher	birch	pitched
richer	church	preached

8. [tʃ] Sentences.

1. The child reached for the teacher's chalk.
2. Charlie had lunch at the beach.
3. Our orchard has many cherry trees.
4. Each of us has watched the church bell chime.
5. Please take this pitcher to the kitchen.
6. Chekov wrote *The Cherry Orchard*.
7. Mitchell, the merchant, was a rich bachelor.
8. The child's speech was wretched.
9. Charlie Chan lit a match and searched for the watch.
10. The chess player watched for a chance to checkmate his teacher.

THE COMBINATION [dʒ]

[dʒ] is a voiced, post-dental, consonant combination, the voiced correlative of [tʃ]. Most typical features: combination of [d] and [ʒ] in a rapid sequence of positions and movements consisting of (1) firm contact of the curved border of the tongue around the entire alveolar ridge, as in the first phase of [d], (2) impounding of air under pressure behind this closure, as in the second phase of [d], (3) sudden assumption of the tongue position for [ʒ], releasing the impounded air. Vocal cord vibration may continue throughout. During the stopped phase the lips usually prepare for [ʒ] by taking a protruded position. The velum is raised.

[dʒ] is spelled typically as in jug, magic, page, lodging, edge, legion, soldier, educate, adjoining. It is found in initial, final and medial positions, and is approximately as frequent as the two or three least common consonant elements. It is one of the ten sounds most frequently defective.

1. Articulating [dʒ] in Isolation.
2. Writing-sounding [dʒ].
3. [dʒ] Nonsense Syllables.

[dʒ-dʒ-i]	[dʒ-i]	[dʒi]	[i-dʒ-dʒ]	[i-dʒ]	[idʒ]
[dʒ-dʒ-e]	[dʒ-e]	[dʒe]	[e-dʒ-dʒ]	[e-dʒ]	[edʒ]
[dʒ-dʒ-ɑ]	[dʒ-ɑ]	[dʒɑ]	[ɑ-dʒ-dʒ]	[ɑ-dʒ]	[ɑdʒ]
[dʒ-dʒ-o]	[dʒ-o]	[dʒo]	[o-dʒ-dʒ]	[o-dʒ]	[odʒ]
[dʒ-dʒ-u]	[dʒ-u]	[dʒu]	[u-dʒ-dʒ]	[u-dʒ]	[udʒ]

[i-dʒ-dʒ-i]	[i-dʒ-i]	[idʒi]
[e-dʒ-dʒ-e]	[e-dʒ-e]	[edʒe]
[ɑ-dʒ-dʒ-ɑ]	[ɑ-dʒ-ɑ]	[ɑdʒɑ]
[o-dʒ-dʒ-o]	[o-dʒ-o]	[odʒo]
[u-dʒ-dʒ-u]	[u-dʒ-u]	[udʒu]

4. [dʒ] Words.

Initial		*Final*		*Medial*	
jack	gem	bridge	age	bridges	agent
jacket	jab	cabbage	badge	edges	imagine
jail	jazz	cage	fudge	engine	legend
jam	jest	carriage	hedge	ginger	legible
jar	jet	change	huge	hedges	logic
jelly	jig	edge	image	magic	majestic
joy	join	language	ledge	manager	major
juice	joke	large	lodge	pigeon	region
jump	judge	orange	oblige	register	unjust
just	jug	page	ridge	soldier	wages

5. Distinguishing [tʃ] from [dʒ].

chin	– gin	cheer	– jeer
chess	– Jess	chump	– jump
chunk	– junk	chill	– Jill
choke	– joke	chest	– jest
char	– jar	breeches	– bridges
chug	– jug	lecher	– ledger
choice	– Joyce	batch	– badge
chain	– Jane	rich	– ridge

6. [dʒ] Blend Words.

[-dʒɹ]	[-dʒd]
badger	judged
lodger	raged
danger	obliged
Roger	hedged
cager	ridged

7. [dʒ] Sentences.

1. She gave a jar of jelly to the soldier.
2. The pigeon jumped into the cage.
3. John jumped the hedge and picked the cabbages.
4. Why, Jim, there is jam on your jacket!
5. Can the bridge hold the fire engine, Jack?
6. Every manager in that region pays unjust wages.
7. Do you know the legend about the soldier, the pigeon and the orange?
8. You must register at the agent's lodge before you cross the bridge.
9. Jumping over the large hedge is no joke.
10. Imagine His Majesty's carriage loaded with huge cabbages.

BIBLIOGRAPHY

1. Barnes, H. G., "A Diagnosis of the Speech Needs and Abilities of Students in a Required Course in Speech Training at the State University of Iowa," *Ph.D. Dissertation, State University of Iowa,* 1932.

2. Brady, L. M., "A Palatographic Study of Superior Articulation," *M. A. Thesis, State University of Iowa,* 1939.

3. French, N. R., Carter, C. W., and Koenig, W., "The Words and Sounds of Telephone Conversation," *Bell System Technical Journal,* 9:290–324 (1930).

4. Hall, M. E., "Auditory Factors in Functional Articulatory Speech Defects," *Journal of Experimental Education,* 7:110–132 (1938).

5. Kenyon, J. S., *American Pronunciation,* George Wahr, Ann Arbor, Mich., 1937.

6. Moses, E. R., Jr., "Palatography and Speech Improvement," *Journal of Speech Disorders,* 4:103–114 (1939).

7. Voelker, C. H., "Phonetic Distribution in Formal American Pronunciation," *Journal of the Acoustical Society of America,* 5:242–246 (1934).

CHAPTER V

PRONUNCIATION

The three preceding chapters have been concerned with the *elements* of spoken language; the vowels, diphthongs and consonants. It is the function of the present chapter to consider the construction of words from these elements, the act referred to as *pronunciation*.

The primary essentials of the correct pronunciation of a word may be enumerated as follows:

1. Correct articulation of the speech sounds.
2. Articulation of all the speech sounds.
3. Articulation of only the required speech sounds.
4. Correct location of accent, or syllabic stress.

Regarding the correct pronunciation of specific words there are three major sources of information.

1. *Spelling.*—The basic rules, taught in any elementary school, will settle many of the simple problems with regard to the speech sounds. Spelling cannot be relied upon to resolve all difficulties, however, as witness the different pronunciations of the same spellings in *cough, bough, tough, though, through,* and the different spellings of the same pronunciations in *speech, speak, niece, deceive, key, machine.*

2. *A good dictionary.*—In spite of the general criticisms of dictionaries by students of speech this is your most important single source, and your pronunciation will be excellent indeed if it is as accurate as that of a modern dictionary.

3. *The pronunciation of persons in your community whose speech is generally respected.*—This source is of particular assistance to the student who is interested in determining preferred pronunciations within a given speech region. It is by this means that you will be able to decide, for example, which of two alternative pronunciations given by a dictionary is the more common

among good speakers in your community. Probably, however, the average person need not confuse himself with such preferences.

Considering the problem of what may be regarded as a pronunciation error, we must recognize, first of all, that certain more or less consistent regional differences in pronunciation, such as the omission of [r] in some dialects, are entirely legitimate. In the second place, it should be remembered that for many words there are acceptable alternative pronunciations, such as [æpər'eɪtəs] and [æpə'rætəs] for *apparatus*. Excluding such variations, we may regard a word as mispronounced if:[1]

1. A sound is substituted, e.g., [gɪt] for [gɛt], *get*.
2. A sound is omitted, e.g., [ɑrtɪk] for [ɑrktɪk], *arctic*.
3. A sound is added or inserted, e.g., [æθəlit] for [æθlit], *athlete*.
4. The accent is misplaced, e.g., [fɔr'mɪdəb]] for ['fɔrmɪdəb]], *formidable*.

This chapter attempts to provide materials which will correct and prevent such pronunciation errors. Two basic considerations have influenced the selection of the practice words: (1) the frequency with which words occur in language; (2) the frequency with which words are mispronounced. E. L. Thorndike in the research cited in the Bibliography has determined the relative frequency of occurrence of the 20,000 most common words of written English, providing thus an approximate index of their frequency in American speech. H. G. Barnes and his students (see Bibliography) have surveyed the frequency with which these most common words were mispronounced by samples of 100 college freshmen. The first two sections of this chapter present all of Thorndike's most frequent 10,000 words which were mispronounced by one or more of Barnes' freshmen, with the exception of proper nouns and the capitalized derivatives thereof. Thus the materials may be said to consider most of the words of

---

[1] In addition to the types listed, errors known as *reversals* sometimes occur. Usually these involve entire syllables, as [kælvərɪ] for *cavalry*. The error heard in [tʃɪldr̩n] for [tʃɪldrən], *children*, frequently is called a reversal, but probably is described more accurately as the substitution of a syllabic [r̩] for [rə], in which [r] is consonantal.

the average vocabulary which present any type of pronunciation problem to adults. They do not, of course, include words which, although infrequent generally, are important and common in the specialized vocabularies of individuals because of such factors as profession and geographical location.

Although Barnes' research did not extend to the specific types of pronunciation errors, it is probable that sound substitutions and errors of accent were the most frequent. It also is likely that the most common sound substitutions concerned the vowels of accented syllables. With these errors in mind, all words of relatively indisputable pronunciation have been classified in the same list (1) according to the number of syllables, (2) according to the syllable having the primary accent, (3) according to the vowel of the accented syllable. This long list composes the first of the following sections. The rest of the words, all of which have definite alternative pronunciations in American speech, are presented in the second section. However, alternatives which are clearly regional are not considered at this point. Words in which such variations occur have been left in the first section, and classified there according to their most probable pronunciations in the General American dialect. Thus, for example, words such as *calf*, *chaff* and *waft*, which usually take [æ] in General American, but are legitimately pronounced with [a] or [ɑ] in some other dialects, are grouped with words such as *sat* which invariably take [æ] in all regions. Especially with respect to the vowels the placement of such words has been arbitrary in many instances, in spite of the use of General American as a constant reference. For these first two sections the 1934 edition of *Webster's New International Dictionary*, of which the *Collegiate Dictionary* is a convenient abridgment for student use, was used as a pronunciation standard. The key-words of the dictionary were interpreted according to what is gauged to be their most frequent pronunciation in General American.

A third section of the materials consists of short lists of words, selected from the first two divisions, but here classified according to the most probable type of error. The balance of the chapter is devoted to alternatives and errors in pronunciation, many of them regional, which are directly related to the phonetic structure of words. Only the final section departs from the researches cited above.

THE LOCATION OF ACCENT; THE VOWELS OF ACCENTED SYLLABLES

Consider each list separately. Note the number of syllables, the location of the accent, the vowel of the accented syllable. Then read the list rhythmically, preserving these three points of similarity in all words of the list. Observe that in certain of the polysyllabic words the location of a secondary accent is mentioned. In such words make the indicated syllable less prominent than that having the primary accent, but more prominent than the unaccented syllables. During your first reading check all words that you do not habitually pronounce correctly and work intensively on these words. It is good practice to scrutinize the spellings, look up the definitions, transcribe the pronunciations and use each word correctly several times.[2]

ONE-SYLLABLE WORDS

[i]	wreathe	whim	stare
cease	ye	wince	steppe
frieze	yeast	wish	weld
lea		with	wept
leave	[ɪ]	wring	whelp
liege	bier		when
mien	film	[ɛ]	whence
pique	fish	breadth	where
plead	mere	get	
seethe	nymph	heir	[æ]
sheath	rift	lens	bade
we'll	sieve	lest	calf
wheels	sit	men	can
wreath	which	slept	caste

[2] The following words have not been classified: *archbishop*, [ˈɑrtʃˈbɪʃəp], with two primary accents; *heterogeneous*, [ˌhɛtɹoˈdʒɪnɪəs]; *laboratory*, [ˈlæbɹ̩əˌtɔrɪ]; *reconciliation*, [ˌrɛkənˌsɪlɪˈeɪʃn̩].

chaff
hast
plaid
quaff
sat
thrash
waft
wrath

[ʌ]

doth
just
must
such

[ɑ]

calm
copse
hearth
snarl
what

[ɔ]

awe
balk
corps
court
dross
fog
gnaw

gourd
lord
pawn
scoff
sore
wharf
wharves

[ʊ]

lure
poor
tour

[u]

groove
hoof
lieu
roof
root
sluice

[ju]

ewe
huge
muse

[oʊ]

clothe
dose
loath

loathe
rogue

[ɑʊ]

cow
crowd
drought
our
ours
rouse
shroud
snout

[eɪ]

ache
bane
baste
bathe
chafe
chaise
chaste
crape
deign
feign
gauge
jade
lathe
mane
neigh

raze
skein
slake
vale
veil

[ɑɪ]

blithe
fire
griped
height
lithe
lyre
rind
scythe
snipe
squire
tithe
vie
while
whine
white
wile
writhe

[ɪ]

scourge
swerve
whirl

TWO-SYLLABLE WORDS

Accent on First

[i]

chieftain
creature
demon

ether
genius
grievous
heathen

legion
meager
precept
precinct

regal
regent
sequel
sequence

species
treatise

[ɪ]

billiard
breeches
brimstone
children
christen
citron
dismal
distaff
era
figure
fissure
gibbet
grisly
insight
instance
instincts
minnows
niggard
pretty
primrose
query
rigor
shrivel
sinew
vicar
victual
villa
villain
visage
whisper
whistle
whither
wintry

zero

[ɛ]

arrant
bevel
brethren
bury
censure
cherub
deluge
despot
destined
entrails
epoch
essence
friendly
gesture
harrow
leaven
legate
leggings
lengthwise
marrow
measured
menace
nestle
nether
parish
penance
pendant
preface
pregnant
prelate
remnant
reptile
resin
revels

second
seraph
sterile
tether
textile
venom
vestige
wherefore
zealous

[æ]

abbey
access
adjunct
annals
anther
antic
aspect
asphalt
athlete
azure
ballast
banquet
chasm
clamber
damsel
facile
falcon
fallow
fathom
fragment
frantic
grandeur
grandsire
hallow
havoc
languish

madam
pageant
palate
plantain
ragged
rapine
sallow
sandwich
sanguine
scabbard
spaniel
statute
tactics
talcum
tassel
tranquil
transient
travail
traversed
valiant
valor
vassal
wrathful

[ʌ]

bustle
comely
comfort
covet
hover
hundredth
luscious
mutter
nothing
nuptials
sculptor
scuttle

subtle
succor
udder

[ɑ]

arctic
ardor
balmy
charcoal
colleague
conscious
consul
contact
contour
contrite
dolphin
farthest
farthing
harlot
hostage
hostile
monstrous
motley
novice
otter
parcel
partner
pollen
pompous
ponder
prostrate
solace
solder
sonnet
wampum
wattle

[ɔ]

altar
bauble
borax
cornice
dogged
foggy
forehead
foreman
forum
gorgeous
offal
orgy
palsy
paltry
proffer
quarry
swarthy
tortoise
washer

[ʊ]

bulwark
pulpit
worsted

[u]

duly
frugal
rooster
ruthless
scruple
steward
tunic

[ju]

bureau
cubit

eunuch
fury
mucous
murals
puny
pupa

[oʊ]

crocus
dotage
froward
grocer
holstein
loathsome
lotus
molten
nomad
notice
ogre
osier
ovule
poem
program
stoic
topaz

[ɑʊ]

dowry
prowess

[eɪ]

aged
alien
brazen
cadence
cambric
chaos
chasten

craven
frailty
heinous
lading
ladle
latent
mason
nature
papal
patron
racial
scraper
slavish
stamen
tabors

[ɑɪ]

bison
client
crisis
divers
fireplace
friar
guidance
heighten
hybrid
libel
lichen
lilac
lion
miter
prior
righteous
typhoid
tyrant
via

whiten
whiteness
whitewash
zion

[r]
borough
burgher
burrowed
colonel
fervent

furtive
kerchief
nurture
pearly
servile
skirmish

surfeit
surly
surplus
thorough
verdure
whirlwind

Accent on Second

[i]
bequeath
bereave
blaspheme
chemise
decease
discreet
fatigue
genteel
intrigued
perceive
receipt
routine
secrete

[ɪ]
austere
desist
eclipse
enlist
evince
herewith
methinks
revere
severe
subsist
therewith
wherein
wherewith

within

[ɛ]
accept
allege
amend
assent
attend
bereft
contemn
dissect
offense
oppress
portend
redress
resent
whate'er
withheld

[æ]
askance
collapse
cravat
enhanced
forbade
harangue
mischance
mishap
supplant
withstand

[ʌ]
confront
consult
rebuff

[ɑ]
catarrh
cretonne
dissolve
garage
guitar

[ɔ]
athwart
because
distort
divorce
exhort
thenceforth
withdraw
withdrawn

[ʊ]
allure

[u]
ado
bamboo
cocoon
endue

ensue
halloo
peruse
protrude
recruit
reproof
uproot

[ju]
amuse
demure
diffuse
misuse
profuse

[oʊ]
deposed
encroach
engrossed
forego

[ɑʊ]
aroused
confound
espouse
resounds
without

[eɪ]
allay

assay
campaign
champagne
crochet
debate
dissuade
efface
estrange
insane
portrayed
restraint
vouchsafe

[ɑɪ]
affright
allied
awhile
baptize
belie
benign
chastise
contrive
deride
descry
espy
expire

malign
prescribe
preside
requite
reside
resign
revile
subside
suffice
whereby

[ɔɪ]
decoy

destroyed
recoil

[ɪ]
absurd
aver
averse
defer
dessert
diverge
immerse
incur
interred
usurp

THREE-SYLLABLE WORDS

Primary Accent on First

No Secondary Accent

[i]
deify
deity
fealty
meteor
theater
theory
vehemence
vehement
wheelbarrow

[ɪ]
chivalrous
cilia
diligent
filament
filial
frivolous

glycerine
hickory
imminent
impious
impotent
impudent
indigo
indolent
infamous
infamy
infancy
inference
infinite
influence
liberate
miracle
mischievous
mitigate
myriad

pitiless
rivulet
sinewy
singular
sinister
symphony
synagogue
timorous
tyranny
vigilance
vigilant
weariness
whimsical

[ɛ]
anyway
arrogance
caramels
cellulose

cherubim
cheviot
credulous
demagogue
deprecate
deputy
designate
desolate
detriment
devastate
ecstasy
embassy
embryo
emphasis
envelope
epitaph
gelatin
heresy
heretic

hesitate
jeopardy
legacy
leprosy
mariner
maritime
metaphor
negligence
paraffin
paragon
paramour
parapet
parentage
pedestal
pendulum
penury
plenteous
precipice
prevalence
prevalent
recognized
recompense
reservoir
residue
retinue
revery
rhetoric
secular
sentinel
sepulcher
sterilize
temperate
temporal
testified
tremulous
venison
venomous

[æ]

accurate
adamant
adjective
aggravate
alkali
anecdote
animate
annual
anthracite
aperture
attitude
avarice
bankruptcy
blasphemy
calculate
canopy
casual
cataract
cavalry
chanticleer
chaperon
chastisement
faculty
frankincense
labyrinth
magistrate
malady
maximum
pancreas
passionate
pastoral
ravenous
sanctify
stratagem
tapestry

[ʌ]

comeliness
company
covetous
culminate
cutlery
government
ruffian
subtlety
suppliant
supplicate
sustenance
ultimate
unctuous

[ɑ]

architect
arduous
artifice
artisan
barbarous
chocolate
cholera
competence
confiscate
contemplate
dominate
guardian
harbinger
ominous
partisan
partnership
politic
populace
popular
prodigal

progeny
prophetess
protestant
soluble
volatile
voluble

[ɔ]

chlorophyl
laureate
oftentimes
orchestra
ordinance
orient
orifice
porcelain
porcupine
sorcerer
sorcery
sorrowful

[u]

cruelty
ludicrous
nucleus
nutrients
rudiment

[ju]

beauteous
mutinous
unison
usury

[oʊ]

copious
grocery
hosiery

overalls
potentate
rotary

[aʊ]

bounteous
counselor
countenance

[eɪ]

atheist
maintenance
patriarchs
satiate
savory

[aɪ]

diadem

diary
dynasty
hyacinth
riotous

[ɔɪ]

boisterous
royalty

[r]

currency
earnestness
earthenware
mercury
personage
turbulent
virtual
virtuous

Primary Accent on Second

No Secondary Accent

[i]

albeit
demeanor
entreaty
ingenious
plebeian
torpedo
unfrequent

[ɪ]

bacillus
capricious
collision
decision
derision
dominion
embitter
epistle
exhibit
familiar
inherent
malicious
malignant
militia

officious
pernicious
persistence
persistent
physician
precision
prodigious
prolific
propitious
provincial
vindictive

[ɛ]

acceptance
ancestral
authentic
barbaric
celestial
confession
contentious
digestion
digestive
director
discretion

disheveled
disparage
eccentric
electric
exchequer
infectious
offender
offensive
oppressive
oppressor
perspective
portentous
possession
preventive
progressive
rebellious
replenish
resemble
stupendous
successful
suspended
together
transgression
umbrella

utensil

[æ]

abandon
assassin
battalion
disaster
disastrous
ecstatic
enamel
enamor
examine
financial
gigantic
piazza

[ʌ]

autumnal
convulsion
eruption
escutcheon
production
sepulchral

[ɑ]

accomplice
demolish
dioxide
embody
imposter
obnoxious
remonstrance

[ɔ]

absorption
discordant
explorer
hydraulic
phosphoric

[u]

consumer
illumine

[oʊ]

component
ennoble
explosive
ignoble
osmosis
precocious

[ɑʊ]

empower

[eɪ]

assailant
capacious
complacent
contagion
equator
gradation
oasis
occasion
persuasive
sagacious

[ɑɪ]

decisive
enliven

environ
horizon
indictment
proviso

[r]

accursed
commercial
conversion
diversion
encircle
paternal
preferment
sojourner
unlearned
unworthy
usurper

Primary Accent on Third

Secondary Accent on First

[i]

guarantee
refugee

[ɪ]

chiffonier
financier

[ɛ]

picturesque
recommends

[æ]

counteract

[ʊ]

premature

[u]

reproduce

[eɪ]

ascertain

Four-syllable Words

Primary Accent on First

No Secondary Accent

[ɪ]
intimacy
lineament
miniature

[ɛ]
despotism

efficacy
heroism
memorable
preferable
reputable
variable
vegetable

[æ]
accuracy
actually
amicable
habitable
lamentable
navigable

practicable

[ɑ]
obstinacy

[ɔ]
formidable

Secondary Accent on Third

[i]
mediator

[ɪ]
kindergarten

[ɛ]
legendary

legislative
meditative
sedentary
speculative

[æ]
adversary
alabaster

capillary
salamander
statuary

[ʌ]
cultivator

[ɑ]
architecture

commentary

[eɪ]
stationary

[r]
mercenary
purgatory

Primary Accent on Second

No Secondary Accent

[i]
expedient
obsequious

[ɪ]
administered
antiquity
assiduous
auxiliary
civility
conspicuous

conspirator
constituent
contributed
diphtheria
ethereal
habitual
illiterate
imperial
indicative
lascivious
nativity

obliterate
oblivion
omnipotent
particular
posterior
precipitous
reiterate
significance
significant
similitude
vicissitude

[ɛ]
accessory
contemptible
contemptuous
dexterity
effeminate
eventual
executive
executor
experiment
extenuate

heredity
impediment
impetuous
incredulous
perpetuate
preeminence
progenitors
receptacle
sincerity
solemnity
supremacy
susceptible
symmetrical
tempestuous

[æ]

audacity
catastrophe
compassionate
immaculate
inadequate

inanimate
infallible
inhabitant
miraculous
potassium
sagacity
theatrical
tyrannical
unanimous

[ʌ]

presumptuous

[ɑ]

abdominal
atrocity
demonstrative
disconsolate
ferocity
hypocrisy
idolatry
impoverish

insoluble
metropolis
phenomenon
prerogative
stenographer
unoccupied

[ɔ]

inaugurate
laborious

[ʊ]

futurity
injurious

[u]

aluminum
credulity
inscrutable
unscrupulous

[ju]

immunity

incurable
unusual

[oʊ]

commodious
erroneous
melodious
pneumonia

[ɑɪ]

annihilate
environment
impiety

[ɔɪ]

embroidery

[r]

absurdity
alternative
diversity
impervious
superfluous

Primary Accent on Third

Secondary Accent on First

[ɪ]

abolition
admonition
beneficial
exposition
inquisition
jurisdiction
panegyric
perseverance
proposition
recognition
supposition

[ɛ]

acquiescence

elemental
energetic
indigestion
peradventure
sentimental
unaffected

[æ]

aromatic
understanding

[ɑ]

antitoxin
apostolic

microscopic
philosophic

[u]

diminution
dissolution

[ju]

persecution

[eɪ]

accusation
adaptation
affectation
compensation
coronation

corporation
degradation
education
emigration
emulation
excavation
exultation
indignation
lamentation
ostentatious
propagation
protestation
provocation
tribulation

Five-syllable Words

Primary Accent on Second

No Secondary Accent	Secondary Accent on Fourth
[ɪ]	[ɛ]
disinterested	preparatory
	unprecedented
[ɛ]	
inevitable	[ɑ]
inexorable	apothecary
[ɑ]	[ɔ]
incomparable	authoritative
intolerable	
[ɹ]	
interminable	

Primary Accent on Third

Secondary Accent on First

[i]	philosophical
intermediate	theological
	zoological
[ɛ]	
architectural	[ɔ]
imperceptible	equatorial
inaccessible	immemorial
indigestible	metamorphosis
[æ]	[u]
liberality	ingenuity
[ɑ]	[aɪ]
animosity	indescribable
curiosity	
periodical	[ɹ]
	indeterminate

Primary Accent on Fourth

Secondary Accent on First	Secondary Accent on Second
[eɪ]	[eɪ]
fertilization	appreciation
fortifications	appropriation
realization	assimilation
representation	pronunciation

ALTERNATIVE PRONUNCIATIONS

Listed below are words that have two or more distinctly different, yet acceptable, pronunciations in American speech. Look them up in a good dictionary and transcribe the alternatives in the spaces provided. Master one correct pronunciation of each word. Although the words are sub-classified to indicate their major variable features, it should be noted that the groups are not mutually exclusive. Alternatives in accent, for example, are frequently accompanied by vowel changes, e.g., [ə'dʌlt], ['ædʌlt], *adult*. Attention also should be called to the fact that some of the alternatives in accent are related to the grammatical functions of the words, e.g., *conflict* is pronounced ['kɑnflɪkt] when used as a noun, [kən'flɪkt] when used as a verb.

In Number of Syllables

ammonia	_____	_____
extraordinary	_____	_____
familiarity	_____	_____
interest	_____	_____
interesting	_____	_____
peculiarity	_____	_____
protein	_____	_____
sovereign	_____	_____
tedious	_____	_____

In Location of Primary Accent

abdomen   _____   _____

abject   _____   _____

accent   _____   _____

adult   _____   _____

advertisement _____   _____

ally   _____   _____

alternate   _____   _____

amateur   _____   _____

aristocrat   _____   _____

augment   _____   _____

canine   _____   _____

chauffeur   _____   _____

confines   _____   _____

conflict   _____   _____

conserve   _____   _____

consummate   _____   _____

contemplate   _____   _____

conversant   _____   _____

convoy   _____   _____

decade   _____   _____

defect   _____   _____

desert   _____   _____

detail   _____   _____

digest   _____   _____

essay   _____   _____

exquisite   _____   _____

extant   _____   _____

ferment   _____   _____

finance   _____

harass   _____   _____

hospitable   _____   _____

illustrate   _____   _____

inquiry   _____   _____

kilometer   _____   _____

mustache   _____   _____

peremptory   _____   _____

perfume   _____   _____

precedent   _____   _____

premise   _____   _____

presage   _____   _____

progress   _____   _____

quinine   _____   _____

recess   _____   _____

resource   _____   _____

romance   _____   _____

sonorous   _____   _____

sultan   _____   _____

surmise   _____   _____

In the Vowel of the Syllable Having Primary Accent

almond   _____   _____

apparatus   _____   _____

bosom   _____   _____

buoy   _____   _____

buoyant   _____   _____

calyx   _____   _____

combatant   _____   _____

creek   _____   _____

cuckoo   _____   _____

data   _____   _____

extol   _____   _____

fount   _____   _____

gape   _____   _____

gratis   _____   _____

hurrah   _____   _____

implacable   _____   _____

isolate   _____   _____

jocund   _____   _____

laurel   _____   _____

patronage   _____   _____

piano   _____   _____

process   _____   _____

promenade   _____   _____

route   _____   _____

salve   _____   _____

satyr   _____   _____

seine   _____   _____

sepal   _____   _____

shone   _____   _____

staunch   _____   _____

tomato   _____   _____

zenith   _____   _____

In the Vowel of an Unaccented Syllable

alpine   _____   _____

cooperative   _____   _____

delegate   _____   _____

dilate   _____   _____

direction _____ _____

economic _____ _____

hurricane _____ _____

imaginative _____ _____

initiative _____ _____

simultaneous _____ _____

tribunal _____ _____

Miscellaneous Alternatives

clothes _____ _____

cordial _____ _____

homage _____ _____

isthmus _____ _____

luxuriant _____ _____

often _____ _____

suite _____ _____

thwart _____ _____

transact _____ _____

trough _____ _____

COMMON TYPES OF MISPRONUNCIATION

The following words are grouped according to the most probable
type of error. As you consider each word make a special attempt
to avoid the specific error indicated. Look up the correct pronunciation of each word and transcribe it in the space provided.

Misplaced Accents

allied _____ chastisement_____

amicable _____ efficacy _____

ancestral _____ executor _____

ascertain _____ formidable _____

chastise _____ impious _____

impotent	_____	mischievous	_____
incomparable	_____	preparatory	_____
infamous	_____	sepulchral	_____
lamentable	_____	superfluous	_____
memorable	_____	vehement	_____

Insertions or Additions

almond	_____	overalls	_____
athlete	_____	prodigious	_____
brethren	_____	propitious	_____
chasten	_____	racial	_____
christen	_____	remnant	_____
film	_____	sinew	_____
forehead	_____	subtlety	_____
frailty	_____	transient	_____
grievous	_____	umbrella	_____
height	_____	villain	_____

Omissions

adjective	_____	must	_____
arctic	_____	particular	_____
chocolate	_____	poem	_____
company	_____	recognized	_____
cruelty	_____	recommends	_____
familiar	_____	rind	_____
friendly	_____	sandwich	_____
government	_____	slept	_____
huge	_____	understanding	_____
mercury	_____	wept	_____

Substitutions

absurd	_____	leave	_____
because	_____	men	_____
can	_____	nothing	_____
complacent	_____	notice	_____
consul	_____	orgy	_____
diphtheria	_____	our	_____
experiment	_____	partner	_____
gesture	_____	such	_____
get	_____	together	_____
just	_____	within	_____

Substitutions of [ɹ] for [rə] or [rɪ]

aggravate	_____	prescribe	_____
children	_____	pretty	_____
hundredth	_____		

"Spelling-pronunciations."—Attempts to pronounce some words exactly as they are spelled frequently lead to errors known as "spelling-pronunciations." Avoid such errors in the following words.

bade	_____	epistle	_____
balmy	_____	gauge	_____
breeches	_____	hearth	_____
bury	_____	heinous	_____
calm	_____	heir	_____
caste	_____	lichen	_____
chaise	_____	mishap	_____
chaos	_____	prelate	_____
comely	_____	receipt	_____
corps	_____	scourge	_____

solder	_____	tortoise	_____
thorough	_____	worsted	_____

ALTERNATIVES AND ERRORS RELATED TO PHONETIC STRUCTURE

Many words differ considerably when pronounced by speakers of different American regional dialects. Most obvious are the changes in pronunciation of [r] words which have been mentioned in the chapter on consonants, but equally real, if perhaps not so striking, are dialect variations that concern vowels. Within the dialects also, certain legitimate vowel variations are heard with considerable consistency. A large body of words, therefore, present acceptable alternative pronunciations based on vowel differences, and in many cases fairly definite phonetic rules can be set down because the variations occur systematically before or after specific consonants. Similarly related to the phonetic structure of words are certain vowel errors, such as the tendency to substitute [i] for [ɪ] before [ʃ] and [ʒ], as in *fish* and *vision*. Alternatives and errors of these types are considered below, the arrangement being according to the vowels concerned.

THE VOWEL [ɪ]

1. Use [ɪ], not [i], before [ʃ] and [ʒ].

ambition	definition	fish	submission
collision	derision	incision	vision
condition	dish	official	visual
decision	division	revision	wish

2. Do not diphthongize [ɪ] before [l] and [n].

bill	fill	pill	till
bin	fin	pin	tin
dill	kill	sill	will
din	kin	sin	win

3. Use either [ɪ] or [i] before [r]. [ɪ] is probably more frequent in connected General American speech.

beer	gear	peer	spear
clear	here	queer	steer
dear	mere	rear	tear
fear	near	shear	year

4. Use either [ɪ] or [i] when final and unaccented. [ɪ] is probably more frequent in connected General American speech.

army	candy	lacy	sleepy
baby	collie	leafy	taxi
badly	cookie	lobby	tiny
bushy	filthy	only	very

The Vowel [ɛ]

1. Use [ɛ], not [eɪ], before [g], [ʃ] and [ʒ].

beg	flesh	measure	pressure
beggar	fresh	mesh	session
depression	keg	peg	special
egg	leg	pleasure	treasure

2. Do not diphthongize [ɛ] before [t], [d], [n], [l] and [r].

bear	care	ken	pen
bed	dead	men	tell
bell	dell	met	ten
bet	den	pear	yell

3. Use either [ɛ] or [eɪ] before [r]. [ɛ] is probably more frequent in connected General American speech.

bear	flare	mare	snare
blare	glare	pear	spare
care	hair	rare	stare
dare	lair	scare	there

4. Use either [ɛ] or [æ] before intervocalic [r], when the spelling is *ar* or *arr*. [ɛ] is probably more frequent in connected General American speech.

baron	carrot	larynx	parry
barrel	carry	marrow	rarity
barrier	charity	marry	sparrow
carol	garret	parish	tarry

The Vowel [æ]

1. Do not diphthongize [æ] before [p], [b], [t], [d], [n] and [l].

bad	gal	mat	pan
cad	lap	nab	rat
can	mad	nap	shall
dab	man	pal	tap

2. Use either [æ], [a] or [ɑ] before [s], [f], [θ] and nasal blends. [æ] is most frequent in General and Southern American; [a] is sporadic throughout America, being fairly common in New England; [ɑ] is heard occasionally in the latter region. Note that [a] is intermediate in sound between [æ] and [ɑ].

bass	calf	laugh	plant
bath	grant	mass	ranch
blanch	lass	pass	slant
branch	lath	path	wrath

The Vowel [ʌ]

1. Use [ʌ], not [ɑ], in the prefix *un*.

unable	uneven	unload	unveil
uncoil	unfair	unpack	unwieldy
undo	unfit	unreal	unwind
unearth	unfold	unused	unworthy

The Vowel [ɑ]

1. Use [ɑ], not [ɔ], before [r], when the vowel is spelled with *a*.

form – farm	court – cart
born – barn	scored – scarred
pork – park	port – part
chores – chars	cord – card
horde – hard	board – bard

bores – bars		force – farce	
stored – starred		cores – cars	
lord – lard		former – farmer	

2. Use either [ɑ] or [ɒ] before [p], [b], [t], [d], [k], [g], or after [w]. [ɑ] is almost universal in General American, and is fairly common in Eastern and Southern speech. In the latter regions, however, [ɒ] is frequently used. Note that [ɒ] is intermediate in sound between [ɑ] and [ɔ]. Before [g] the vowel [ɔ] is more frequent than [ɑ] or [ɒ] in General American; see [ɔ], below, for such words.

bob	nod	rock	top
dock	pod	shod	wan
dot	pop	shop	was
knot	rob	sob	watt

THE VOWEL [ɔ]

1. Use either [ɔ], [o] or [oʊ] before [r]. [ɔ] is probably most frequent in connected General American speech.

bore	for	pore	sore
core	lore	roar	store
door	more	shore	tore
floor	nor	snore	wore

2. Use [ɔ], [o] or [oʊ], not [ɑ], before [r] plus a consonant, when *o* appears in the vowel spelling.

farm – form		card – cord	
barn – born		bard – board	
park – pork		bars – bores	
chars – chores		starred – stored	
hard – horde		lard – lord	
cart – court		farce – force	
scarred – scored		cars – cores	
part – port		farmer – former	

3. Use either [ɔ] or [ɑ] before intervocalic [r], when the spelling is *or*, *orr* or *arr*. [ɔ] is probably more frequent in connected General American speech.

borrow	forest	quarry	sorry
coral	horrid	sorority	tomorrow
forehead	moral	sorrel	torrent
foreign	quarrel	sorrow	warrant

4. Use either [ɔ], [ɒ] or [ɑ] before [g], [ŋ], [s], [θ], [f] and [ʃ]. [ɔ] is almost universal in General American; [ɒ] is fairly common in other regions, however, especially in New England; [ɑ] is heard occasionally.

boss	fog	long	song
cough	gong	loss	toss
doff	hog	moss	wash
dog	log	moth	wrong

The Vowel [ʊ]

1. Use either [ʊ] or [u] before [r]. [ʊ] is probably more frequent in connected General American speech.

alluring	insurance	mooring	sure
assure	lure	plural	tour
boor	mature	poor	tourist
detour	moor	poorly	your

The Vowel [u]

1. Use [u], not [ju], when *o* appears in the vowel spelling.

doom	lose	noose	soon
loom	mood	route	soup
loop	moon	shoes	too
loose	noon	shoot	tooth

2. Use [u], not [ju], after [l] and [r], regardless of the vowel spelling. Pronunciation of [ju] after these consonants is exceedingly difficult, and usually is not attempted by good American speakers.

lucid	lunar	lute	ruin
lucrative	lunatic	ruby	rule
Luke	lure	rude	ruler
lunacy	lurid	rudiment	ruse

3. Use either [u] or [ju] after [t], [d], [n], [s], [z] and [θ], except when *o* appears in the vowel spelling. [u] is probably more frequent in connected General American speech.

deuce	dune	nude	thews
dude	dupe	sued	tube
dues	news	sues	tune
duke	newt	suit	Zeus

4. Use either [u] or [ʊ] in the following words and their derivatives. [u] is said to be "preferred," but [ʊ] is quite frequent.

broom	hoof	roof	root
coop	hoop	room	soot

BIBLIOGRAPHY

1. Barnes, H. G.; see Meredith, L., Gould, W. S., Bergh, F., Danielson, A. O., Henderson, L. E., "Pronunciation Drills for College Freshmen, Parts I, II, III, IV, V," *M.A. Theses, State University of Iowa*, 1936–1938.

2. Gray, G. W., and Wise, C. M., *The Bases of Speech*, Harper & Brothers, New York, 1934.

3. Kenyon, J. S., *American Pronunciation*, George Wahr, Ann Arbor, Mich., 1937.

4. Krapp, G. P., *The Pronunciation of Standard English in America*, Oxford University Press, New York, 1919.

5. Thorndike, E. L., *A Teacher's Word Book of the Twenty Thousand Words Found Most Frequently and Widely in General Reading for Children and Young People*, Teachers College, Columbia University, New York, 1932.

6. *Webster's Collegiate Dictionary*, G. and C. Merriam Company, Springfield, Mass., 1936.

7. *Webster's New International Dictionary*, A Guide to Pronunciation, G. and C. Merriam Company, Springfield, Mass., 1934, 2nd ed.

CHAPTER VI

BREATHING

Breathing during speech must accomplish two ends: (1) It must oxygenate the blood for the maintenance of life. (2) It must supply the energy for the production of speech sounds. In undisturbed vegetative or life breathing, inspiration is active but expiration passive. The two phases are of approximately equal duration, and are characteristically rhythmical. On the average, 15 to 20 inspiration-expiration cycles are completed every minute. Life is maintained, however, even with wide deviations from this typical process. Thus in speech (1) both inspiration and expiration are active, (2) inspiration is more rapid, (3) expiration usually is prolonged and (4) the inspiration-expiration cycles are less rhythmical. The one important limitation is that, over a period of time, an adequate amount of oxygen must be exchanged for carbon dioxide. From the vegetative standpoint it is probably satisfactory to breathe either shallowly and frequently, or deeply and infrequently.

In good speech this process of lung ventilation affords no problem, because pauses are frequent, and each pause gives an opportunity to breathe. In general, if a speaker pauses as often as he should, and if he utilizes these pauses to ventilate his lungs, he will never "run out of breath," nor will he need to create a special pause for breathing alone. Furthermore, it is easier to take a shallow breath than a deep one. And since inspirations may be frequent in average speech, they also may be shallow.

Inspiration is accomplished through enlargement of the thoracic (chest) cavity, in both the horizontal and vertical dimensions, by action of the chest muscles and diaphragm, respectively. This does not involve raising the chest as a whole. The shoulders and upper chest should remain relatively fixed, while the lower chest and abdomen expand. The gross expiratory movements, on the other hand, are functions chiefly of the abdominal muscles. These muscles work in opposition to the inspiratory group. They lower the ribs, and thus decrease the size of the chest in the horizontal plane. Their contraction also compresses the viscera and forces the domes of the diaphragm upward, thus shortening the chest cavity vertically.

By this means, air, admitted to the lungs by action of the chest muscles and diaphragm, is forcibly expelled by the abdominal muscles. The expulsion is controlled by the coordination of the antagonistic action of these two groups of muscles. As the abdominal muscles contract, the chest muscles and diaphragm relax slowly. The result of this balanced opposition is a constant state of tonicity, or tension, during expiration, and the air in the lungs is kept steadily under pressure even as it decreases in amount.

During the speaking of a phrase there are superimposed upon this gradual inward contraction smaller movements, or pulses, for the individual syllables. They probably are produced by the smaller thoracic muscles, since the large abdominal muscles do not follow the rapid individual bursts of air necessary to speech at high speed.

Mastery and habitual active use of these coordinations are fundamental to efficient speech breathing. In general the skills to be developed are three in number.

1. *Expansion and contraction in the proper regions of the torso.* —The predominant region of expansion determines what is known as the "breathing type," and is a point of much controversy. It is mentioned here as an essential because, while there probably is no one "right way" to breathe, there is one "wrong way" which should be avoided. This "wrong way" is clavicular or high-chest breathing, in which the structures of the extreme upper chest, and sometimes even the shoulders, are elevated. There are three chief reasons why this is an inefficient way to breathe for speech: (a) It is fatiguing, (b) it increases throat and laryngeal tension and (c) you have poor control over expiration. Apart from this type, use the method that is easiest

and most comfortable for you. This means that your expansions and contractions will be in the general region of the lower chest and abdomen.

2. *Controlled expiration.*—Use progressive contraction of abdominal and chest muscles accompanied by coordinated tension of all the breathing muscles. There is evidence to show that this contraction is steady in good voice usage, jerky in poor.

3. *Inspiration during the natural pauses of your speech.*—Learn to coordinate inspiration with phrasing so that you need not make special breathing pauses.

EXPANSION-CONTRACTION

1. Sitting erect in a chair, place your hands so that the thumbs touch the lower ribs at the sides and the fingers extend over the abdomen. Exhale as much as possible, squeezing in the lower ribs and abdomen with the hands. Then inhale as much as possible, letting the ribs and abdomen move outward against the pressure of your hands. Then exhale, forcing the air out with steady contraction in the region of the ribs and abdomen. Repeat 20 such cycles without stopping. Make the first inspiration approximately as long as the first expiration, but as you go on gradually speed up inspiration and slow down expiration until the former is very rapid and the latter very slow.

2. Repeat, with the right hand in the same position, but with the left hand flat on the chest at the point where the clavicles join the sternum. Preserve the movement in the lower chest and abdomen, but inhibit movement of the upper chest.

3. Repeat, without the aid of your hands. Attend to the sensation of movement or lack of movement in the regions concerned.

CONTROLLED EXPIRATION

Preserve the expansion-contraction technique throughout these drills, if possible without the aid of your hands.

1. Whisper [ɑ] as long as possible, using slow, steady expiration.

2. Repeat with phonated [ɑ].

3. Produce staccato whispered [ɑ] as many times as possible on one breath, with a small, rapid, firm contraction on each [ɑ], and a gradual contraction throughout the breath.

4. Repeat with staccato phonated [ɑ].

5. Articulate [p] as many times as possible on one breath.

6. Laugh as long as possible on [hɑ], contracting for each [hɑ]. Repeat for [hɔ] and [ho].

7. Count in a whisper as far as possible on one breath.

8. Count, using normal phonation, as far as possible on one breath.

9. Shout "help" three times on one expiration, contracting for each shout. Repeat, using "hey," "wait," "stop," "fire."

10. Some persons allow more breath to escape at the beginning of a phrase than toward the end, while still others expire a large fraction of their breath immediately after inspiration before beginning the phrase, or on the first word. Checking expiration with your hands as you keep these errors in mind, expire gradually and steadily as you read each of the following sentences.

He slammed the door shut with a loud bang.

I ran all of the way to the railroad station carrying two large suitcases.

The news commentator spoke fifteen hundred words in less than five minutes.

I studied diligently at my desk until half past two in the morning.

The little boy rode on the merry-go-round fifteen times trying to catch the gold ring.

INSPIRATION AT NATURAL PAUSES

The technique to learn here is to inspire only during pauses between phrases and to create no special pauses for this purpose. Preserve the expansion-contraction and controlled-expiration methods drilled above. Consult Phrasing for drills on that skill.

1. One way in which the following paragraph may be phrased is indicated by vertical lines, which mark pauses between

phrases. Each of these pauses affords an opportunity to inspire, although you probably will not require so many inspirations as that. Typical breathing pauses are indicated by asterisks. Note that all agree with interphrasal pauses. Read, observing these markings.

*|The necessary art of punctuation |cannot be relied upon |as a satisfactory guide for vocal phrasing. *|Although it sometimes happens |that pauses coincide with punctuation marks, |no definite generalizations can be made. *|Punctuation helps to indicate the structure of the sentence |to the eye and to the mind. |Vocal phrasing, |on the other hand, *|allows the meaning of the sentence |to become clear to the mind |through the ear. *|There are times when the punctuation mark is slighted |as a guide to phrasing, *|and at other times |phrasing is necessary |even though the writer has found no need for any punctuation whatsoever. *|

2. The following paragraph is marked with interphrasal pause lines only. After several trial readings, mark the pauses that you will use for breathing. Read, observing your marks.

|Many misunderstandings have arisen regarding the role of breathing in speech. |An early belief, |now rejected by most modern students, |was that the training of breathing |is the most important single aspect of any kind of voice improvement. |Great emphasis was placed on deep breathing |and exercises were given to increase the lung capacity. |In those days, also, |bitter controversies arose |over whether the so-called "diaphragmatic" breathing |is superior to the so-called "intercostal" breathing, |the terms referring to the regions of greatest expansion. |Recent evidence, however, |seems to indicate that an enormous lung capacity |is not an essential attribute of the superior speaker, |and that the two types of breathing that were mentioned |are equally satisfactory for speech. |

3. Following the method of the above two drills, mark inter-

phrasal pauses and indicate which are to be breathing pauses, in the following paragraph. Read, observing your marks.

In the act of breathing many parts of a complex mechanism are set into motion. Several groups of muscles work both together and in opposition to make this possible. Breathing for speech, as one might suppose, is far more complex than normal vegetative breathing. In breathing for speech both inhalation and exhalation are active, whereas in vegetative breathing only inhalation is active. Of all of the so-called "overlaid" functions, breathing is the most definite example for the reason that during all speaking we alter this basic biological function. Breathing is closely related to general bodily conditions, and with such a relationship it is to be expected that strong emotional reactions alter breathing and, consequently, speech. In fact, emotions not otherwise shown sometimes are betrayed by a person's speech.

4. Using the same techniques, but without marking, read the following long sentence.

In the production of speech, air, which is put under pressure by the action of muscles compressing the thoracic cavity, forces apart the vocal cords and causes them to vibrate, whereupon, the vibrations of the cords are transmitted upward through the cavities of the throat, mouth and nose, are modified and amplified, and emerge from the mouth as speech sounds.

GENERAL

1. Inspire fully and hold your breath. Tense the muscles of your abdomen and check with your hand. Count to 10 silently while holding the breath, expiring rapidly on the count of 10. Repeat, counting to 20, then to 30. The important thing here is abdominal tension.

2. Inspire, hold, tense, as in 1. Slap your abdomen in front, just below the ribs, with the flat of your hand. Gradually increase the force of the slaps until they are as hard as you can endure.

3. As you lie in bed at night before you go to sleep, turn on your back and complete ten inspiration-expiration cycles slowly and steadily. Inspire as fully as possible. Use the expansion-contraction technique. Repeat every night.

4. As you walk, count your footsteps silently. Inspire on steps 1 and 2. Then expire steadily for the next ten steps. Then repeat the process. Inspire rapidly. Use steady torso contraction during expiration. Preserve abdominal tension.

BIBLIOGRAPHY

1. Bloomer, H. H., "A Roentgenographic Study of the Mechanics of Respiration," *Speech Monographs*, 3:118–124 (1936).

2. Gray, G. W. (editor), "Studies in Experimental Phonetics," *Louisiana State University Studies*, No. 27, 1–164 (1936).

3. Huyck, E. M., and Allen, K. D. A., "Diaphragmatic Action of Good and Poor Speaking Voices," *Speech Monographs*, 4:101–109 (1937).

4. Stetson, R. H., "The Breathing Movements in Singing," *Archives Néerlandaises de Phonétique Expérimentale*, 6:115–164 (1931).

5. Stetson, R. H., and Hudgins, C. V., "Functions of the Breathing Movements in the Mechanism of Speech," *Archives Néerlandaises de Phonétique Expérimentale*, 5:1–30 (1930).

CHAPTER VII

TIME

The duration of tones and pauses, and the arrangements in which they occur along the time dimension, compose this attribute of voice. All parts of the speech mechanism exercise control over the time aspects, as is seen clearly if we mention only three of the ways in which a phonation may be ended, namely, exhaustion of the breath supply, separation of the vocal cords, closure of the mouth and nose.

The most common errors of time are:

1. Too rapid rate.
2. Too slow rate.
3. Staccato phonations.
4. Prolonged phonations.
5. Monotony.
6. Jerkiness.
7. Faulty phrasing.
8. Time patterns.

Although stuttering is reflected primarily in the time aspects of speech, this subject is not considered here because of the highly specialized methods that have been developed for treatment of this disorder. Some of the materials of this chapter, however, especially those on phrasing and rhythm, may prove to be helpful auxiliary devices.

The most common causes of disorders of time are (1) poor motor control, (2) faulty sense of rhythm, (3) emotional mal-adjustment, (4) faulty learning. As a matter of convenience the drills of this chapter have been written primarily from the point of view of disturbances of the latter type. However, they are easily adapted to fit other causes.

RATE

Rate refers to the speed of speech. Your rate should be slow enough to render your speech intelligible, should at the same time be neither too slow nor too rapid, and should suit the material spoken in the situation in which it is spoken. It may be conveniently measured in words per minute.

1. Measure your reading rate. The 300-word Test Passage for Measurement of Reading Rate below has been constructed to approximate typical reading material. In frequency of occurrence and in number of syllables the words that compose it agree closely with the long samples analyzed by Skalbeck (see Bibliography). The sentences are of approximately average length and difficulty. To measure your reading rate, read the passage as well as you are able as if to a group of 15 to 25 persons, and time the reading in seconds. It is preferable to do this from a phonograph or dictaphone record, or to have someone else time you. Your rate in words per minute is equal to 60 times the number of words read divided by the reading time in seconds. In the case of the 300-word passage, therefore, simply divide your reading time in seconds into 18,000 (i.e., 60 × 300) to get words per minute, or refer to Table 1 in which some of the values have been worked out.

Having computed your rate, look up the corresponding percentile in Table 2, which is from the work of Darley (see Bibli-

TABLE 1.—DETERMINATION OF RATE IN WORDS PER MINUTE FOR THE 300-WORD TEST PASSAGE FROM THE TOTAL READING TIME IN SECONDS

Reading Time in Seconds	Words per Minute	Reading Time in Seconds	Words per Minute
75	240	130	139
80	225	135	133
85	212	140	129
90	200	145	124
95	189	150	120
100	180	155	116
105	171	160	113
110	164	165	109
115	157	170	106
120	150	175	103
125	144	180	100

TABLE 2.—PERCENTILES CORRESPONDING TO VARIOUS RATES OF ORAL
READING OF THE 300-WORD TEST PASSAGE

Percentile	Rate	Percentile	Rate
100	222	45	164
95	196	40	162
90	190	35	161
85	185	30	159
80	181	25	157
75	177	20	155
70	175	15	153
65	172	10	148
60	170	5	140
55	168	0	129
50	166		

ography), who measured the rates of college freshmen reading the test passage. If, for example, your rate is at the seventy-fifth percentile, you may interpret this to mean that you read more rapidly than approximately 75 per cent of college freshmen. Now plot the value for the measurement of your rate in words per minute on the graph of Figure 1, at the proper point in the column for the first trial. Record the date. By plotting successive trials on the same graph and connecting the points, you may draw a curve of improvement.

Although preferences vary, the research of Franke, cited in the Bibliography, has shown that in such a reading situation, with material comparable to the test passage, critical listeners are almost certain to find your rate too rapid if it exceeds 185 words per minute, or too slow if it is less than 140 words per minute. These limits are indicated by heavy horizontal lines in Figure 1. However, rates within this range are *not necessarily* satisfactory; they still may be judged as too rapid or too slow. Consider, for example, two persons who read the same material at the same rate of 175 words per minute. If one of them employs considerably longer pauses between phrases than does the other, he can equal the rate of the other only by accelerating his rate *during phrases*. But if he does this, observers will judge him to be reading more rapidly than the other person on the basis of the rapid rate within phrases, although actually his output in words per minute over many phrases and pauses is equal to that of the other individual who employs shorter pauses and a slower rate within phrases. Similarly, the individual who uses short pauses between phrases and a slow rate within phrases may be judged as reading too slowly, while another person with an identical general rate may be judged as satisfactory because his pauses are longer and his rate within phrases more rapid.

If your rate is too rapid, therefore, you will not achieve a more favorable rate solely by lengthening your pauses, or, if your rate is too slow, by shortening them. This tendency is common, however; if it operates in your case refer to the drills in Variations in the Rate of Phrases and Variations in the Duration of Pauses Between Phrases, in addition to the drills of this section.

2. If your rate is too rapid or too slow set up an improvement program, following the procedure outlined in drill 1 and using the test passage provided. Attempting to decrease or increase your rate as the case may be, make five consecutive trials on the first day, plot the points on the graph and connect them. Repeat the test at weekly intervals thereafter (more often if desired), recording the date under each point plotted. Attempt to bring your curve as quickly as possible into the middle range, and continue until you have kept it there for at least six consecutive weekly trials. Remember to read as well as possible from all standpoints each time.

3. Read simple, factual materials of your own choosing, attempting to employ the same general rate that you used successfully in drill 2. Measure these performances also if possible.

4. Along with the practice for normal rate in drill 2, make two additional attempts each week, one to approximate 125 and the other 225 words per minute. Plot curves for these attempts also on the graph in Figure 1.

5. General rate varies in different situations, even if the same material is spoken or read. In the presence of large audiences rate tends to be slow. Read the test passage above as if reading in such a situation.

6. Read the passage as if to three persons five feet away. Note

Test Passage for Measurement of Reading Rate

Your rate of speech will be adequate if it is slow enough to provide for clearness and comprehension, and rapid enough to sustain interest. Your rate is faulty if it is too rapid to accomplish these ends. The easiest way to begin work on the adjustment of your speech to an ideal rate is to measure your present rate in words per minute in a fixed situation which you can keep constant over a number of trials. The best method is to pick a page of simple, factual prose to be read. Read this page in your natural manner, timing yourself in seconds. Count the number of words on the page, divide by the number of seconds, and multiply this result by sixty to calculate the number of words per minute. As you attempt to increase or retard your rate, repeat this procedure from time to time, using the same reading material, to enable you to check your success.

A common accompaniment of rapid rate is staccato speech, in which the duration of words and syllables is too short, whereas in slow speech the words and syllables frequently are over-prolonged. When the person with too rapid rate tries to slow down, he tends to make the error of keeping the duration of his tones short, and of attempting to accomplish the slower rate solely by lengthening the pauses between phrases and by introducing new pauses. On the other hand, the person who is working to speed up his rate tends to do this by shortening the pauses alone and retaining his prolonged tones. It is impossible at the present time to set down in rules the ideal relation between the duration of tones and pauses in speech. Further research is needed before this can be done with any great accuracy.

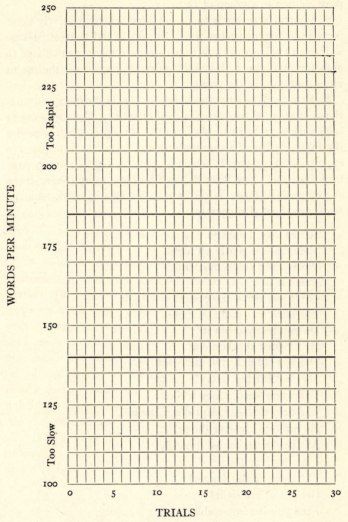

Figure 1.—Chart for Improvement Curve of Rate in Words Per Minute.

that your rate may be more rapid even than in drill 1, where you were reading to a group of 15 to 25.

7. General rate tends to be retarded where relatively complete audience comprehension is the aim. Read the test passage as if to an audience of 15 to 25 persons, in a manner calculated to give the audience a thorough understanding of all the major ideas contained in the passage.

8. Rate tends to vary also in relation to the meaning and emotional content of the material read or spoken. Conscious use of such variations helps to reinforce the ideas presented. Consider the following list of sentences with this in mind. Note that the expression of meaning is helped in some by a rapid rate, in some by a slow rate. Using R for Rapid, S for Slow, mark the sentences as you analyze them. With these indications in mind, read the sentences aloud. Exaggerate.

It was long, long ago.
She dreamed gently all night.
Please keep still a moment.
There it is!
Can't you drive any faster?
The lawn was cool and damp.
Do you really mean it?
He plodded slowly along.
She was old and thin and worn.
My, but it's hot today!
They whispered a long while.
The driverless car leapt down the hill.
He ran quickly over the grass.
All the flowers folded drowsily.
I'm very lazy today.
But think of the danger!
Get out of my sight!
I tell you it's impossible!
Why do you do things like that?
The sun rose slowly through the haze.
You'll be an hour late.

Well, now, I don't know.
The stream murmurs sad songs.
You can make it if you run.
The dawn was hushed and lovely.
This is a sleepy day.

9. In the expression of emotion rate is an important tool. Simulate grief as well as you are able in reading the following passage. Use a very slow rate, in the neighborhood of 120 words per minute, and many long pauses.

GRIEF

A man has forced his son to leave him alone on a deserted island. Out of his grief, the son speaks:

SON: Goodbye, father. Your wish is that I go and leave you here beside your warrior's barrow. Because of that wish, and that alone will I go. But in all the years of my life I shall remember you living alone upon this deserted island. And although my mind and body travel to the ends of the earth, my heart will be forever on this shore, a lonely bleeding thing without a father's love to return it to my breast. The mornings now will be like nights, emptied of the moon and stars, holding only the cold and fearful dark. And each tomorrow will be a dull mirror to reflect my yesterdays. How can I be happy there in the cold Northland of our fathers? How can you send me there? No, father, don't ask me again to remember our faith and our love for God; don't ask me if I can drown my sorrow in working for the church. And don't ask me to smile at our farewell. I can't do that! Don't you understand? *There is no other answer. You've asked me that question a thousand times and my reply has always been the same. It always will be the same.* Leaving you will break the heart within me. Yet I know that staying is impossible. Your own heart is set on the course you have set for me and I must obey. That is my only destiny.

10. Simulate fear as you read the following passage, using a rate of approximately 210 words per minute.

Fear

A boy in his teens has been sentenced to die for murder. At dawn of the day of his execution, as his cell slowly becomes gray and he knows that the time is not long, he is suddenly seized with a fit of uncontrollable terror. He cries:

THE BOY: Oh, God! Please don't let them take me away now. Let me have one more day—one more hour—to live. I don't deserve hanging for the thing I did. I didn't know then that a man's life meant so much. But I know now, I know, and please forgive me. I don't know how it happened. Honest I don't. One minute he was standing there, and the next minute there was a smoking gun in my hand. I don't know how it got there. You've got to believe me this time, God, if you never did before. You've got to believe it in time to keep them from hanging me. Every night you ask me how it happened. But I don't know! I don't know! I can't remember! *There is no other answer. You've asked me that question a thousand times and my reply has always been the same. It always will be the same.* You can't figure out things like that. They just happen. And afterwards you're sorry. I'm that way now. I'm sorry. Oh, God, stop them—quick—before it's too late.

11. It will be noticed that three sentences (italicized) are duplicated in both speeches. Using these sentences only, express grief and fear. Experimental study of these two emotions shows that when actors are highly successful in portraying grief, they employ a total duration of approximately 13 seconds for the three italicized sentences. For fear the value is close to seven seconds. Time your own portrayals and check them against these figures.

DURATION OF TONES

The aim of this series of drills is to habituate the use of words and syllables that are neither too short nor too long in duration, and to develop control over this factor so that variations can be produced at will. Although your approach to these drills will vary, you can use the same materials whether your tones are staccato or prolonged. For consideration of variations in duration as they relate to meaning see Chapter XI, on stress.

1. Read the following word list, making each word extremely staccato.

get	feet	ape	mitt
mud	lout	yes	go
law	jug	sick	camp
peat	house	cot	hay
lit	door	came	full
hat	at	wish	loot
set	shoe	man	wise
toot	lie	why	red

2. Read the list, prolonging each word.

3. Read the list, giving normal duration to each word.

4. Count from 1 to 25, making each word extremely staccato. Repeat with extreme prolongations. Repeat with normal duration.

5. Repeat the letters of the alphabet, making each syllable extremely staccato. Repeat with extreme prolongations. Repeat with normal duration.

6. Working on the words of drill 1, above, make each word in turn (a) staccato, (b) prolonged, (c) normal.

7. Read the following passage, (a) making the words extremely staccato, (b) prolonging the words, (c) using normal duration.

Vocal sounds may be grouped into three general classes on the basis of their durations. First of all there is normal duration of tones. Unemotional conversation provides a typical example. Secondly we have staccato speech, in which the tones are of very short duration. Such tones frequently are heard in expressions of anger and fear. In the third place we find tones which are prolonged, and such prolongation of vocal tones is common in the expression of the more pleasant emotions. Experimental studies of speech inform us that effective speakers tend to have a longer average duration of words than do poor speakers. It would seem, therefore, that staccato speech is a more frequent error among poor speakers than is the undue prolongation of tones. Observation would appear to confirm this conclusion. If we exclude the deliberate use of staccato tones as a technique, we can say with some certainty that tones which are too short in duration should be avoided.

8. Read the following three selections with the idea of reinforcing the meaning of each by using, as indicated, staccato tones, prolonged tones, tones of normal duration.

STACCATO TONES

If you'd run your home like a man runs his office there wouldn't be any need for getting off for a late start at every blasted dinner date we have. —Yes, I shaved, and the car's already warmed up. Hand you your stockings? You haven't got your stockings on yet? —Sure, I know I smoke too much, but it's the sitting around and waiting that makes me do it. It's a wonder I don't drink myself to death! Shall I phone and tell them we'll be half an hour late so you can wash your hair too? Don't—all right, hurry up, hurry up, hurry up!

PROLONGED TONES

The old orator was a pleasant, if somewhat sentimental character, from a school of speech that has almost gone. We often sat in the pleasant glow of a late autumn afternoon with the sun lighting up the old gray head. "Your youth," he would say, "reminds me of the past." He would often tell me of the glorious days of his own young strength, days when he rose rapidly in the esteem of his countrymen. It was a great experience to hear him speak out the memories of a long-forgotten yesterday.

TONES OF NORMAL DURATION

Normal duration of vocal sounds is to be expected in ordinary conversational situations. Unusually long or short duration of speech sounds should be reserved for special effects. If the speaker does not use normal duration in casual conversations and factual speeches he may be accused of attempting to set himself apart from other speakers. Extreme variations of duration should be used very cautiously by the average speaker.

9. Simulate contempt as you read the following passage. Use prolongation of tones as a deliberate technique to aid your expression.

CONTEMPT

If Judas Iscariot had betrayed Christ to the Romans, instead of to the Jews, a Roman officer might have sneered as follows:

OFFICER: Here they are, Iscariot. Thirty pieces of silver, thirty shining discs of money covered with a friend's blood. For this paltry sum I have bought a man's life. I thank you for making my task so easy, and my bargain so cheap. So pick up your money, contemptible dog, and begone before the very air becomes foul with the stench of such a deed. Glad as I am to end my search, I can hold nothing but loathing for a man who betrays his friend. You two washed your hands in the bowl together. Often you have kissed his face. And now you give him into our hands. What will we do to your "Master"? You should have considered that before you sold him. We'll catch him and kill him, Jew. *There is no other answer. You've asked me that question a thousand times and my reply has always been the same. It always will be the same.* Your friend will die, and I'll be given a city for catching him. And you have thirty pieces of silver. So take the ransom which your greed has earned, and hie you to some place where traitors are welcome.

10. Simulate fear, using the passage above under Rate, drill 10. Use staccato tones.

PHRASING

As it is used in this book, the term phrasing refers simply to the act of dividing words spoken or read into groups, by the device of introducing into the time sequence pauses which are long enough in duration to perform this function. This objective conception has several implications, of which three may be mentioned. (1) Phrasing refers to *what the speaker does at the moment of speaking*, not to any preconceived idea of what he ought to do. (2) There is *no one right way to phrase or group words*. The fact that phrases frequently coincide with single ideas does not mean necessarily that they must so coincide. Good speakers continually group several ideas together into what is called a phrase in this sense; just as frequently do they split one idea into several phrases. This may be regarded as entirely justifiable as long as the phrasing helps to reinforce the meaning. Whenever phrased examples are presented in this book it is understood, therefore, that one way, but not the only way, of phrasing is marked. (3) Any series of words can be phrased in a *large number of different ways*. Consider the following extreme example, in which the four-word sentence, "I shall go now," is phrased in eight different ways. |I shall go now.| |I| shall go now.| |I shall| go now.| |I shall go| now.| |I |shall| go now.| |I shall |go| now.| |I |shall go| now.| |I |shall| go |now.|

The aim of these drills is to teach you to group your words into phrases which reinforce the meaning of what you are saying.

1. Read the following sentences for which phrasing has been marked arbitrarily. Observe the marks.

|If you will get the steaks, |the bread, |and the pickles, |we are ready to start.|

|The words that he read |fell into two groups.|

|He could see me |and I could see him, |so there wasn't any use in running away.|

|I could see him do it, |but I couldn't help him.|

|He marked off the sentences, |largely on the basis of the meaning.|

|The rancher dug a well two hundred feet deep, |only to find that there was no water.|

|In spite of the bad weather, |several of our most prominent alumni attended the reunion.|

|The audience was bored by his performance |and hissed him off the stage.|

|Swimming is excellent exercise, |but it can be harmful |if carried to an extreme.|

|You may do it either way, |according to your desire as a speaker.|

2. Read the following sentences in one phrase each.

Breathe quickly.

This is a phrase.

Phrases may be short.

This is the way to breathe.

Long phrases are not very frequent.

Phrases may be thought of as breath groups.

Emphasized words should be held longer than usual.

Phrases usually are marked off by long or short pauses.

One may look upon these pauses as chances to breathe.

Breathe for the next phrase while you pause after the last one.

During each pause you should be thinking ahead and filling your lungs.

The speed with which a phrase is spoken or read depends upon the meaning.

It is conceivable that a single phrase could have a length of fifty or sixty words.

It is possible to speak a long phrase in as little time as a short one.

The logical phrases of average speech are so short that one should never find himself out of breath.

But even with phrases as long as these you can see that you need not necessarily run out of breath.

And in the phrase which you are now reading it would not affect the meaning to pause slightly after "reading."

3. Break each of the above sentences into two logical phrases. Mark with vertical lines and read.

4. Now break the same sentences into as many phrases as you think necessary for logical expression. Avoid over-phrasing. Mark and read.

5. Read the following paragraph as marked, noting especially the fact that adjacent phrases may vary considerably in length, and that this increases interest.

|Phrasing, |as used by the speaker, |is the splitting up of the sentences spoken |into groups of words |separated by pauses which are longer than those |ordinarily found between words. |These phrases may vary in length |according to the desire of the speaker. |Since their main purpose is to add to the forcefulness of speaking, |they do not depend entirely upon the construction of the sentence |as determined by the student of grammar. |Because of this fact, |the number of ways in which a selection may be phrased |is very large. |A good speaker, |by careful use of phrasing, |can bring out important parts of the passage spoken |which might not be properly emphasized by the poor speaker. |Thus, phrasing is one of the basic principles |of the speaker's art.|

6. Read the following paragraph as marked, noting this time the *location* of the pause marks.

|We speak in phrases, |not in words; |in thought units, |not in parts of speech. |A more or less obvious phrase is spoken quickly |and with reduced emphasis |so that the important phrases stand out clearly, |strongly |and with real contrast. |The length of phrases varies, |because speakers vary in their habits of speech |and in the meaning which they wish to give to phrases. |In other words, |phrasing depends upon the meaning of what you say |and also upon your whims as a speaker. |And although there is an element of logic in the process, |there are no definite rules.|

7. For an example of illogical phrasing, in which pauses occur at "wrong" places, read the same paragraph as it is marked below.

|We speak in phrases, not |in words; in |thought units, not in parts |of speech. A more or |less obvious phrase |is spoken quickly and |with reduced |emphasis so that |the important phrases stand out |clearly, strongly and with real |contrast. The length of phrases |varies, because speakers vary in |their habits |of speech and in the meaning |which they wish to give to phrases. In other words, |phrasing depends upon the meaning of |what you say and also |upon your whims as a speaker. And |although there is an element |of logic in the process, there |are no definite rules.|

8. After several readings, indicate your own best phrasing of the following paragraph with pause marks such as those used above.

In dividing language into phrases, the method of the speaker differs greatly from that of the student of grammar. While the student of grammar merely divides the various sentences up into parts according to the more or less definite rules of composition, the speaker chooses those divisions which will give most emphasis to the more important parts of his sentences. The number of ways in which a speaker may phrase a spoken sentence is very large, because his phrasing is determined only in part by the construction of the sentence and mainly by his own judgment. The phrases of speech usually are thought of as being thought groups, preceded and followed by longer pauses than those within the groups. Phrases may vary in length from one word to a large number of words, according to the selection read and the desire of the speaker.

9. Read the following paragraph without marking, once silently and then orally. If possible have another student mark on a duplicate copy the interphrasal pauses which you made during the first oral reading. Study these pauses and revise your phrasing until it satisfies you.

It is evident that phrasing is one of the most important tools of the speaker. Properly used it adds unity, coherence and emphasis to the passage spoken. On the other hand, improper phrasing may cause speech or reading to be disconnected, incoherent and monotonous. Daniel Webster and other great orators who are recorded in history mainly because of their ability as speakers were undoubtedly masters of the art of phrasing. Although the average student of speech may never have occasion to deliver a great oration, the technique of adequate phrasing will always be valuable to him in ordinary speaking and reading situations.

10. Read, study and mark the following paragraph until you can read it so that a listener can get at least a little meaning out of it.

Esau Wood sawed wood. Esau Wood would saw wood. All the wood Esau Wood saw Esau Wood would saw. In other words, all the wood Esau saw to saw Esau sought to saw. Oh, the wood Wood would saw! And oh, the wood-saw with which Wood would saw wood. But one day Wood's wood-saw would saw no wood, and thus the wood Wood sawed was not the wood Wood would saw if Wood's wood-saw would saw wood. Now, Wood would saw if Wood's wood-saw would saw wood. Now, Wood would saw wood with a wood-saw that would saw wood, so Esau sought a saw that would saw wood. One day Esau saw a saw saw wood as no other wood-saw Wood saw would saw wood. In fact, of all the wood-saws Wood ever saw saw wood Wood never saw a wood-saw that would saw wood as the wood-saw Wood saw saw wood would saw wood, and I never saw a wood-saw that would saw as the wood-saw Wood saw would saw until I saw Esau saw wood with the wood-saw Wood saw saw wood. Now Wood saws wood with the wood-saw Wood saw saw wood.

VARIATIONS IN THE RATE OF PHRASES

This is one means of giving your speech desirable variety. Your variations, however, should be related to the meaning of what you are saying. In general, this means that you will speak important phrases at a slow rate, while unimportant phrases, or phrases which are purely connective in function, can be spoken rapidly. For the time being ignore variations within the phrase.

1. Read the following sentences. Note that it is logical to read the italicized phrase more rapidly than the others in the same sentence. Observe this difference as you read.

"Over-phrasing," *as it is called*, results from too many pauses.

He can fool the rest of the class, but he can't fool me.

You are right, but I certainly pity her poor listeners.

The real reason, *in case you want to know*, is that I just don't like it.

A phrase, *so to speak*, is a group of words.

2. Read the following phrased paragraph. Note the mark S, F or E above each phrase. It means that the rate of the phrase is relatively Slower than, Faster than, or approximately Equal to the *preceding phrase*. (These are merely arbitrary indications, of course, which appear to suit the logical expression of this example.) Read the paragraph with these indications in mind. Exaggerate.

         S   F

|In grammar |the term "phrase" |refers to a group of

                                   E

words that form a fragmentary thought unit |or have the

                       F   F

properties of a part of speech |such as an adverb |or an ad-

       S   F   S

jective. |The phrases of speech, |however, |are arbitrary

                    S   E

groupings of words |by the speaker |as he is speaking

F

|which may or may not agree with his grammatical phrases.

S

|Grammarians have developed methods and rules for sentence

               E

analysis |that define and limit phrases in a relatively exact

           F   **F**   **S**

manner. |But the speaker, |on the other hand, |creates his

own rules as he goes along. |

3. Consider the following paragraph carefully. Mark your phrasing of it and indicate the relative rates of the phrases as above. Read.

> In speaking, the contents of a phrase, or of any other thought group must be relatively simply stated and restricted to a reasonable length. If this is not done, the audience and even the speaker himself may become confused. The writer has an advantage over the speaker in that the symbols used in writing are recorded more or less permanently and can be read and reread by his readers. The speaker, on the other hand, deals with auditory symbols which are transitory in nature. This means that anything that the speaker can do to promote immediate understanding on the part of his listeners will be done, if he is a good speaker. One way to achieve understanding in speech is, of course, repetition. But because the speaker cannot be forever repeating himself, he must do the next best thing and phrase his speech simply with due regard to the characteristics of auditory symbols.

VARIATIONS IN THE DURATION OF PAUSES BETWEEN PHRASES

This factor of time usage is related to the expression of meaning in a manner not wholly understood, but is another means of securing variety. Generally speaking, a long pause after a phrase indicates relative finality, while a short pause indicates incompleteness of the idea. This is dependent upon intonation, however. If the phrase preceding a long pause ends with a downward intonation the effect of finality mentioned is obtained, and the emphasis is turned back, as it were, upon the preceding phrase.

But if an upward intonation has been used, the long pause tends to emphasize the following phrase by withholding it after the rising intonation has caused it to be anticipated.

1. In the following examples interphrasal pause length is shown arbitrarily by the number of vertical lines. Short, medium or long pauses are indicated, respectively, by one, two or three lines. Read these examples, observing the differences.

SHORT

If you are in a hurry,	then I'll come at once.
If you can buy at that price,	buy at once.
He hit my brother	and then disappeared completely.
It's a sunny day	with a gentle breeze.
Hit him again, Charley,	he's still breathing.

MEDIUM

That's my guess,		but I really don't know.
We're glad to have you;		come again soon.
Try your best;		that's quite enough in this case.
This is one phrase,		and this another.
Do it right;		time is no object.

LONG

I go,			but I will return.
Now listen to me:			I won't have it.
There are two important things about any job:			speed and concentration.
To be or not to be,			that is the question.
Money is worth a lot,			but not the price some people pay.

2. Read all of the above sentences with a short pause at each break, then with a long pause. Note the differences in meaning.

3. The following sentences are phrased arbitrarily. Analyze them for pause length, and then add marks at each break to indicate the length of the pauses. Read, observing your marks.

Run quickly,	and don't wait for me.
I doubt it,	but I am willing to be shown.
Either you are very wise,	or very foolish.
Happiness is something,	but not everything.
Speak vigorously,	and pause often.
Of course you can stay;	it is only ten.
If you think you really know,	why don't you do something about it?
I tried fifty times,	but each time with absolute failure.
It cost me twenty dollars,	and that's quite enough.
At last he ran away;	it will kill his poor old mother.
We went to get a "coke,"	but the drug-store was closed.
That statement makes a fool of me,	and it doesn't help you either.
We couldn't find a hotel,	so we went to an auto camp.
If you want to fight,	we'll go down to the gym.
Go see Mr. Jones;	he has plenty of money.

4. Phrase the following paragraph and indicate pause length by the above method. Read.

There are no data available to furnish an objective answer to the question: "What is the optimum length of a pause?" And it is probable that when experiments have been performed they will show pause length to be influenced by so many factors that few generalizations can be made. A little evidence on the point comes from a study which compared the pauses of trained speakers to those of poor speakers. It was found that the pauses of the better speakers were longer, on the average, than those of the other group, and that there was considerably more variability in their length. It would appear from this that the beginning speaker should avoid especially pauses that are too short and too similar in duration.

RHYTHM

Rhythm is that aspect which has to do with the periodic recurrence in time of similar patterns of pitch, loudness, duration or quality. The tick of a watch is an example of nearly perfect rhythm, while the reports of firecrackers on July 4th are unrhythmical or aperiodic. Rhythm should vary with the material spoken and the goal. A limerick requires highly rhythmical utterance, while factual prose demands a relatively unrhythmical reading. It will be seen, then, that good *verse* rhythm is not necessarily good *prose* rhythm. In fact, it rarely is. In speech, too much rhythm is monotonous. Jerkiness, on the other hand, has too little rhythm. In most situations, the best rhythm is found somewhere between these two extremes, and at a point which best suits the situation.

It will be noted that we are not using the term rhythm as it sometimes is used, when an attempt is made to infer the "rhythm of the thought processes" or the "rhythm with which the speech mechanism operates" by listening to the speech. We are concerned instead solely with those objective characteristics of the stimulus itself which are stated above. Thus we are not forced into the equivocal position of characterizing the relatively irregular time usage of the good speaker as rhythmical.

The following drills aim to make you conscious of the varying degrees of rhythm which may be found or used in language.

1. As you read the following examples in order, note that they become progressively less rhythmical if your reading follows the presumable intent of the authors.

Highly Rhythmical

When a man hath no freedom to fight for at home,
Let him combat for that of his neighbors;
Let him think of the glories of Greece and of Rome,
And get knock'd on his head for his labors.

To do good to mankind is the chivalrous plan,
And is always as nobly requited;
Then battle for freedom wherever you can,
And, if not shot or hang'd, you'll get knighted.

Byron.

RHYTHMICAL

Thou wast not born for death, immortal bird!
No hungry generations tread thee down;
The voice I hear this passing night was heard
In ancient days by emperor and clown:
Perhaps the self-same song that found a path
Through the sad heart of Ruth, when, sick for home,
She stood in tears amid the alien corn;
The same that oft-times hath
Charm'd magic casements, opening on the foam
Of perilous seas, in faery lands forlorn.

Keats.

LESS RHYTHMICAL

No habitation can be seen; but they
Who journey thither find themselves alone
With a few sheep, with rocks and stones, and kites
That overhead are sailing in the sky.
It is in truth an utter solitude;
Nor should I have made mention of this dell
But for one object which you might pass by,
Might see and notice not. Beside the brook
Appears a straggling heap of unhewn stones!
And to that simple object appertains
A story—unenriched with strange events,
Yet not unfit, I deem, for the fireside,
Or for the summer shade.

Wordsworth.

UNRHYTHMICAL

The three selections presented above demonstrate roughly how rhythm may vary in language. The first example was chosen to illustrate highly rhythmical verse, while the rhythm of the second poem is still very apparent but somewhat less obvious than that of the first. The third selection approaches the temporal irregularities of the present paragraph. This graded series will provide you with a general idea of the various degrees of rhythm and of the way in which the rhythm of poetry is related to that of prose.

2. Read the examples again with *maximum* rhythm. Exaggerate.

3. Write out the first three selections in prose form. Preserve the identical words and word sequences, but change punctuation and capitalization to suit the prose version. Read with as little obvious rhythm as possible (i.e., attempt to approach your reading of the fourth selection).

4. Now read the selections *from their verse forms* as printed, but attempt a compromise between maximum rhythm and lack of rhythm.

5. In the first stanza of *America* following you have not only a highly rhythmical and rhymed selection, but also one with which are associated definite melodic sequences. Read this stanza from the verse form with maximum rhythm. If you sing, sing the stanza first.

> My country, 'tis of thee,
> Sweet land of liberty,
> Of thee I sing.
> Land where our fathers died,
> Land of the Pilgrims' pride,
> From every mountainside
> Let freedom ring.

6. Write out the stanza in a prose form as indicated above. Attempt to read it as prose with no obvious rhythm.

7. Copy the lyric of a current dance tune. Read it with maximum rhythm, then with no obvious rhythm.

8. Read the prose passage headed Unrhythmical, drill 1, with maximum rhythm. Using words as your rhythmical units, give each word equal duration, pitch and loudness, and make all pauses between words of equal duration.

9. Mark an extremely regular phrasing of the passage. This time, using phrases as your rhythmical units, give each phrase

equal duration, loudness and pitch pattern, and make all inter-phrasal pauses of equal duration.

10. Rephrase the passage as well as you can. Read with avoidance of extreme rhythm in a manner that will best express the meaning.

BIBLIOGRAPHY

1. Brigance, W. N., and Henderson, F. M., *A Drill Manual for Improving Speech*, J. B. Lippincott Company, Philadelphia, 1939.

2. Cowan, M., "Pitch and Intensity Characteristics of Stage Speech," *Archives of Speech*, Supplement, 1–92 (1936).

3. Darley, F. L., "A Normative Study of Oral Reading Rate," *M.A. Thesis, State University of Iowa*, 1940.

4. Franke, P., "A Preliminary Study Validating the Measurement of Oral Reading Rate in Words per Minute," *M.A. Thesis, State University of Iowa*, 1939.

5. Hoaglin, L. W., "The Duration Aspects of Emotional Speech," *M.A. Thesis, State University of Iowa*, 1937.

6. Murray, E., and Tiffin, J., "An Analysis of Some Basic Aspects of Effective Speech," *Archives of Speech*, 1:61–83 (1934).

7. Skalbeck, O. M., "A Statistical Analysis of Three Measures of Word Length," *M.A. Thesis, State University of Iowa*, 1938.

8. Snidecor, J. C., "Experimental Studies of the Pitch and Duration Characteristics of Superior Speech," *Ph.D. Dissertation, State University of Iowa*, 1940.

CHAPTER VIII

PITCH

The pitch of a tone refers to its position on the musical scale, and is related to the frequency of sound-wave repetition. In voice production the fundamental sound-wave frequency is directly determined by the frequency of vibration of the vocal cords.

The most frequent pitch disorders are the following:

1. Too high pitch.
2. Too low pitch.
3. Inflexibility of pitch.
4. Pitch patterns.

The drills of this chapter have been designed to correct these disorders and to lay the foundation for skilled pitch usage.

The most common specific causes of pitch defects are (1) faulty pitch discrimination, (2) poor tonal memory, (3) poor motor control, (4) emotional maladjustment, (5) faulty learning. The drills are written primarily with causes of the fifth type in mind. Since pitch differences can be perceived and produced by the majority of students, the form of the drills assumes these abilities. But the same procedures can be adapted very simply for use with cases where the abilities are lacking, or where other causes obtain.

PITCH LEVEL

During most speech the pitch of the voice varies almost constantly throughout a comparatively wide range. Over a period of time the pitches that are used by a good speaker distribute themselves relatively normally and continuously within this range, about a central pitch that is used and, consequently, heard more frequently than the pitches above and below it. The entire distribution can be located along the musical scale and, if this central, most frequently used pitch is known, the pitch level of the sample as a whole can be given satisfactory general description in terms of a single value. It is in this statistical sense that the term *pitch level* is used in this book. Pitch level should be a matter of concern to any speaker, because, in addition to being of obvious importance itself, it exerts a direct effect upon voice quality, loudness and pitch variability. Although the primary emphasis of this section is upon determining and training the most effective pitch level, as such, it is intended that the student consider also its influence upon the other aspects of voice.

The term *habitual pitch level* is applied to the pitch used most frequently by a given speaker. It is also proposed that each speaker has a certain individual pitch level, determined by the characteristics of his mechanism, at which that speaker's voice is most efficient for speech. This is referred to herein as the *natural pitch level*. In most cases it is desirable for a speaker to use his natural level habitually. Methods for determining the two levels and for habituating the natural level are described below. In certain instances, however, the natural pitch is so high in comparison to the average level of other speakers of the same sex that listeners find it unpleasant. It is unwise, of course, to train the use of such a level, and it is recommended that the problem be approached experimentally. Usually this means that a certain amount of vocal efficiency should be sacrificed in favor of a somewhat lower, more pleasant level. Contrary to prevailing opinion, however, lowering the pitch of a voice that is not too high rarely improves it. The pitch tends to become more inflexible, the voice quality is affected unfavorably and the production of adequate loudness becomes more difficult.

1. Determine your *habitual pitch* as follows. Read the following prose passage at the pitch level which you use habitually and listen to the pitch of your voice. After you pass the first pair of vertical lines in the passage, begin *gradually* to compress your range as you read until you are chanting in a monotone. Sustain

this last tone on [ɑ]. Note: Narrow the range both from above and below, attempting to end up on the tone which you use *most frequently*, not on the lowest tone which you use. The tendency here is to end finally on a tone that is slightly lower than the habitual pitch unless instructions are followed with care. If you have performed correctly, this tone is, or is close to, your habitual pitch level. Now locate this level with respect to the lowest tone of your *singing* range, as follows. Using the habitual pitch as *do*, sing down the scale to your very lowest tone, counting the notes as you go. Don't stop with the lowest pleasant, easy or loud tone that you can produce, but go down as far as you can identify a pitch. For example, if you sing *do, ti, la, so, fa, mi, re*, the last note, *re*, is the seventh note down, counting *do* as the first. Now refer to Table 3, below, and look up 7, the number of the lowest note, *re*, in the second column. Then look across to the third column to find the *number of musical tones* that lie between *re*, your lowest tone, and your habitual pitch, the *do* from which you began to sing down the scale. This shows you how far up from the bottom of your range the pitch which you use most frequently lies. In the case of the example cited, the table shows this value to be 5.0 tones.

TABLE 3.—DETERMINATION OF HABITUAL PITCH LEVEL IN TONES
ABOVE LOWEST NOTE

Name of Lowest Note	Number of Lowest Note	Habitual Pitch Level in Tones
do	1	0
ti	2	.5
la	3	1.5
so	4	2.5
fa	5	3.5
mi	6	4.0
re	7	5.0
do	8	6.0
ti	9	6.5
la	10	7.5
so	11	8.5
fa	12	9.5
mi	13	10.0
re	14	11.0
do	15	12.0

Selection for Determination of Habitual Pitch

When the sunlight strikes raindrops in the air, they act like a prism and form a rainbow. The rainbow is a division of white light into many beautiful colors. These take the shape of a long round arch, with its path high above, and its two ends apparently beyond the horizon. There is, according to legend, a boiling pot of gold at one end. People look, but no one ever finds it. When a man looks for something beyond his reach, his friends say he is looking for the pot of gold at the end of the rainbow.

Throughout the centuries men have explained the rainbow in various ways. Some have accepted it as a miracle without physical explanation. To the Hebrews it was a token that there would be no more universal floods. | |The Greeks used to imagine that it was a sign from the gods to foretell war or heavy rain. The Norsemen considered the rainbow as a bridge over which the gods passed from earth to their home in the sky. Other men have tried to explain the phenomenon physically. Aristotle thought that the rainbow was caused by reflection of the sun's rays by the rain. Since then physicists have found that it is not reflection, but refraction by the raindrops which causes the rainbow. Many complicated ideas about the rainbow have been formed. The difference in the rainbow depends considerably upon the size of the water drops, and the width of the colored band increases as the size of the drops increases. | |The actual primary rainbow observed is said to be the effect of superposition of a number of bows. If the red of the second bow falls upon the green of the first, the result is to give a bow with an abnormally wide yellow band, since red and green lights when mixed form yellow. This is a very common type of bow, one showing mainly red and yellow, with little or no green or blue.

2. Determination of the *natural pitch level*. According to the researches of Pronovost and Snidecor (see bibliography) the pitch levels of superior adult male speakers are located very close

to C₃, one octave below middle C on the musical scale, while those of superior adult female speakers approximate G♯₃, two tones below middle C. Although these values may be recommended as the *optimum* or *best* pitch levels for the two sexes, they cannot be enforced rigidly with all speakers, because of individual structural variations. The most satisfactory method that has been devised thus far for the calculation of the *natural* pitch level of an individual involves the determination of that pitch which lies 25 per cent of the way up that individual's total singing range including falsetto. Directions for finding this level are given in the following paragraph. Even this method, however, is unsatisfactory in certain instances; apparently the best procedure in such cases is to try various levels until one is found that gives the desired result. This is especially true of women's voices.

Estimate your *natural pitch* as follows. Sing down to your very *lowest* tone. Letting this tone be *do* of the musical scale, sing up the scale to your *very highest tone including falsetto*. Repeat this several times to be sure that you are covering your maximum range. Count the notes as you go. Research has shown that, following these instructions, superior speakers have average total singing ranges including falsetto of approximately 22 to 24 notes, or 18 to 20 musical tones. Refer now to Table 4 below, and locate your highest note by number in column 2. The value opposite this in column 3 is the *number of musical tones* in your total singing range. Now move directly across to column 4 which tells you in musical tones approximately how far your natural pitch level lies above your lowest tone. In other words, this last value is a measure of your *natural* pitch level in musical tones above the lowest note of your range. In case you have access to a piano you can locate exactly the various pitches used in this process.

Compare your natural pitch level directly to your habitual pitch level in musical tones, as measured in the previous drill, and determine whether or not you should raise or lower your pitch level and by what amount. Plot both highest and lowest pitches, and both natural and habitual pitch levels on the graph of Figure 2. Consult Pitch Range, drill 1, below, for the method.

If the difference is only one or two tones you are using a close enough approximation to your natural level. Even in such a case, however, experiment with the indicated adjustment to find out if it improves your voice. If the difference is more than two tones you should begin a program to habituate the new level. Consult the following drills.

TABLE 4.—CALCULATION OF NATURAL PITCH LEVEL IN TONES ABOVE LOWEST NOTE, BY DETERMINING 25 PER CENT OF TOTAL RANGE

Name of Highest Note	Number of Highest Note	Range in Musical Tones	Natural Pitch Level in Tones	Name of Natural Pitch Level
do	1	0		
re	2	1.0		
mi	3	2.0		
fa	4	2.5		
so	5	3.5		
la	6	4.5	1.1	re
ti	7	5.5	1.4	re
do	8	6.0	1.5	mi
re	9	7.0	1.8	mi
mi	10	8.0	2.0	mi
fa	11	8.5	2.1	mi
so	12	9.5	2.4	fa
la	13	10.5	2.6	fa
ti	14	11.5	2.9	fa
do	15	12.0	3.0	so
re	16	13.0	3.3	so
mi	17	14.0	3.5	so
fa	18	14.5	3.6	so
so	19	15.5	3.9	so
la	20	16.5	4.1	la
ti	21	17.5	4.4	la
do	22	18.0	4.5	la
re	23	19.0	4.8	la
mi	24	20.0	5.0	ti
fa	25	20.5	5.1	ti
so	26	21.5	5.4	ti
la	27	22.5	5.6	ti
ti	28	23.5	5.9	do
do	29	24.0	6.0	do
re	30	25.0	6.3	do
mi	31	26.0	6.5	re
fa	32	26.5	6.6	re
so	33	27.5	6.9	re
la	34	28.5	7.1	re
ti	35	29.5	7.4	re
do	36	30.0	7.5	mi

3. Refer again to Table 4 and locate the row corresponding to your total singing range. The last column gives the name of the note up to which you should sing to reach your natural pitch. For example, if you can sing 22 notes of the scale, you have a total singing range of 18 musical tones, your natural pitch is calculated to lie 4.5 musical tones up from your lowest tone, and you can find this level by singing up the scale to *la*, beginning with your lowest tone as *do*. Using this method, sing up to your natural pitch and sustain a good [ɑ] at this level as long as possible. Repeat ten times, singing up each time and listening carefully to the pitch.

4. Without singing up, attempt now to strike this same tone spontaneously. Check your accuracy by singing down the scale to your lowest tone. Look up in Table 3 the name of the note which you reach at your lowest tone, read the corresponding value in musical tones, and compare this to your natural pitch level in musical tones. Repeat the sustaining of spontaneous tones until the two values agree.

5. Sing up to your natural pitch level and *chant* the following list of words.

neat	sod	wheeze	length
guess	chime	mute	bite
jig	quoit	yet	feed
hatch	code	sigh	judge
book	gown	palm	blob
spoon	shun	crown	sick
chuck	much	range	eight

6. Repeat, *speaking* the words this time.

7. Sing up to your natural level and read the following sentences. Use your natural level as the dominant pitch, but read the sentences naturally about this level.

I dropped the jug.
He came and went.
Don't you think so?
Pop goes the weasel.

You can't have it because I need it.
Do you really like it, but don't want to say so?
Come in if you wish, but I'd rather be alone.
Keep it up, you can't miss.
He is as thin as a rail.
It is a shame that he can't come.
Do you like chocolate pudding?
It will thaw, if spring ever comes.

8. Read the test passage for habitual pitch, drill 1, as follows. Having sung up to your natural level, chant the first part of the passage slowly at this level until you reach the first pair of vertical lines. Then, without stopping, gradually spread out your inflections until you are reading normally at your natural level. Continue in this manner until you reach the second pair of vertical lines. Then, still without stopping, compress your range gradually until you are chanting at your natural pitch. When you finish the passage sustain [ɑ] at this pitch. Determine how well you have succeeded in preserving your natural pitch throughout the reading by singing down to your lowest note and comparing as in drill 4, above.

9. Read the passage at a high pitch level. Repeat at a low level.

10. Simulate fear as you read the following passage. Use a high pitch level as a deliberate technique to aid your expression.

FEAR

A boy in his teens has been sentenced to die for murder. At dawn of the day of his execution, as his cell slowly becomes gray and he knows that the time is not long, he is suddenly seized with a fit of uncontrollable terror. He cries:

THE BOY: Oh, God! Please don't let them take me away now. Let me have one more day—one more hour—to live. I don't deserve hanging for the thing I did. I didn't know then that a man's life meant so much. But I know now, I know, and please forgive me. I don't know how it happened. Honest I don't. One minute he was standing there, and the next minute there was a smoking gun in my hand. I don't know how it got there. You've got to believe me this time, God, if you never did before. You've got to believe it in time to keep them from hanging me. Every night you ask me how it happened. But I don't know! I don't know! I can't remember! *There is no other answer. You've asked me that question a thousand times and my reply has always been the same. It always will be the same.* You can't figure out things like that. They just happen. And afterwards you're sorry. I'm that way now. I'm sorry. Oh, God, stop them—quick—before it's too late.

11. Simulate indifference as you read the following passage, using a low pitch level as a deliberate technique to aid your expression.

INDIFFERENCE

Johnson receives a matter-of-fact, unemotional, business letter from a publisher friend. The letter follows:

JOHNSON (reading): Dear Johnson: Your letter of last Thursday is at hand. At your request I am sending under separate cover two dozen copies of the magazine. You will notice that the format has been changed, and that we now publish a critical article a month instead of the many short stories which used to appear in these pages. Our changed policy was determined by the fact that Americans are becoming interested in the implications of our national literature. We believe that people are analytical now instead of superficial, as they were in the preceding decade. This is also the reason why we have not started publication of poetry. Once more you have requested me to change my mind. Once more, as a matter of policy, not inclination, I must refuse. *There is no other answer. You've asked me that question a thousand times and my reply has always been the same. It always will be the same.* As editor of a commercial journal, I cannot undertake publication of material which will not yield appreciable profit. Sincerely yours, . . .

PITCH RANGE

By total pitch range is meant that pitch interval which separates the lowest and highest tones used in any given sample of speaking or reading. Ordinarily it is expressed in musical scale units such as the semi-tone, the tone or the octave. The most recent evidence shows that good speakers employ speaking ranges of slightly less than two octaves in factual reading, that this range is located in the lowest fraction of the total singing range, and that it may extend lower than the lowest sung tone to include pitches that are used only momentarily. Poor speakers employ narrower ranges on the average. It has been demonstrated experimentally that raising the pitch level tends to produce a concomitant increase of the range, while the latter tends to be reduced as the level is lowered. If your pitch is inflexible, therefore, compare your habitual and natural pitch levels carefully. It will be easier for you to achieve more flexibility if you use a pitch level that is higher than the one you are using at present.

1. If you are judged as inflexible, determine first if your mechanism in its present condition can produce an adequate range of pitches. A study of superior speakers showed them to have total singing ranges including falsetto of approximately 20 tones, although they used only the lower fraction of these ranges in speech. If your range is less than 15 tones, make a systematic attempt to increase it by daily drill. From a point three or four notes above your lowest tone, sing down the scale as far as possible, then sing back up to the starting point and go on down again. Repeat this process six or eight times, attempting to extend your range downward. Then attempt to add notes to the top of your range by reversing the same method. Do not strain as you drill. Assume a good posture and use a medium loudness. If possible, use a piano so that you may locate the limits of your range very definitely. Graph your progress on the chart of Figure 2.

The vertical axis of this chart is range in tones, while the horizontal axis represents your daily trials. If you have no piano or other means of determining exactly what note you are singing,

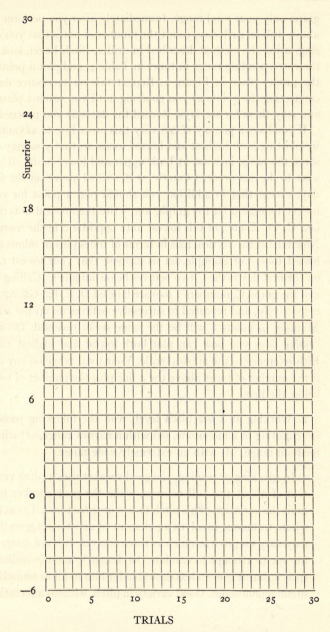

TRIALS

Figure 2.—Chart for Improvement Curve of Range in Musical Tones.

graph only your total range. Immediately after you perform the above drill on each day, count the number of notes that you can sing, using the method described in drill 2, Pitch Level, look up the corresponding range in tones in Table 4, and plot a point at the proper place in Figure 2. Repeat this on successive days, connecting the points as you go along until you reach a plateau and stay there for six days. Record the dates as you proceed.

If you have a piano you can vary this procedure to advantage by plotting both highest and lowest tones, so that you may observe the range increase at both upper and lower limits. If you wish to do this proceed exactly as described above on the first day, except that in addition you should plot a point for your lowest tone at o on the graph, and write the musical notation, i.e., C, D, E, etc., of this lowest note opposite o in the margin. Now relabel the vertical axis in terms of tones plus or minus this lowest tone. For example, let us suppose that your lowest tone on the first day is the C two octaves below middle C. Calling the o of the graph C, numbers 1 to 6 are labeled D, E, F♯, G♯, A♯, C, respectively, and repeated in successive octaves on up the scale. Minus 1 to minus 6 will be the same series reversed. On successive days you now can plot both lowest and highest tones with reference to the musical scale. Your total range on any day is the number of tones above the o line plus the number of tones below the line.

2. Working at a *low* pitch level, read the following passage (a) chanting in a monotone, (b) with a narrow range, (c) with a medium range, (d) with an extremely wide range.

In speaking or reading, the good speaker uses a pitch variation of about two full octaves, while the poor speaker may limit the variation of his pitch to two or three tones. The actor, whose technique involves an element of artistic exaggeration, may vary his pitch as much as three octaves. It is not desirable for one to attempt to emulate the dramatic actor in ordinary speech, but it is even less desirable for him to allow himself to sound monotonous. Good variety in pitch, without affectation, gives a sense of vitality and variety to any type of speech or reading.

3. Repeat the four readings of the passage, employing the pitch ranges specified but at *high* pitch levels.

4. Repeat but at your *natural* pitch level.

5. Read the following passage, beginning with a chant and increasing your range gradually until you end by reading with an extremely wide range.

A recent experiment indicates that there is a definite relationship between pitch variability and pitch level. In this experiment a group of superior readers recorded uninstructed readings of a test passage and then listened to the records of their own performances. They then were instructed to read with greater flexibility, and this second performance was compared to the first by means of objective measurements. It was found in each case that the second reading not only was more flexible, but also was higher in pitch level than the first. When a like comparison was made between normal readings and less flexible readings, it was found that the pitch level was lowered. In order to establish more definitely the relationship between pitch level and flexibility the procedure was reversed by having the readers listen again to their normal readings and then read at higher and lower pitch levels. Measurements of these performances also were made, and it was found that at higher pitch levels the readers had increased flexibility, while it had been decreased at lower levels.

6. Read the passage again, but reverse the above process.

7. Simulate anger as you read the following passage, using a wide pitch range as a deliberate technique to assist your expression. Note that a *high* pitch level also will help the portrayal.

Anger

The General is exceedingly angry at the continued demands of a certain man to grant clemency to a soldier who has been condemned to death for treason. The man again forces his way in to the General. The latter shouts:

GENERAL: But, sir, this is war! You come to me and ask pardon for a traitor—you whom I was recently compelled to pardon against my will. You have the audacity to return again and again and beg the life of one against whom the world cries "death!" You wonder why I will not commit him to the ranks and let him die in battle—fighting—since die he must. I said that I could but abide by what was the law—the law of war. You wrote to me—you besieged me with letters, and when I did not reply you attempted to bribe my orderly to get your message through to me. Failing that you watched my door, and now at this opportunity you force yourself upon me! You stand before me as if I were facing judgment! You flay me with vicious accusations, and defy me to repeat what I have said before. *There is no other answer. You've asked me that question a thousand times and my reply has always been the same. It always will be the same.* Thank God that you are free, but do not think that your freedom is the price with which to free the other traitors in this war. What love you have for this doomed man I will not attack, but if you loved your country half as well, you, too, would say that those who love it not deserve death.

8. Simulate contempt as you read the following passage, using a wide pitch range in combination with a generally *low* pitch level as a deliberate expressive technique.

CONTEMPT

If Judas Iscariot had betrayed Christ to the Romans, instead of to the Jews, a Roman officer might have sneered as follows:

OFFICER: Here they are, Iscariot. Thirty pieces of silver, thirty shining discs of money covered with a friend's blood. For this paltry sum I have bought a man's life. I thank you for making my task so easy, and my bargain so cheap. So pick up your money, contemptible dog, and begone before the very air becomes foul with the stench of such a deed. Glad as I am to end my search, I can hold nothing but loathing for a man who betrays his friend. You two washed your hands in the bowl together. Often you have kissed his face. He loved you—as much as a Jew can love anyone but himself. And now you give him into our hands. What will we do to your "Master"? You should have considered that before you sold him. We'll catch him and kill him, Jew. *There is no other answer. You've asked me that question a thousand times and my reply has always been the same. It always will be the same.* Your friend will die, and I'll be given a city for catching him. And you have thirty pieces of silver. So take the ransom which your greed has earned, and hie you to some place where traitors are welcome.

SHIFTS OF PITCH

When a change in pitch occurs between the terminal pitch of a given phonation and the initial pitch of the following phonation, that jump in pitch is termed a *shift*. Shifts occur both within and between phrases, the latter usually being of wider extent. Upward shifts usually exceed downward shifts both in extent and in number. This is another means of introducing desirable variety into your pitch usage.

   1. Read the following two-word sentences, making a barely perceptible pause between the two words and a definite upward shift to the second word.

He went.	Winter comes.
Move fast.	How many?
Bill jumped.	Fish swim.
Shut up.	What happened?
Go home.	Believe me.
Dogs bark.	Who won?
Understand it?	Write this.
Wake up.	Help yourself.

   2. Repeat, using a downward shift to the second word.
   3. Read the following two-phrase sentences, shifting upward or downward or not shifting at all as the arrows indicate.

If he does that, |↓|I'll kill him.
His car is black, |↓|and mine is blue.

She learned that tears failed to influence anyone, |↑| least of all her father.

Come into the house, |↑|dinner's ready.

He ran to the corner |→| and came right back.

In other words, |→|the blue car is mine.

4. Read the following examples, shifting upward or downward or not at all as the meaning seems to indicate. After a trial mark your decisions with arrows. Exaggerate.

You can't lose, | |take a shot.

If you don't get an answer, | |write him.

The sign said, | |"For Sale."

Come to think of it, | | I do know the answer.

Do you, | |or do you not?

If you can't do it, | |I can do it.

Phrase it carefully, | |as if you meant it.

Your honor, | |I am guilty.

5. Phrase the following passage, indicating the direction of shifts between phrases by arrows as above. Read.

For the most part, shifts in pitch between phonations occur in an upward direction. Inflections, or changes of pitch without cessation of phonation, occur relatively more often in a downward direction. Although based upon sound research, these conclusions are of no great practical help to the student who wishes to consider individual pitch changes in phonations or in shifts, for almost every case must be considered as an individual problem. However, the exercises of this section illustrate certain general principles of pitch usage and indicate a number of specific ways in which pitch and logical meaning are related. The student should remember that it is not only the words that the speaker says, but also the pitch changes that he uses, which convey his meaning to his listeners.

INFLECTIONS

When pitch changes without interruption of phonation the change is termed an *inflection*. Inflections may be upward or downward, the latter usually exceeding the former in extent and number. Frequently they are combined into complex inflections. This aspect of pitch usage has been shown experimentally to be very closely related to the expression of meaning and emotion. That the use of inflections of varying extents and directions is an important determinant of pitch flexibility has likewise been demonstrated.

1. Each of the following words is followed by a phrase in parentheses and accompanied by an arrow or arrows to indicate inflection. After analysis of the corresponding phrase and arrows, reach each word *alone*, using the indicated inflection to express the meaning of the phrase. Exaggerate. Do not read the phrases aloud.

Well↘	(I didn't expect to find you here.)
My↘	(That's fine.)
George↘	(Stop right now.)
Ruth↗	(Is she here?)
Oh↘	(Is that so?)
Stop→	(Don't move.)
Oh↘	(That hurts.)
Red↗	(Do you mean he bought a red car?)
Go↘	(Leave at once.)
Cute↗	(Is she cute?)
Say↘	(That's swell.)
Rot→	(I mean it's all rot.)
Now↘	(I mean right now.)
Fire↗	(Do you mean there's a fire?)
Fool↘	(I think you're a fool.)
Carl↘	(You're a dear, Carl.)

2. In a similar manner attach an emotion or situation to each of the following words and write a phrase for each like those above. Experiment with the expression of the meaning of each phrase by means of inflecting the word alone and diagram the inflections decided upon. Read with exaggeration.

yes	what	well	when	why
no	where	don't	oh	good
please	shame	who	there	wait

3. To each of the above words *in turn* give (a) a narrow, (b) an average, (c) a wide *downward* inflection.

4. Repeat, giving to each word (a) a narrow, (b) an average, (c) a wide *upward* inflection.

5. Another important aspect of the inflection is the rate at which pitch changes take place. Two inflections of the same extent may differ in this regard if their durations are different. Using *wide downward* inflections throughout read each of the above words one at a time, (a) with slow rate of pitch change, (b) with rapid rate of pitch change.

6. Repeat, using only *wide upward* inflections.

7. Read the passage for simulation of anger under Pitch Range above, using wide inflections with rapid pitch change as a deliberate technique.

INTONATION

Intonation is the term reserved here for the *general* pitch movement during a number of phonations. It may include numerous shifts and inflections. The intonation of phrases merits special consideration, since pitch patterns frequently consist of the repetition of similar types of intonations, employing the phrase as the unit of repetition.

Since general pitch movement is closely related to the meaning, it is apparent that a pitch pattern violates the general principle that voice usage reinforces the meaning in good speech.

1. Simple statements of fact (affirmative sentences) or commands (imperative sentences) usually take a downward intonation. Read the following examples with this in mind. Exaggerate. Note the arrows; we shall use this marking system to indicate the general course of intonation during a phrase.

I am going home↘.

Good night↘.

This is the end↘.

Turn around↘.

I am ready↘.

Do it now↘.

Carry the large case↘.

Feed the dog at ten↘.

Get me some pencils↘.

That's a good remark↘.

Stand still↘.

Call him tomorrow↘.

He didn't see me↘.   Go home↘.
Bring me the books↘.   He saw Henry↘.
Go to bed↘.   I did that↘.
That's not at all true↘.   That's the way↘.

2. The second basic American intonation is found in questions
which can be answered with "yes" or "no." These so-called
general questions typically are given *upward* intonations. Read
the following examples with this in mind. Exaggerate.

Are you coming↗?   Have you seen her↗?
Do you think so↗?   Did you get it↗?
Did it arrive↗?   Will you tell him↗?
Do you recognize him↗?   Coming, Jim↗?
Do you mean it↗?   Do you like it↗?
Wasn't it good↗?   Will it cost too much↗?
Will you leave↗?   Will it hold together↗?
Can't you just see it↗?   Did you go↗?
Won't he be jealous↗?   Will you wash the dishes↗?
Will you please hurry↗?   Did you see him↗?

3. Not all questions take upward intonations. Where the expected answer is in the form of a statement, rather than the
simple affirmative or negative, the question usually takes a
downward intonation. Such a question has been called a *special*
question. Read the following with downward intonations.

Where are you going↘?
Why won't you tell me↘?
Who is that↘?
What is the date↘?
How do you know that↘?
What did he tell you↘?
Who is fooled now↘?
Who is there↘?
Why didn't you say so↘?
Why do you know that↘?
What time is it↘?
How well does she know it↘?

Why don't you go\?
How well do you like him\?
How did he answer your question\?
How much does it cost\?
Who took my book\?
Who shot cock-robin\?
Why not shoot the traitor\?
How many gallons, please\?

4. As an example of what intonation can do to meaning read the simple sentences of drill 1, above, with *upward* intonations. Note that they are converted into general questions, answerable with "yes" or "no."

5. Now read the general questions of drill 2 with *downward* intonations. Note that extremely complex meanings are added. In some cases scepticism or sarcasm or some other attitude is expressed. (Do you mean it\?) In others the question becomes an affirmation (Won't he be jealous\?), or a command (Will you please hurry\?).

6. Now read the special questions of drill 3 with upward intonations. Note that the effect is one of irritability, excitement, impatience, or that it can be simply a request that a previous statement be repeated (Who is that/?).

7. When a statement having a downward intonation is followed in the same sentence by a question, a change in the direction of intonation of the question can change the implication of the entire sentence. If an *upward* intonation is given to the question, the sentence becomes a request for information. "He is speaking, isn't he/?" "Yes." In effect the speaker asks, "Is he speaking?" But if a *downward* intonation is given to the question, the speaker asks the listener to confirm or deny the statement in the first part of the sentence. "He is speaking, isn't he\?" "Yes" (e.g., it sounds like it), or "No" (e.g., I don't think he is speaking). The question has become "I think he is speaking; do you or do you not agree?" Read the following examples with this distinction in mind.

He doesn't have ten dollars, does he↗?
He doesn't have ten dollars, does he↘?

He isn't washing the car, is he↗?
He isn't washing the car, is he↘?

They are different, aren't they↗?
They are different, aren't they↘?

You are going to the country, aren't you↗?
You are going to the country, aren't you↘?

Joe didn't steal the book, did he↗?
Joe didn't steal the book, did he↘?

They and Elmer saw the show, didn't they↗?
They and Elmer saw the show, didn't they↘?

It won't cost me fifty dollars, will it↗?
It won't cost me fifty dollars, will it↘?

8. Where words or phrases are listed one after the other a special intonation problem arises. The following examples are marked typically as if the speaker knows in advance all the items that he is going to list. Note that each item takes an upward intonation, except the last, which takes a downward movement. Read as marked. (Note: In these examples level intonations have much the same effect as upward intonations.)

He came↗, he saw↗, he conquered↘.
Bring me the knives↗, the forks↗ and the spoons↘.
The garden contained hollyhocks↗, violets↗, daffodils↗, daisies↘.
He spoke in the name of justice↗ and decency↘.
I will buy the vegetables↗, groceries↗ and meat↘.
I can give you seventeen cents↗, five old keys↗ and a dozen pawn tickets↘.
There were several men in the race: Milton↗, Brown↗, Shaw↗ and Stevens↘.
Of the people↗, by the people↗, and for the people↘.

9. The same sentences now are marked as if each list of items is incomplete. Note the effect of uncertainty as you read.

He came↗, he saw↗, he conquered↗.
Bring me the knives↗, the forks↗ and the spoons↗.
The garden contained hollyhocks↗, violets↗, daffodils↗, daisies↗.
He spoke in the name of justice↗ and decency↗.
I will buy the vegetables↗, groceries↗ and meat↗.
I can give you seventeen cents↗, five old keys↗ and a dozen pawn tickets↗.
There were several men in the race: Milton↗, Brown↗, Shaw↗ and Stevens↗.
Of the people↗, by the people↗, and for the people↗.

10. Now the sentences are marked as if the speaker doesn't know as he goes along how many items he is going to list, but is conscious of the fact that a downward intonation indicates completeness and is providing for this on each item in case he can't think of another item to add at any time. Note also that the same patterns can be used as a deliberate technique to give special prominence to each item in turn. Read as marked.

He came↘, he saw↘, he conquered↘.
Bring me the knives↘, the forks↘ and the spoons↘.
The garden contained hollyhocks↘, violets↘, daffodils↘, daisies↘.
He spoke in the name of justice↘ and decency↘.
I will buy the vegetables↘, groceries↘ and meat↘.
I can give you seventeen cents↘, five old keys↘ and a dozen pawn tickets↘.
There were several men in the race: Milton↘, Brown↘, Shaw↘ and Stevens↘.
Of the people↘, by the people↘, and for the people↘.

11. Note that the differences in effect mentioned above are true also for certain consecutive phrases which are not part of a list. Read the following phrased examples using on each example the three intonation patterns marked in drills 8, 9 and 10.

I am going to town, |and I expect to return.
He will buy the house, |and that won't help matters.
You can go, |or you can stay right here.
He hit my brother, |and then disappeared completely.
You are right, |and I am wrong.
He said he will graduate, |and he expects to graduate.

12. As another illustration of ways in which intonation can change meaning consider the following questions in which alternatives are presented to the listener. Using the same words you can call for a simple "yes" or "no," or demand a specific choice. "Have you read Byron↗ or Keats↗?" "Yes." "Have you read Byron↗ or Keats↘?" "Byron." Read as marked.

Are you going to the beach↗ or to the mountains↗?
Are you going to the beach↗ or to the mountains↘?

Will you take vanilla↗ or chocolate↗?
Will you take vanilla↗ or chocolate↘?

Will he buy a Ford↗ or Chevrolet↗?
Will he buy a Ford↗ or Chevrolet↘?

Will they be here↗ or there↗?
Will they be here↗ or there↘?

Does she wear green↗, or blue↗, or yellow↗, or red↗?
Does she wear green↗, or blue↗, or yellow↗, or red↘?

Can she cook↗ or sew↗?
Can she cook↗ or sew↘?

13. The above drills make it apparent that it is poor speech to impose the same type of intonation on all phrases. When this is done too frequently the defect is termed a *pitch pattern*. Possible logical intonations are marked for each phrase of the following paragraph. Read with attention to the marks. (Note: It is, of course, impossible to describe all the pitch changes which occur during a phrase with a single arrow. The following marks indicate only the *general* directions of the intonations.)

|The accurate pronunciation of words→| is not the only thing that constitutes good oral reading\.| The emotions and meanings conveyed through words→| are conditioned by the way in which the voice is used\| as the words are read\.| For example↗,| the sentence→,| "That's a lovely gown"→,| if spoken one way↗| may mean that the gown truly is lovely\,| or that you agree with another's opinion→| concerning the loveliness of the gown\.| Spoken in another way↗| the same phrase can mean that this particular gown is lovely\,| but that the gown that the person wore yesterday→| was not such a lovely gown\.| It is even possible to reverse completely↗| the obvious meaning of the words\| so that a listener understands→| that you consider this gown to be definitely unlovely\.| Because of this dependence of meaning upon voice→| one of the most important tasks of the oral reader↗| is to determine exactly what the writer means\| and then to read in such a manner→| that the subtle meanings\,| in addition to the obvious ones→,| will be clearly expressed to his listeners\.|

14. Read the following phrased selection with a downward intonation on each phrase.

|In addition to relating their variations in pitch to the meaning ,|good speakers employ flexibility of pitch for another reason ,|namely, to avoid monotony .| A speaker uses many phrases |which may take any one of several different intonations |without distorting the meaning .| If he is alert |he will take advantage of such options |to employ intonations which differ from those immediately preceding or following .| To be more specific ,|let us suppose that you are about to speak a sentence composed of three phrases .| Let us assume further |that the most natural direction of intonation for each of these three phrases |is downward .| As you form the sentence in your mind ,|however ,|you note that the second phrase |might be given an upward intonation |without changing the essential meaning of the sentence .| So you speak the phrase in that manner ,|thus avoiding the triple repetition of the same downward pattern .| This is a

simple illustration |of one technique used by superior speakers |to avoid monotony of pitch usage .|

15. Read the above selection with an upward intonation on each phrase.

16. Read the above selection with a level intonation on each phrase.

17. Now analyze the selection to determine the most logical intonation of each phrase and mark with arrows.

18. The complex word-to-word variations and inflectional patterns which are superimposed upon the general intonational trends are so intimately related to meaning that a consideration of these phenomena has been reserved for the chapter on stress. Listening, however, to these variations, reread the selections presented in drills 13 and 14 and draw above each phrase a *pitch curve* which diagrams as many of the pitch fluctuations as you can hear in your voice as you read.

19. In addition to the intonation patterns of phrases, another means of reinforcing meaning is to contrast the general *pitch level* of consecutive phrases. An outstanding example of this is the parenthetical phrase, which is spoken typically at a lower pitch level than adjacent phrases as a device to mark it as an unimportant qualification of what is said, or to indicate that it is merely the speaker's comment on what he is saying. Read the following marked sentences with this in mind.

The science of phonetics is laying, *although in an irregular manner*, the foundation of an objective approach to the problem of speech.

It's a long road, *so they say*, that has no turning.

That text, *in case you are interested*, is a fine summary.

He hit the ball, *it seemed*, with a perfect stroke.

Good speech, *to Henry*, is unimportant.

Phonetics, *to the man on the street*, is a much misunderstood subject.

It is a shame, *I said*, that he didn't get a fair chance.

He had just finished eating, *my uncle remarked*, when the hurricane struck the house.

The boss, *in a moment of weakness*, gave Henry a raise.

It is true, *in the main*, that sound principles are not arrived at by guessing.

BIBLIOGRAPHY

1. Cowan, M., "Pitch and Intensity Characteristics of Stage Speech," *Archives of Speech*, Supplement, 1–92 (1936).

2. Curry, E. T., "An Objective Study of the Pitch Characteristics of the Adolescent Male Voice," *Ph.D. Dissertation, State University of Iowa*, 1939.

3. Fairbanks, G., "Recent Experimental Investigations of Vocal Pitch in Speech," *Journal of the Acoustical Society of America*, 11:457–466 (1940).

4. Fairbanks, G., and Pronovost, W., "An Experimental Study of the Pitch Characteristics of the Voice During the Expression of Emotion," *Speech Monographs*, 6:87–104 (1939).

5. Lewis, D., and Tiffin, J., "A Psychophysical Study of Individual Differences in Speaking Ability," *Archives of Speech*, 1:43–60 (1934).

6. Lynch, G., "A Phonophotographic Study of Trained and Untrained Voices Reading Factual and Dramatic Material," *Archives of Speech*, 1:9–25 (1934).

7. McIntosh, C. W., Jr., "A Study of the Relationship between Pitch Level and Pitch Variability in the Voices of Superior Speakers," *Ph.D. Dissertation, State University of Iowa*, 1939.

8. Pronovost, W., "An Experimental Study of the Habitual and Natural Pitch Levels of Superior Speakers," *Ph.D. Dissertation, State University of Iowa*, 1939.

9. Snidecor, J. C., "Experimental Studies of the Pitch and Duration Characteristics of Superior Speech," *Ph.D. Dissertation, State University of Iowa*, 1940.

CHAPTER IX

LOUDNESS

Loudness refers to the magnitude of an auditory sensation. It is
to be distinguished from *intensity*, which is its chief physical
determinant, and from *volume*, which is more closely related to
pitch than to intensity, and which is a property referring to the
auditory perception of spatial extent, e.g., broad tones vs. thin
tones.

The degree of loudness of a vocal tone is the result of two
factors: (1) the amplitude of excursion of the vocal cords, and
(2) the amount of amplification of the tone by the resonators.
The former is determined by the relations between breath pressure and vocal cord tension, the latter by the number of resonators used, the tension of the resonator walls, the duration of the
vocal cord tone, and other factors. The cause of a loudness defect
may be sought somewhere in these two processes.

The chief disorders of loudness are:

1. Too loud level.
2. Too soft level.
3. Monotony.
4. Over-flexibility.
5. Loudness patterns.

The following drills provide materials which may be used in
correcting these defects.

LOUDNESS LEVEL

We refer here to the *gross* loudness of a sound or series of sounds
as loudness level. Obviously, a loudness level of sufficient magnitude to insure audibility is of primary concern. An important

technique which should be mastered is that of adjusting the loudness level to suit the particular room situation.

Apart from poor judgment in adjusting loudness level to particular situations, the ability of the mechanism to produce adequate loudness is significantly affected by two factors which should be investigated before any retraining is attempted, namely, (1) laryngeal pathology, and (2) the influence of other variables. If your voice is weak the first step in your procedure should be to check and drill the following functions. (1) *Pitch level.*—Investigate your natural pitch level with care (see Pitch for the method). Many cases of weak voice are caused by pitch levels which are *too low*. Even if you are using your natural pitch you will be able to produce a louder tone by raising the pitch to a point above that level. (2) *Duration of tones.*—Make certain that your tones are of sufficient duration to give your mechanism a chance to produce adequate loudness. See Time for drills. (3) *Breathing.*—Scrutinize particularly your region of expansion and contraction, and your control over expiration. See Breathing for drills. (4) *Voice quality.*—If you are also breathy or hoarse set up a program to work on loudness and quality conjointly, since the two frequently are related.

1. If your voice is weak work first on sustained (sung) tones. Set an arbitrary loudness level which is reasonably difficult for you, objectifying it if possible by using an intensity meter. Sustain a steady [ɑ] of good quality at your *natural pitch* as long as possible. After several such trials, time the duration of the tone in seconds. Plot this value on the graph of Figure 3. Making such a measure at the same loudness level on consecutive days as long as you are working on your loudness, plot each on the graph and connect the points. Record the dates. In this procedure you are holding loudness relatively constant and measuring the "output capacity" of your voice, so to speak, as a function of duration. This is not entirely satisfactory but is the best that can be done in most situations. The average person with adequate loudness can sustain a loud tone for 20 to 25 seconds.

Another method of approaching this problem is possible if the

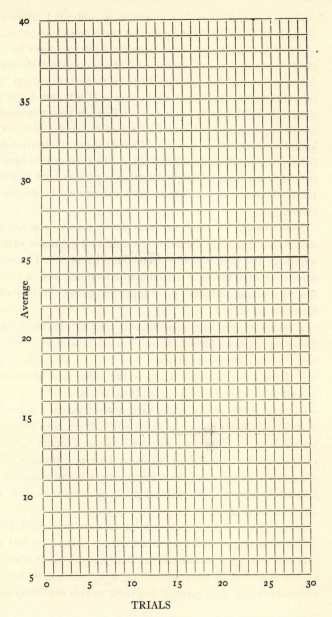

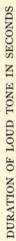

Figure 3.—Chart for Improvement Curve of Duration of Loud Tone in Seconds.

"volume control" on your amplifier is calibrated. Here your measure of intensity is the point on the volume control dial to which it is turned *when your loudest possible sustained tone just barely activates the needle on the meter*. For example, if the tone is not very intense the control will have to be "turned up" considerably before the meter needle moves at all, and if you now were to leave the control alone as you increase your loudness the needle would move up onto the face of the meter dial. At the louder level, therefore, you would have to turn the control down to keep the needle at its original place. The amount by which you turn it down from its original setting is proportional to the intensity increase of your voice. Such values may be graphed as above.

Note: In any of these methods which involve the use of a meter your measures are worthless unless all are made with the mouth at the same distance from the microphone. The easiest way to arrange this is to fasten a wire loop one foot in front of the microphone and place your upper lip against this loop every time you phonate.

2. Sustain [ɑ] as long as possible at your natural pitch, at the following loudness levels: (a) soft (avoid breathiness), (b) medium, (c) loud (avoid harshness).

3. Repeat with [i] and [u]. Note the differences between the vowels as to ease of producing all three levels.

4. Sing up an octave scale, each note of which is a good [ɑ] sustained *as loudly and as long* as possible. Begin with your natural pitch as *do*. Note that you can produce a louder tone with each successive raise. Observe this on a meter if possible. When you get to the top *do* of the scale, reverse without stopping and sing back down to your natural pitch, *still trying to make each tone as loud as possible*.

Note: This drill and that following are very important. If you follow directions carefully you are almost certain to find that you can produce a louder tone at your natural pitch when you return to it. This is the coordination which you should attempt to preserve and anticipate. Come back to this drill frequently.

5. Now repeat drill 4, but immediately after you finish read the following paragraph as loudly as possible at approximately your natural pitch.

It goes without saying that a voice that is audible is of basic importance to anyone. A speaker's articulation may be flawless, his use of pitch and time expressive and his voice quality superb, but if his listeners can't hear him he might just as well say nothing at all. Some day all of us may be outfitted with pocket public address systems, so that we can go around whispering into lapel microphones and turning little knobs to make our listeners hear. But until that great day comes we shall have to struggle along without the aid of high-powered amplification and use the old-fashioned system of making our voices louder.

6. Repeat at your natural pitch as many staccato examples of the word [tɑp] as possible on one breath, at the following levels: (a) soft, (b) medium, (c) loud.

7. Repeat, using [tip] and [tup].

8. Sustain [ɑ] at your natural pitch for at least ten seconds, beginning at a loud level and producing a smooth diminuendo (decrease in loudness) throughout the tone to the point where it is barely audible by the time you are out of breath. Keep pitch constant. Use a meter.

9. Repeat, beginning at a soft level and producing a smooth crescendo (increase in loudness).

10. Repeat, with a diminuendo on the first half and a crescendo on the last half of the tone.

11. Reverse 10 with a crescendo-diminuendo.

12. Now read the paragraph above in drill 5 four times, producing (a) diminuendo, (b) crescendo, (c) diminuendo-crescendo, (d) crescendo-diminuendo.

13. In addition to developing your voice so that it is loud enough for normal use you should learn to adapt it to various distances and rooms, and to produce variations in level in these situations. Imagining a listener 10 feet away, read the following paragraph three times so that to *him* it will sound (a) soft, (b)

medium, (c) loud. Repeat at imaginary distances of 20, 40 and 80 feet. If possible actually use these distances.

One can speak, if he chooses, with equal loudness in all speaking situations and for all phrases of a given speech. Such a course of action disregards completely two essential principles of loudness usage. First of all, different speaking situations demand different general levels of loudness. An intimate chat by the fireside demands a very low loudness level. An oration delivered in a large auditorium must be delivered with many times the loudness of the fireside conversation. These extreme examples suffice to illustrate the fact that general levels of loudness do vary from situation to situation. In the second place, loudness should vary from phrase to phrase within a given speech or speaking situation. If this second procedure is not followed, all of the speaker's ideas, both important and unimportant, will tend to be given the same relative vocal emphasis.

14. Repeat, imagining the following room situations: (a) A small, highly reverberant room, (b) an average living room, (c) a small auditorium, (d) a large auditorium.

LOUDNESS VARIATIONS

1. Read the following lists of two-syllable words. The words of the first group are stressed on the first syllable, while those of the second group are stressed on the second syllable. Observe that the stressed syllable is louder (also, of course, longer and frequently higher pitched) than the unstressed syllable. Exaggerate this difference.

First Syllable Stressed		Second Syllable Stressed	
loudness	longing	begin	reward
going	fitted	sustain	disease
blacking	reading	cajole	depend
sickness	nasty	report	cafe
goodness	coffee	garage	arouse
sorrow	fellows	deplore	receive
island	signpost	bewail	enrich

2. Read the following two-word sentences. Taking each in turn, stress first the second word, then the first word, by making the stressed word louder.

He went.	Winter comes.
Move fast.	How many?
Bill jumped.	Fish swim.
Shut up.	What happened?
Go home.	Believe me.
Dogs bark.	Who won?
Understand it?	Write this.
Wake up.	Help yourself.

3. Read the following repeated commands. Note that it is a common technique to reinforce the meaning of such repetitions by making the second louder than the first. Go ahead; **go ahead!** Observe this as you read.

Go ahead, **go ahead.**
Hurry up, **hurry up.**
Come here, **come here.**
Hit him again, **hit him again.**
Don't laugh, **don't laugh.**
Dry up, **dry up.**
Let me alone, **let me alone.**
Catch it, **catch it.**
Drop it there, **drop it there.**
Get back, **get back.**
Pull him in, **pull him in.**
Grab it, **grab it.**

4. Read the following two-sentence speeches. Taking each in turn, make the second sentence louder than the first, then the first louder than the second.

I can't believe it. I won't believe it!
This is your answer. I'll never do it!
Come on in. The water's fine.
Speak softly at first. Then speak loudly.

I try not to worry. But I can't help it.
My left lung is gone. But the right one's O.K.
My reply is always the same. It always will be the same.
It's the truth. Even if you don't think so.
Can you hear me? Can you hear me now?
This is the end. This is the finish.

5. In a similar manner the relative prominence of phrases in context can be indicated. In the following phrased paragraph the marks above the line, **S, L** and **E**, indicate arbitrarily for each phrase whether it should be Softer than, Louder than, or Equal in loudness to the *preceding* phrase. Read, observing these marks.

                                                       E

Loudness differences between the phrases of speech |are

                               E   **E**

determined for the most part |on a logical basis. |The

                        E

chief factor here |is the relative importance of the phrases.

S   **L**   **L**

|For example, |consider the sentence |"It's a long road,

S   **L**   **S**

|so they say, |that has no turning." |The parenthetical

            L   **E**

phrase |"so they say" |ordinarily would be spoken at a

                      E   **S**   **L**

lower loudness level, |to set it off, |so to speak, |from the

                      S

rest of the sentence |as a means of indicating that it is of

                      L   **L**

lesser importance. |If, however, |the speaker wishes to

                      S

emphasize the phrase, |perhaps in order to imply disbelief

                  L   **S**

of the proverb, |then one method of doing this |would be

<pre>
            L   E
to speak |"so they say" |at a louder level than the other
                           S
phrases of the sentence. |It is interesting to note as this
               E
paragraph is read |that whenever "so they say" is re-
                                                 E
peated out of its context in the example given, |there is a

tendency to use this louder level.
</pre>

6. Analyze the following paragraph, phrasing it and marking each phrase according to the method used above. Read with attention to these marks.

Many speakers, especially those who speak over-precisely on the theory that such a practice is more correct, tend to give approximately the same loudness to all words. Superior speakers, on the other hand, usually make the important words relatively more prominent than others by increasing the loudness of such words. It has been shown experimentally that loudness differences are related to the grammatical parts of speech. The adverbs, adjectives, nouns and verbs, words that carry most of the meaning, usually are given much more loudness by good speakers than are other parts of speech, such as pronouns, prepositions, conjunctions and articles. The implications of this evidence should be considered seriously by all students of speech.

7. Read the paragraph in the preceding drill twice, using on each phrase (a) a crescendo, (b) a diminuendo. The latter is the most common loudness pattern.

8. Now analyze the paragraph and indicate a logical loudness usage for each phrase by diagramming above the line. Read with attention to the marking. Loudness variations of this sort are not so amenable to classification as are intonations. It is probable that they are most closely related to the problem of individual word stress, for which see Stress.

BIBLIOGRAPHY

1. Cowan, M., "Pitch and Intensity Characteristics of Stage Speech," *Archives of Speech,* Supplement, 1–92 (1936).

2. Lewis, D., and Tiffin, J., "A Psychophysical Study of Individual Differences in Speaking Ability," *Archives of Speech,* 1:43–60 (1934).

3. Lynch, G., "A Phonophotographic Study of Trained and Untrained Voices Reading Factual and Dramatic Material," *Archives of Speech,* 1:9–25 (1934).

4. Murray, E., and Tiffin, J., "An Analysis of Some Basic Aspects of Effective Speech," *Archives of Speech,* 1:61–83 (1934).

5. Steer, M. D., and Tiffin, J., "A Photographic Study of the Use of Intensity by Superior Speakers," *Speech Monographs,* 1:72–78 (1934).

6. Stout, B., "Harmonic Structure of Vowels in Singing in Relation to Pitch and Intensity," *Journal of the Acoustical Society of America,* 10:137–146 (1938).

7. Van Riper, C., *Speech Correction Principles and Methods,* Prentice-Hall, Inc., New York, 1939.

8. West, R., Kennedy, L., and Carr, A., *The Rehabilitation of Speech,* Harper & Brothers, New York, 1937.

9. Wolf, S. K., Stanley, D., and Sette, W. J., "Quantitative Studies on the Singing Voice," *Journal of the Acoustical Society of America,* 6:255–266 (1935).

CHAPTER X

VOICE QUALITY

Quality is that attribute of tone which is determined by the composition of the sound wave, and which enables us to discriminate between two sounds which are alike in pitch, duration, and loudness, but yet are different. If a speaker pronounces the seven words *beat, bit, bet, bat, bought, but, boot,* giving to each the same pitch, duration, loudness, and consonant articulation, a listener makes the distinction between the words primarily on the basis of *vowel quality.* If seven speakers, however, all pronounce the word *beat,* and all keep all of the attributes, *including vowel quality,* constant, a listener tells the difference between the speakers on the basis of *voice quality.*

Two factors determine voice quality: (1) the original tone as initiated by the vocal cords, and (2) the selective modification of this tone by the resonance cavities. Disorders of quality have their bases in one of these two functions, the most common defects being:

1. Nasal quality.
2. Breathy quality.
3. Harsh quality.
4. Hoarse quality.

The first is a disorder of resonance, the others are defects of the initial tone produced by the cords. It will be observed that the so-called "muffled," "metallic" or "strident," and "denasal" qualities are omitted from the list. It is not denied that such vocal phenomena exist or that they are qualitative in character. However, they probably are not *voice* quality disorders in the same sense as those listed. There is research evidence which suggests that they are articulatory in nature. In brief, muffled quality, so called, is characteristically a slighting of consonants and a neutralization of vowels; metallic quality probably is systematic substitution, or tendency toward substitution, among front vowels of vowels higher in tongue position; denasal quality is the reduction or prevention of nasal consonants.

The test of the existence of a voice quality disorder is whether or not the quality that is heard is independent of phonemes, or, in other words, whether or not the phenomenon heard can be superimposed upon a good example of a voiced sound. This criterion has been applied repeatedly to so-called muffled, metallic and denasal quality defectives by attempting to discern the qualitative disorder when a *typical example of a given vowel is sustained*. In all but a few cases the "quality defects" disappeared when the good vowel was produced. The few exceptions were cases of high-pitched harshness which had been misdiagnosed as metallic or strident. Furthermore, the cases found it impossible to superimpose their "quality defects" upon *good* vowels even when they tried. The muffled and metallic cases invariably made a frank substitution or distorted the vowel so much that it became ambiguous, while every denasal case was definitely bewildered. In nasal, breathy, harsh and hoarse cases, however, both the good vowel quality and the voice quality deviation are heard at the same time.

This distinction is of practical importance since it indicates the direction of the improvement program. It is recommended that the defects known commonly as "muffled, metallic or strident, and denasal voice quality disorders" be treated frankly as articulatory disorders, and that the first step be an extremely detailed speech sound description to be followed by correction procedures similar to those used for any other articulatory defect. In the case of muffled speech the consonants, particularly the plosives, and all the vowels should have special scrutiny. In metallic or strident speech the front vowels are especially important. In denasal speech the three nasal consonants should have most of the attention, although in such cases there usually is a nasal obstruction which must be removed before nasal consonants are possible.

In all cases of nasality, breathiness, harshness and hoarseness two general causal factors should be studied thoroughly. These factors are (1) laryngeal pathology, or, in nasality, oral and nasal pathology, and (2) the influence of other variables. A few general suggestions are listed here and others will be mentioned as we proceed. (1) *Pitch level.*—There is research which shows that voice quality defectives are lower in pitch level on the average than other speakers, and other evidence which demonstrates that quality defectives tend to have habitual pitch levels which are lower than their own calculated natural pitch levels. This is sufficient indication of the importance of scrutinizing pitch level in all cases of voice quality deviation. Consult Pitch Level for the method. Strangely enough, there is no evidence to support the popular belief that high pitch and poor quality are related. (2) *Duration of tones.*—Be certain that your tones are of sufficient duration to give your mechanism a chance to produce good quality. See Time for drills. (3) *Breathing.*—Scrutinize especially your region of expansion and contraction, and your control over expiration. See Breathing. (4) *Loudness.*—If study shows your voice quality and loudness to be related drill them together.

For the average speaker, normal, pleasant quality is the goal. This quality best can be defined by saying that it does not have the attributes of the defective qualities. In this section the general principle will be to achieve what we want by getting rid of what we do not want. The drills are written from the standpoint of relearning, but with the complete understanding that organic limitations are exceedingly frequent in this type of disorder, and that in such cases the procedure will and should be adapted.

NASAL QUALITY

Nasal quality, or nasality, is characterized by undue nasal resonance in non-nasal voiced sounds. It is particularly evident in vowels. The chief general causes are two: (1) organic pathologies such as velar insufficiency, cleft palate or velum, paralysis of velar muscles, anterior nasal obstructions; (2) faulty oral habits such as lowered velum, too small mouth opening, tongue elevated in the rear of the mouth. Of the first class there are two types. Most typical is the type in which there is complete opening of the nasal passages. In the second type there is free posterior passage but obstruction or constriction anteriorly. The most frequent instance of faulty oral habits is assimilated nasality in which the characteristics of the nasal consonants are carried over into the adjacent vowels. This is especially marked in words where the vowel precedes the nasal consonant, when the oral positions for the nasal tend to be anticipated and begun before the vowel is completed.

1. The following paired sentences are constructed so that the first member of each pair favors the production of non-nasal quality and the second member favors the production of nasal quality. Read the sentences as you normally would without attempting at this point to eliminate nasality. Your aim as you read is to learn to distinguish nasality from normal quality. Listen especially to the vowels. Reread until you hear the difference.

> You put the foot rule above the law books.
> Jane rang the triangle and the cranky men came.

> Cookies with soup get awfully soggy.
> Signs of rain changed my mind.

> Shoot until you shoot up to the stars.
> Men and hounds ran madly in the morning.

> "Sup with cute Sue," suggested Ruth.
> "I am in the chain gang," exclaimed angry Dan.

> Look above you; that cloud covers up the stars.
> Dangling antecedents in slangy sentences mean many long
> and lengthy changes.

2. To develop the sensation of using a larger mouth opening speak the following nonsense routine, which brings most of your oral articulators into play in extreme movements. Read and

reread, rapidly and rhythmically as indicated, exaggerating the dropping of the jaw for [ɑ].

[pɑ-pɑ-pɑ]   [tɑ-tɑ-tɑ]   [sɑ-sɑ-sɑ-sɑ-sɑ-sɑ-sɑ]

3. Still attending to size of mouth opening read the following sentences rapidly.

Jack laughed as Bobby fell, but Bobby had the last laugh.
Ask the cop whether Popeye or Pluto played at the Palace.
Pop robbed a hock shop as his pals watched.
The Japs attacked Kavala at dusk.
Cabs cross Paris as fast as bicycles.
Ted stopped Paul as Paul tackled the cop at Bob's party.
Bobby bought pop bottles at Roberts' Hot Dog Shop.
Water rotted the beautiful poplar that stood above the public park.
Pat taught his daughter to bake hot pop-overs.

4. Work now to perceive velar position and movement. Assume the tongue position for [k] and build up air pressure behind the closure in the usual manner, but do not release the [k]. Now, keeping the tongue in the same position, lower the velum rapidly so that the air "explodes" through the nose with a noticeable voiceless click. Repeat many times in succession, attending to the velar sensations.

5. Repeat, using [t] and [p].

6. Attending still to the velar action go through the following nonsense routines many times. Work especially on maintaining a raised velum, as in the plosive position, during the vowels. Listen and check all nasality in the vowels.

[ki-ku-ki-ku-ki-ku-ki]
[ti-tu-ti-tu-ti-tu-ti]
[pi-pu-pi-pu-pi-pu-pi]

7. Read the following word list. Keep the velum raised all the time and produce non-nasal vowels.

cook	coat	cuff	toot	tote	tuck
coos	cope	cut	twos	taupe	tut
coot	coke	cup	tooth	toast	tough

pooch	pope	puff
poof	poke	pup
poop	post	puck

8. Pinch your nostrils firmly between your thumb and first finger and produce a series of examples of the vowel [æ] on one breath. On every other example lower your velum, so that in the series you have alternate nasal and non-nasal examples of [æ]. Keep the vowel the same each time, merely adding and subtracting nasality by lowering and raising the velum. Keep the nostrils closed throughout. Repeat with [ɑ] and [ɔ].

9. Sustain a normal [ɑ] as long as possible. As you phonate, close and open your nasal passages by pinching and releasing your nostrils alternately with your finger and thumb. If your [ɑ] is non-nasal there will be no perceptible quality change.

10. Pinching your nostrils throughout, read the following words. There should be no quality change.

feet	lap	look	pie	say
bit	soup	ask	house	low
pot	toss	gap	yet	cube
buck	had	tub	seek	seat

11. Pinching your nostrils throughout, read the following sentences. There should be no quality change.

Ruth cut up the fish swiftly.
The rude pup roughed up the rug.
The butcher hooked a cookie.
Sue bought a box of dull books.
Sock the cop with a boat hook.
Bobby the bookie bought a butchered duck.
Pop took the tots to Dot's.

12. The aim of the following routine is to assist you to construct nonsense syllables from nasal consonants and vowels without assimilating nasality to the vowels. Produce the nasal, pause for a second or two, then produce the vowel. Repeat with a shorter pause. Repeat with no pause, but sustaining both nasal and vowel slightly. Lastly, repeat with normal duration and joining.

[m]	long pause	[i]
[m]	short pause	[i]
[mi]	sustain both	
[mi]	join normally	

Combine [i], [e], [ɑ], [o] and [u] each with [m], [n] and [ŋ] preceding in this manner.

13. Reverse the above order, as:

[i]	long pause	[m]
[i]	short pause	[m]
[im]	sustain both	
[im]	join normally	

Combine [i], [e], [ɑ], [o] and [u] each with [m], [n] and [ŋ] following in this manner.

14. Place the vowel now in the medial position, as:

[m]	long pause	[i]	long pause	[m]
[m]	short pause	[i]	short pause	[m]
[mim]	sustain both			
[mim]	join normally			

Combine [i], [e], [ɑ], [o] and [u] each with [m], [n] and [ŋ] both preceding and following in this manner.

15. Read the following "word triplets" one row at a time. The words in each row of each column are arranged in ascending order of difficulty. Work to make the vowel of the third word as non-nasal as that of the first.

PRECEDING	FOLLOWING
pack – back – Mac	cap – cab – cam
pate – bait – mate	tap – tab – tam
pet – bet – met	cat – cad – can

	PRECEDING			FOLLOWING	
tot	– dot	– knot	late	– laid	– lain
tip	– dip	– nip	rack	– rag	– rang
tote	– dote	– note	rick	– rig	– ring

PRECEDING AND FOLLOWING

pop	– bob	– mom
pap	– Bab	– ma'am
toot	– dude	– noon
tight	– died	– nine
Tutt	– dud	– nun
tat	– dad	– Nan

16. The words of the following list increase in difficulty as you read. Preserve in all the non-nasality which you should be able to attain in the first few.

put	face
tip	meet
cup	gong
toot	wren
sought	pan
house	man
fight	ma'am

17. The following sentences decrease in difficulty from top to bottom. Read from *bottom to top* preserving in all the quality of the first few read. Then reverse order.

Banging, clanging, hair-raising gongs rang deafeningly to warn the remaining gangs.

The mangled remains of mammals make many museums memorable.

Our ancestors founded a new nation, as Lincoln mentioned on a not unknown occasion.

About to die, Ryder sighed, and cried for his wife, his eye glass, violets and Life.

"Ouch!" he shouted as he bowed and backed into the mouse trap.

The Beach League repeats by dealing complete defeat to the Beasley Speeders.

The shock of the flogging robbed John of his bodily strength.

Peggy said Ned wrecked several red sleds.

The bowsprit of the boat was ripped in two, but quick-witted Kit fixed it.

The bit was nicked by hitting it quickly and vigorously with a stick.

Joe Blow, the local show-off, posed as a rider at the rodeo.

The cook forsook the book to look at the rook who was hooking a cookie.

18. The following sentences *alternate* in difficulty. Read, preserving the same good quality in all.

Chang rang the wrong gong and mangled his ankle.

The lucky cook put the cookies in the cup.

Maidens and men came in their prime.

Bustles were tucked away with shoes and rugs.

"I am the wrong man!" exclaimed Dan.

Bitter and swift is the death of a spy.

The clanking of chains rang madly in the rain.

Sip this juicy piece of fish swiftly.

19. Negative Learning. Repeat any of the above drills exaggerating nasality consciously.

BREATHY QUALITY

Breathy quality results when the vocal cords fail to approximate completely as they vibrate, and a steady stream of air rushes audibly through the glottis and resonance cavities. Common causes of this condition are laryngeal pathology, and improper coordination between breath supply and vocal cord tension. The exact nature of the normal coordination is not known, and as far as breathy quality is concerned it may be said only that there apparently is a condition of optimum vocal cord tension in relation to a given amount of breath pressure below the cords, which optimum relationship is violated in this disorder. Under certain conditions either over-tension or under-tension may result in breathiness. Weakness of voice and breathiness are closely related, for it is impossible to produce extremely loud tones with breathy quality. In such cases the two problems may be drilled conjointly. High chest breathing and poor control over expiration frequently cause functional breathiness. The typical error here is to expire too passively and too rapidly. Sometimes, however, an inefficient relationship between phrasing and the number and location of inspirations produces breathy quality. See Breathing for drills. A pitch level that is lower than the natural level also leads to this disorder with some frequency. In this connection it is interesting to observe the modern tendency in some circles to regard this combination of low pitch and breathiness as good voice usage, particularly in women.

1. Attempting to hear the difference between breathy and non-breathy quality, read the following paired sentences. On each pair whisper the first sentence, then read the second as well as possible and try to eliminate all traces of the quality heard in the whispered example.

Sitting on a stool, the youth stopped to tie a loop in the loom.
The wrecking helped the men wedge the deck of the vessel.

Bully beef cooked over a sooty flame looked good to the footsore rookie.
The dam ran across the jagged valley where the campers had their shacks.

Walter stalked along haltingly without talking.
Generous exercise helped the fellow render himself well again.

Soapy Joe moaned and moped dolefully over his home-grown shoat.
The laggard tagged along waving a ragged sack.

The troop hooted, tooted, and blew, while guns boomed.
Nell set the letter against the desk and let her guests guess the contents.

2. Force yourself to economize breath by exhaling rapidly as much as possible, then inhaling a *very small* amount of air and beginning immediately to sustain [ɑ]. Hold it as long as possible, which should not be long if you have followed directions. Concentrate on getting as much sound as possible per unit of breath.

3. Checking your lower ribs and abdomen with one hand and your upper chest with the other, inhale and exhale silently several times until your region of expansion is not in the upper chest. Then, using the same coordination and avoiding breathiness, sustain [ɑ] as long as possible.

4. Repeat, reading the following sentences.

As the bugler blew the first call, the men came out of their tents rapidly and washed for breakfast.

Come again soon, bring your wife with you, and stay for two or three weeks.

Alice sent the gift with a long note explaining that she did not care to accept it in view of the fact that she did not feel that she deserved it.

The teacher praised the student because he had written a very fine theme on American literature, her favorite subject.

The judge fined the speeder fifty dollars and lectured to him at great length on the dangers of driving at a high rate of speed in a thickly populated residential district.

5. Some persons sound particularly breathy at the beginning of a phrase because they allow more breath to escape at the beginning than toward the end. Still others allow a large fraction of their breath to escape immediately after inspiration, before they begin the phrase or on the first word. Checking expiration with your hands and avoiding these errors by expiring gradually and steadily, read the above sentences.

6. Beginning with your natural pitch as *do*, sing up an octave scale each note of which is a sustained [ɑ], as *loud*, as *long* and as *non-breathy* as possible. When you get to the upper *do* reverse immediately and sing back down to your natural pitch, still making each tone loud, long and non-breathy. The chances are good that elimination of breathiness will be easier as you ascend

the scale and that you can retain the non-breathy quality to a certain extent as you descend.

7. Repeat 6, but immediately after you finish read the following paragraph, preserving the same good quality.

Adequate tone quality comes, in large part, from a proper balance of tension and control of the breathing and phonating mechanisms. Breathy quality is an example of poor balance in these mechanisms. In view of the fact that a very loud voice cannot at the same time be breathy, it would seem that from loud speaking a proper relationship between vocal cord tension and breath pressure might be learned. Of course it is not desirable to speak with extreme loudness all of the time, but by so speaking it usually is possible to illustrate speech without breathiness. Furthermore, a person with breathy quality frequently can habituate an efficient coordination by daily drill at loud levels.

8. Reread the above paragraph as *loudly* as possible for the first few lines, exerting every effort to eliminate breathiness. Then reduce your loudness gradually as you proceed until you are using a normal loudness but have retained the non-breathy quality. Note: This is a very valuable drill. Return to it from time to time.

9. Sustain a whispered [ɑ]. Gradually add phonation to the whisper and increase the loudness at the same time until you are phonating loudly and without breathiness. Listen carefully as you do this.

10. Repeat with a series of staccato productions of [tɑp].

11. Read the following word pairs. For the first member of each pair exert no control over breathiness, letting it carry over into the vowel if it has a tendency to do so. For the second member, however, use an abrupt initial "attack" on the vowel. Exaggerate the difference.

heat – eat	hod – odd	hail – ail	hark – ark
hate – ate	hit – it	hair – air	harm – arm
hat – at	had – add	heel – eel	Helen – Ellen
hem – em	ham – am	hand – and	helm – elm

12. Experiment with varying degrees of laryngeal tension. Sustaining [ɑ], use an even expiration of air and vary tension. Search for the optimum degree of tension. Don't strain.

13. Repeat the above experimentation but this time hold tension constant at the optimum point established above and vary the rapidity with which you expire air. Search for the optimum rate of expiration in relation to optimum tension.

14. Read the following words rapidly and without breathiness.

team	call	which	line
from	mode	whole	fact
two	bead	plain	course
hand	book	sense	thus
worth	from	weed	slow
skill	such	thought	still
said	rule	page	strike

15. Read the following paragraph without breathiness.

Because whispering is used typically when a speaker wants to limit the audibility of his speech to one listener or to a small group, it has acquired a symbolic value that makes it useful as an attention-getting device. But certain speakers overwork this technique until they fall into the habit of using on all occasions a breathy quality that approaches a whisper. They develop a "now-I'm-going-to-tell-you-a-big-secret" type of voice in which the near-whisper has lost all its attention value. They are like the boy in the fable who cried "Wolf! Wolf!" too many times. One teacher of speech has sarcastically dubbed this habit as "that delightfully confidential manner of speaking."

HARSH QUALITY

Harsh quality is characterized by a noisy, rasping, unmusical tone. When low pitched it frequently is described as "guttural"; when high pitched the term "strident" sometimes is applied. According to our present information the location of the disorder always is in the larynx, it may be organic or functional in nature, and the two most common causes are laryngeal pathology and hyper-tension. Frequently the latter cause is an effect of the strain to produce adequate loudness, particularly at low pitches. Like breathiness this disorder sometimes is caused by poor co-ordination of vocal cord tension and breath supply, especially if the individual wastes breath on expiration and avoids breathiness by increasing cord tension. Conversely, harshness sometimes occurs when the breath supply is limited and cord tension increased for that reason. A common accompaniment of harshness is the habitual use of glottal stops or clicks at the initiation of vowels. Whenever any one of the variables described appears to be operating, and this will be true in almost every case, other sections of this book should be used in conjunction with the drills which follow.

1. Attempt to produce and hear the difference between harsh and non-harsh quality as you read the following pairs of sentences. On each pair make the first sentence harsh and the second non-harsh.

The wrecking helped the men wedge the deck of the vessel.
Sitting on a stool, the youth stooped to tie a loop in the loom.

The dam ran across the jagged valley where the campers had their shacks.
Bully beef cooked over a sooty flame looked good to the footsore rookie.

Generous exercise helped the fellow render himself well again.
Walter stalked along haltingly without talking.

The laggard tagged along waving a ragged sack.
Soapy Joe moaned and moped dolefully over his home-grown shoat.

Nell set the letter against the desk and let her guests guess the contents.
The troop hooted, tooted, and blew, while guns boomed.

2. Sustain a whispered [ɑ]. Add phonation gradually and easily

at your natural pitch until the tone is average in loudness. Avoid harshness.

3. Repeat, using discrete examples of the word [loʊn] with longer than average duration.

4. Read the following paragraph, beginning with a whisper and adding phonation gradually until you are working at a normal loudness.

Harsh quality in the human voice, as with harsh quality in a violin, detracts from the pleasure of the listener. If the habitual pitch of your voice is low, watch for what is termed "guttural" quality. On the other hand, in case your pitch is high, listen for "stridency." Sometimes organic conditions in the larynx produce harshness. In other cases, too much tension and poor balance between breath control and phonation may contribute to such a condition. Constant drill on the initiation of tones with emphasis on just the right amount of tension should do much to modify an undue amount of harshness.

5. In the following list of word pairs the first member of each pair, beginning with [h], is favorable for a gradual initiation of the vowel. Read the pairs with this problem of initiation in mind. Attempt to carry over the gradual vowel initiation in the first word to the vowel of the second word in each pair. Avoid an abrupt glottal "attack."

heat – eat	hod – odd	hail – ail	hark – ark
hate – ate	hit – it	hair – air	harm – arm
hat – at	had – add	heel – eel	Helen – Ellen
hem – em	ham – am	hand – and	helm – elm

6. Read the following list of words without an abrupt glottal initiation of the vowels.

eat	egg	up	ought	edge
imp	at	on	ooze	own
ouch	ire	is	etch	isle
ate	oil	eke	out	ape

7. Reread the paragraph under drill 4 above with as little harshness as possible.

HOARSE QUALITY

Hoarseness is the typical voice quality of the individual who has acute or chronic laryngeal infection or irritation. The locus of the disorder is the larynx and the above are the most frequent organic causes. Sometimes hoarse quality results as a secondary effect of infections of the superior respiratory tract, and on other occasions irritation is produced by vocal strain. Functional hoarseness is rare, since such laryngeal strain leads to organic impairment. Medical examination and treatment is of special importance in this disorder and should be the first corrective step in all cases.

From both acoustical and causal points of view hoarseness combines the features of breathiness and harshness. It is subject also to the influence of the variables which produce and perpetuate these disorders. Therefore, specific drills for hoarseness, which would duplicate materials presented elsewhere in the book, are not provided. It is recommended instead, subject to modification in individual cases, that the student's program include all drills in the sections on breathy quality, harsh quality, pitch level and breathing, with additional reference to other chapters, such as Chapter IX, Loudness, when the need arises.

BIBLIOGRAPHY

1. Johnson, D. L., "An Analysis of the Voice and Articulation Abilities of Students Registered in a Required Course in Speech and Dramatic Art," *M.A. Thesis, State University of Iowa*, 1938.

2. Kelly, J. P., "Studies in Nasality," *Archives of Speech*, 1:26–42 (1934).

3. Laase, L. T., "The Effect of Pitch and Intensity on the Quality of the Vowels in Speech," *Archives of Speech*, 2:41–60 (1937).

4. McIntosh, C. W., Jr., "An Auditory Study of Nasality," *M.A. Thesis, State University of Iowa*, 1937.

5. Russell, G. O., *Speech and Voice*, The Macmillan Company, New York, 1931.

6. Stout, B., "Harmonic Structure of Vowels in Singing in Relation to Pitch and Intensity," *Journal of the Acoustical Society of America*, 10:137–146 (1938).

7. Talley, C. H., "A Comparison of Conversational and Audience Speech," *Archives of Speech*, 2:28–40 (1937).

8. Van Riper, C., *Speech Correction Principles and Methods*, Prentice-Hall, Inc., New York, 1939.

9. West, R., "Recent Studies in Speech Pathology," *Proceedings of the American Speech Correction Association*, 6:44–49 (1936).

10. West, R., Kennedy, L., and Carr, A., *The Rehabilitation of Speech*, Harper & Brothers, New York, 1937.

CHAPTER XI

STRESS

The terminology related to this aspect of voice usage is in a highly confused state. To avoid ambiguity certain terms will be employed according to the following definitions. *Stress* is used in a generic sense to refer to the relative prominence given to a sound, syllable or word by any vocal means and for any purpose whatever. *Emphasis* is logical stress for the purpose of expressing meaning and pertains primarily to words. *Accent* is syllabic stress, referring thus to the relative prominence of syllables. The adjectives *unstressed*, *unemphasized* and *unaccented* pertain to conditions of relative lack of prominence.

A definitive experimental study of stress has not yet been made, and until that has been done statements concerning the relative importance of the various vocal attributes will not be possible. The present evidence makes it quite clear, however, that no single attribute performs the function of rendering sounds more or less prominent, but that duration, loudness and pitch all take part. A stressed word tends to be louder and longer than adjacent words. With respect to pitch the information is not so definite. Stressed sounds are slightly higher in pitch, on the average, than others, but are lower in many instances, while pitch curves indicate that the pitch of unstressed syllables and words tends to follow that of adjacent sounds. The data on inflections of pitch are more conclusive, showing that stressed words tend to have inflections of wider extent. Whenever directions are given in the following drills to stress or unstress a word or syllable, the combined use of duration, loudness and pitch is implied.

The present chapter is entirely devoted to logical stress, or emphasis, accent having been considered under Pronunciation.

1. Nouns, verbs, adjectives and adverbs, words which are of primary importance to the meaning of what is said, customarily are given more stress than other parts of speech. Each of the following groups of sentences has been selected to exemplify one part of speech. In each group examples of that part of speech are in bold-face type. As you read the sentences stress the words so indicated, stressing only the stressed syllable of polysyllabic words. Note that the words marked in any sentence may not be the only words to which stress is given.

Nouns

It is a **book**.
The **man** came back.
Joan saw the **dog**.
She comes from **France**.
Jack is tired.
Henry Clay was an **orator**.
Curiosity is a **virtue**.
Honesty is the best **policy**.
It filled the **space**.
He pushed through the **crowd**.
He saw a **herd** of **sheep**.
The **party** is over.

Verbs

Stop, look and **listen**.
I **gave** him the box.
You **eat** too much.
Jack **polished** the car.
The man **objected**.
Stop him.
I **doubt** it.
Mary **completed** the task.
I **thought** so.
They **wondered** about it.
He **came** before I **telephoned**.
Look before you **leap**.

ADJECTIVES

Massa's in the **cold, cold** ground.
She collected **smooth, round, white** stones.
There were **good** ones and **bad** ones.
Stress the **long** word.
We saw **several** rabbits.
Make a **second** choice.
Two men in **white** uniforms walked by.
We went on **numerous** occasions.
You take the **high** road.
Western jackrabbits have **long** ears.
Take the **next yellow** car.
Pick **two green** ones and a **black** one.

ADVERBS

They ran **fast**.
You can do it **easily**.
Begin **slowly**.
He smiled **playfully**.
They swam **often**.
Yesterday it rained.
He will go **far**.
The ship is **homeward** bound.
Certainly I will.
Johnson **also** ran.
That is **especially** true of America.
Henceforth and **forevermore**.

2. Exceptions to the above principle are inevitable. One of the most notable is the case of auxiliary verbs, which ordinarily are not emphasized. In the following sentences the auxiliaries are italicized. Unstress them as you read.

AUXILIARY VERBS

I *am* going.   The bird *has* flown.
A dog *is* barking.   The bells *will* ring.

You *are* playing.   That *can* wait.
It *was* raining.   The men *had* moved.
The men *were* working.   Night *must* fall.
All *have* died.   Jack *should* come.

3. Pronouns, prepositions, conjunctions and articles, words which are largely connective in function, usually are unstressed. In the following sentences these parts of speech are italicized. Unstress them as you read.

PRONOUNS

He kicked *me*.   Throw *them* out.
John knew *it*.   *I* came back.
We went home.   Show *him* the way.
Go if *you* can.   The dog bit *her*.
They fell down.   *She* ran back.
Please call *us*.   *I* want to.

PREPOSITIONS

All roads lead *to* Rome.   I'll be *at* home.
United States *of* America.   *To* the right.
From noon *till* night.   *From* Monday *to* Friday.
Not *since* yesterday.   Look *on* the table.
Late *in* July.   He is *at* liberty.
On the top *of* the hill.   *With* Malice *Toward* Some.

CONJUNCTIONS

You *and* I.   Injured *but* living.
Red, white *and* blue.   Dangerous *but* passable.
One *or* the other.   Wealthy *yet* unhappy.
To be, *or* not to be.   I want to, *yet* I can't.
Neither here *nor* there.   I shall do it, *for* I must.
Neither willing *nor* able.   Jack barks, *for* he is a dog.

ARTICLES

The man ran.   *A* clock struck.
The whistle blew.   Take *a* cab.

Jump *the* fence.　　　　Here's half *a* dollar.
The apple is red.　　　　*An* echo answered.
Give me *the* orange.　　　He is *an* Eskimo.
What is *the* answer?　　　Make *an* effort.

4. Exceptions to the principle of drill 3 occur most notably for purposes of special emphasis. As you read the following sentences stress the bold-face words and note the changes in meaning.

It is **the** thing to do.　　　She **and** her dog.
You **and** I.　　　　　　　**You** are going.
Look **under** the table.　　　She wore black **and** brown.
He kicked **me**.　　　　　Jump **over** the fence.
One **or** the other.　　　　I like him.
It is **in** the desk.　　　　I like **him**.

5. Compound nouns afford interesting examples of the importance of stress. In the word "blackbird," for instance, stress is the only clue, apart from the context, which enables a listener to decide whether a speaker is referring to one of a large number of different kinds of birds which are black in color or to one of a particular species known as blackbirds (black bird vs. blackbird). Read the following paired examples with this in mind. Bold-face type again signifies increased stress.

black bird	**black**bird	all ready	**already**
green house	**green**house	write up	**write**-up
copper head	**copper**head	work out	**work**out
break down	**break**down	put out	**put**-out
blue bell	**blue**bell	high brow	**high**-brow
fool's cap	**fool**scap	cross word	**cross**word
green land	**Green**land	hook up	**hook**up
white house	**White** House	over head	**over**head

6. Certain sentences may be given entirely different meanings depending upon emphasis. Consider the sentence "These are some examples." If emphasized "**These** are some **examples**," the statement can be taken at its face value. If emphasized

"These are **some examples**," the speaker may be expressing sarcastic disapproval of the examples. Study the following "examples" with this problem of complete change in meaning in mind, reading them as indicated.

> **What intelligence!**
> **What** intelligence?
>
> How **good!**
> **How** good?
>
> Now, **John!**
>
> Why, **John!**
> **Why,** John?
>
> Now, **we** can go **home.**
> **Now** we can go **home.**
>
> It is the **city** which has the largest houses.
> It is the **city** which has the **largest houses.**
>
> Feed it to the **black dog.**
> Feed it to the **black** dog.
>
> She is **unhappily married.**
> She **is,** unhappily, **married.**
>
> She **barely saw** the **man.**
> She **barely saw** the man.
>
> She **thought** he came **back.**
> She **thought** he came back.
>
> He **won't live** a **year** if he does that.
> He **won't live** a **year** if he **does** that.
>
> I **supposed** he was **finished.**
> I **supposed** he was finished.
>
> He could **see** an improvement.
> He could **see** an **improvement.**

7. Considering the following sentences one at a time, emphasize each word of the sentence in turn. Note the changes in meaning.

Today is a fine day.
Say it this way.
Go very slowly down the street.
Keep still a moment.
You may be right.
Do you really mean it?
Did you see what I saw?
You can do that.
How do you know that?
Her name was Ann.

8. In typical reading or speaking, a word is to a phrase as a syllable is to a word. Just as within a word certain syllables are stressed and others are unstressed, so within a phrase the words are given various degrees of prominence. The following sentences are phrased and certain words are marked arbitrarily for emphasis. Read, observing the marks.

The **words** of a **phrase** |should be **emphasized** in **accordance** with the **meaning** that the **speaker** **wishes** to **convey.**

The **meaning** of a **sentence** |can be **changed** **radically** |simply by a **change** in **emphasis** |from **one** **word** to **another** **word.**

Increasing the **duration** of a **word** |is **one** **way** of **emphasizing** it.

We **know** from our **observation** |that an **excited** **command** |tends to have **increased** **loudness** on the **stressed** **words** of the **command.**

The **process** of **analyzing** a **phrase** |is a **valuable** **approach** to the **problem** of **emphasis.**

The **study** of **emphasis** |is **useful** in **overcoming** the **peculiar** **patterns** of **stress** in our **speech.**

The **repetition** of an **emphasis** **pattern** |may be **monotonous** in the **extreme.**

A **speaker** who is **over-precise** in his **emphasis** |may **not** **allow** for a **normal** **difference** in the **importance** of **words.**

Attempt to **shift** the **emphasis** |from **one** **word** to **another**

word in a **given phrase** |and **see what differences** in the **meaning** may be **conveyed.**

The **student** who is **interested** in **experimentation** |might **well consider** the **problem** of **stress** |as a **field** of **investigation.**

9. Reread the above sentences, paying special attention to un-stressing the words so indicated.

10. Phrase the following sentences and underline the words to be stressed. In doing this take the attitude that you propose to stress only the essential words. It is as if you were writing a tele-gram, for example, and wished to economize as much as possible but still make the meaning clear. Read, observing your marks and attending to both stressed and unstressed words.

Every student is familiar with the term accent, which refers here to syllabic stress.

Some writers feel that as many as five factors are related to the problem of emphasis.

One experiment showed that thirty-nine per cent of the stressed words were, on the average, higher in pitch than the same words when unstressed.

Eighty per cent of the stressed words, however, had a greater magnitude of inflection than the same words when unstressed.

In the same experiment it was shown that stressed words have definitely greater intensity than have the average words of a sentence.

When words are stressed in one reading of a sentence and unstressed in a second reading of the same sentence, it has been shown that the stressed words are longer in duration al-most every time.

Emphasis usually is achieved by a combination of factors rather than by one factor alone.

It is not to be expected that there is any single correct way of achieving emphasis.

It should seem evident to the student of speech that em-phasis needs more study on an objective basis.

An important aspect of rhythm is the regular recurrence of stress.

11. Phrase and mark the following paragraph for stress. If your procedure is correct you will underline only approximately one-half of the words. Read the paragraph three times as follows. (a) Read only the underlined words. Do not read the others. Make the meaning clear to a listener by means of inflection and pause, which is not at all impossible. (b) This time omit all of the underlined words and read only those not underlined. The result should be a meaningless series of unimportant words. (c) Now read the paragraph as well as you are able, with the best possible relative stress.

When a foreigner learns English his speech is distinguished by characteristics which are not typical of the speech of persons for whom English is the native language. The popular term for these characteristics, as well as for the characteristics of regional American speech, is "accent." Thus, a German speaking English is said to have a "German accent" and a Georgian speaking in the Middle West is charged with having a "Southern accent." Upon closer inspection, however, we find that the term "accent," which refers to syllabic stress, is inadequate, for the differences which exist are not only those of accent. The greatest difference probably is in articulation and is a matter of speech sound substitutions for the most part. Time and pitch differences represent a second major aspect of foreign speech, for the ear alone tells us that such differences unquestionably exist. Finally, there are stress differences that may be observed, and such differences include not only distortions of accent, but also deviations in word emphasis. From these considerations it is apparent that "accent," used in this sense, should be replaced in the vocabulary of the student of speech by a more inclusive term, and the word "dialect" suits this need admirably. We may speak then of "foreign dialects" and "regional dialects" without employing a label which gives a false and limited impression of the speech characteristics to which we refer.

BIBLIOGRAPHY

1. Ortleb, R., "An Objective Study of Emphasis in Oral Reading of Emotional and Unemotional Material," *Speech Monographs*, 4:56–68 (1937).

2. Parmenter, C. E., and Blanc, A. V., "An Experimental Study of Accent in French and English," *Publications of the Modern Language Association of America*, 48:598–607 (1933).

3. Schramm, W. L., "The Acoustical Nature of Accent in American Speech," *American Speech*, 12:49–56 (1937).

4. Tiffin, J., and Steer, M. D., "An Experimental Analysis of Emphasis," *Speech Monographs*, 4:69–74 (1937).

BIBLIOGRAPHY

1. Ortleb, R., "An Objective Study of Emphasis in Oral Reading of Emotional and Unemotional Material," *Speech Monographs*, 4:56-68 (1937).
2. Parmenter, C. E., and Blanc, A. V., "An Experimental Study of Accent in French and English," *Publications of the Modern Language Association of America*, 48:598-607 (1933).
3. Schramm, W. L., "The Acoustical Nature of Accent in American Speech," *American Speech*, 12:49-50 (1937).
4. Tiffin, J., and Steer, M. D., "An Experimental Analysis of Emphasis," *Speech Monographs*, 4:69-74 (1937).

INDEX